The South Pole an Account of the Norwegian Antarctic Expedition in the

Roald Amundsen, John Murry

BIBLIOLIFE

THE SOUTH POLE

ROALD AMUNDSEN IN POLAR KIT.

AN ACCOUNT OF THE NORWEGI
ANTARCTIC EXPEDITION IN THE "FRA
1910–1912

BY ROALD AMUNDSEN

TRANSLATED FROM THE NORWEGIAN BY
A. G. CHATER

WITH MAPS AND NUMEROUS ILLUSTRATIONS

IN TWO VOLUMES
VOL. II

35

20.

LONDON
JOHN MURRAY, ALBEMARLE STREET, W.
1912

CONTENTS OF VOL. II

LIST OF ILLUSTRATIONS TO VOL. II

LIST OF MAPS AND CHARTS

THE SOUTH POLE

CHAPTER X

THE START FOR THE POLE

At last we got away, on October 19. The weather for the past few days had not been altogether reliable; now windy, now calm—now snowing, now clear: regular spring weather, in other words. That day it continued unsettled; it was misty and thick in the morning, and did not promise well for the day, but by 9.30 there was a light breeze from the east, and at the same time it cleared.

There was no need for a prolonged inquiry into the sentiments of the party. " What do you think ? Shall we start ?"—" Yes, of course. Let's be jogging on." There was only one opinion about it. Our coursers were harnessed in a jiffy, and with a little nod—as much as to say, " See you to-morrow "—we were off. I don't believe Lindström even came out of doors to see us start. " Such an everyday affair: what's the use of making a fuss about it ?"

There were five of us—Hanssen, Wisting, Hassel, Bjaaland, and myself. We had four sledges, with thirteen dogs to each. At the start our sledges were very light, as we were only taking supplies for the trip to 80° S., where all our cases were waiting for us ; we could therefore sit on the sledges and flourish our whips with a jaunty air. I sat astride on Wisting's sledge, and anyone who had seen us would no doubt have thought a Polar journey looked very inviting.

Down on the sea-ice stood Prestrud with the cinematograph, turning the crank as fast as he could go as we went past. When we came up on to the Barrier on the other side, he was there again, turning incessantly. The last thing I saw, as we went over the top of the ridge and everything familiar disappeared, was a cinematograph ; it was coming inland at full speed. I had been engaged in looking out ahead, and turned round suddenly to throw a last glance in the direction of the spot that to us stood for all that was beautiful on earth, when I caught sight of—what do you think ? A cinematograph. " He can't be taking anything but air now, can he ?"—" Hardly that." The cinematograph vanished below the horizon.

The going was excellent, but the atmosphere became thicker as we went inland. For the first twelve miles from the edge of the Barrier I had been sitting with Hassel, but, seeing that Wisting's dogs could manage two on the sledge better than the others, I moved. Hanssen drove first ; he had to steer by compass alone, as the weather had got thicker. After him came Bjaaland, then

Hassel, and, finally, Wisting and I.   We had just gone up
a little slope, when we saw that it dropped rather steeply
on the other side; the descent could not be more than
20 yards long.   I sat with my back to the dogs, looking
aft, and was enjoying the brisk drive.   Then suddenly
the surface by the side of the sledge dropped perpendicularly, and showed a yawning black abyss, large
enough to have swallowed us all, and a little more.   A
few inches more to one side, and we should have taken
no part in the Polar journey.   We guessed from this
broken surface that we had come too far to the east,
and altered our course more westerly.   When we had
reached safer ground, I took the opportunity of putting
on my ski and driving so; in this way the weight was
more distributed.   Before very long it cleared a little,
and we saw one of our mark-flags straight ahead.   We
went up to it; many memories clung to the spot—cold
and slaughter of dogs.   It was there we had killed the
three puppies on the last trip.

We had then covered seventeen miles, and we camped,
well pleased with the first day of our long journey.   My
belief that, with all in one tent, we should manage our
camping and preparations much better than before was
fully justified.   The tent went up as though it arose out
of the ground, and everything was done as though we
had had long practice.   We found we had ample room
in the tent, and our arrangements worked splendidly the
whole time.   They were as follows: as soon as we

halted, all took a hand at the tent. The pegs in the valance of the tent were driven in, and Wisting crept inside and planted the pole, while the rest of us stretched the guy-ropes. When this was done, I went in, and all the things that were to go inside were handed in to me— sleeping-bags, kit-bags, cookers, provisions. Everything was put in its place, the Primus lighted, and the cooker filled with snow. Meanwhile the others fed their dogs and let them loose. Instead of the "guard," we shovelled loose snow round the tent; this proved to be sufficient protection—the dogs respected it. The bindings were taken off all our ski, and either stowed with other loose articles in a provision-case, or hung up together with the harness on the top of the ski, which were lashed upright to the front of the sledge. The tent proved excellent in every way; the dark colour subdued the light, and made it agreeable.

Neptune, a fine dog, was let loose when we had come six miles over the plain; he was so fat that he could not keep up. We felt certain that he would follow us, but he did not appear. We then supposed that he had turned back and made for the flesh-pots, but, strangely enough, he did not do that either. He never arrived at the station; it is quite a mystery what became of him. Rotta, another fine animal, was also set free; she was not fit for the journey, and she afterwards arrived at home. Ulrik began by having a ride on the sledge; he picked up later. Björn went limping after the sledge.

Peary was incapacitated; he was let loose and followed for a time, but then disappeared. When the eastern party afterwards visited the depot in 80° S., they found him there in good condition. He was shy at first, but by degrees let them come near him and put the harness on. He did very good service after that. Uranus and Fuchs were out of condition. This was pretty bad for the first day, but the others were all worth their weight in gold.

During the night it blew a gale from the east, but it moderated in the morning, so that we got away at 10 a.m. The weather did not hold for long; the wind came again with renewed force from the same quarter, with thick driving snow. However, we went along well, and passed flag after flag. After going nineteen and a quarter miles, we came to a snow beacon that had been erected at the beginning of April, and had stood for seven months; it was still quite good and solid. This gave us a good deal to think about: so we could depend upon these beacons; they would not fall down. From the experience thus gained, we afterwards erected the whole of our extensive system of beacons on the way south. The wind went to the south-east during the day; it blew, but luckily it had stopped snowing. The temperature was −11·5° F., and bitter enough against the wind. When we stopped in the evening and set our tent, we had just found our tracks from the last trip; they were sharp and clear, though six weeks old. We were glad to find them, as we had seen no flag for some time, and were beginning to get near the ugly trap, forty-six and a half miles from the house, that had been found on the last depot journey, so we had to be careful.

The next day, the 21st, brought very thick weather : a strong breeze from the south-east, with thick driving snow. It would not have been a day for crossing the trap if we had not found our old tracks. It was true that we could not see them far, but we could still see the direction they took. So as to be quite safe, I now set our course north-east by east—two points east was the original course. And compared with our old tracks, this looked right, as the new course was considerably more easterly than the direction of the tracks. One last glance over the camping-ground to see whether anything was forgotten, and then into the blizzard. It was really vile weather, snowing from above and drifting from below, so that one was quite blinded. We could not see far ; very often we on the last sledge had difficulty in seeing the first. Bjaaland was next in front of us. For a long time we had been going markedly downhill, and this was not in accordance with our reckoning ; but in that weather one could not make much of a reckoning. We had several times passed over crevasses, but none of any size. Suddenly we saw Bjaaland's sledge sink over. He jumped off and seized the trace. The sledge lay on its side for a few seconds, then began to sink more and more, and finally disappeared altogether. Bjaaland had got a good purchase in the snow, and the dogs lay down and dug their claws in. The sledge sank more and more—all this happened in a few moments. "Now I can't hold it any longer." We—Wisting and I—had just come up. He was holding on convulsively, and resisting with all his force, but it was no use— inch by inch the sledge sank deeper. The dogs, too, seemed to understand the gravity of the situation; stretched out in the snow, they dug their claws in, and resisted with all their strength. But still, inch by inch, slowly and surely, it went down into the abyss. Bjaaland was right enough when he said he couldn't hold on any longer. A few seconds more, and his sledge and thirteen dogs would never have seen the light of day again. Help came at the last moment. Hanssen and Hassel, who were a little in advance when it happened, had snatched an Alpine rope from a sledge and came to his assistance. They made the rope fast to the trace, and two of us—Bjaaland and I—were now able, by getting a good purchase, to hold the sledge suspended. First the dogs were taken out; then Hassel's sledge was drawn back and placed across the narrowest part of the crevasse, where we could see that the edges were solid. Then by our combined efforts the sledge, which was dangling far below, was hoisted up as far as we could get it, and made fast to Hassel's sledge by the dogs' traces. Now we could slack off and let go : one sledge hung securely enough by the other. We could breathe a little more freely.

The next thing to be done was to get the sledge right up, and before we could manage that it had to be unloaded. A man would have to go down on the rope, cast off the lashings of the cases, and attach them again for drawing up. They all wanted this job, but Wisting had it; he fastened the Alpine rope round his body and went down. Bjaaland and I took up our former positions, and acted as anchors; meanwhile Wisting reported what he saw down below. The case with the cooker was hanging by its last thread; it was secured, and again saw the light of day. Hassel and Hanssen attended to the hauling up of the cases, as Wisting had them ready. These two fellows moved about on the brink of the chasm with a coolness that I regarded at first with approving eyes. I admire courage and con- tempt for danger. But the length to which they carried it at last was too much of a good thing; they were simply playing hide-and-seek with Fate. Wisting's in- formation from below—that the cornice they were standing on was only a few inches thick—did not seem to have the slightest effect on them; on the contrary, they seemed to stand all the more securely.

" We've been lucky," said Wisting; " this is the only place where the crevasse is narrow enough to put a sledge across. If we had gone a little more to the left "—Hanssen looked eagerly in that direction— " none of us would have escaped. There is no surface there; only a crust as thin as paper. It doesn't look very inviting down below, either; immense spikes of ice sticking up everywhere, which would spit you before you got very far down."

This description was not attractive; it was well we had found "such a good place." Meanwhile Wisting had finished his work, and was hauled up. When asked whether he was not glad to be on the surface again, he answered with a smile that "it was nice and warm down there." We then hauled the sledge up, and for the time being all was well. "But," said Hassel, "we must be careful going along here, because I was just on the point of going in when Hanssen and I were bringing up the sledge." He smiled as though at a happy memory. Hassel had seen that it was best to be careful. There was no need to look for crevasses; there was literally nothing else to be seen.

There could be no question of going farther into the trap, for we had long ago come to the conclusion that, in spite of our precautions, we had arrived at this ugly place. We should have to look about for a place for the tent, but that was easier said than done. There was no possibility of finding a place large enough for both the tent and the guy-ropes; the tent was set up on a small, apparently solid spot, and the guys stretched across crevasses in all directions. We were beginning to be quite familiar with the place. That crevasse ran there and there, and it had a side-fissure that went so and so—just like schoolboys learning a lesson.

Meanwhile we had brought all our things as far as possible into a place of safety; the dogs lay harnessed to reduce the risk of losing them. Wisting was just going over to his sledge—he had gone the same way several times before—when suddenly I saw nothing but his head, shoulders and arms above the snow. He had fallen through, but saved himself by stretching his arms out as he fell. The crevasse was bottomless, like the rest. We went into the tent and cooked lobscouse. Leaving the weather to take care of itself, we made ourselves as comfortable as we could. It was then one o'clock in the afternoon. The wind had fallen considerably since we came in, and before we knew what was happening, it was perfectly calm. It began to brighten a little about three, and we went out to look at it.

The weather was evidently improving, and on the northern horizon there was a sign of blue sky. On the south it was thick. Far off, in the densest part of the mist, we could vaguely see the outline of a dome-like elevation, and Wisting and Hanssen went off to examine it. The dome turned out to be one of the small haycock formations that we had seen before in this district. They struck at it with their poles, and—just as they expected—it was hollow, and revealed the darkest abyss. Hanssen was positively chuckling with delight when he told us about it; Hassel sent him an envious glance.

CREVASSED SURFACE ON THE BARRIER.

By 4 p.m. it cleared, and a small reconnoitring party, composed of three, started to find a way out of this. I was one of the three, so we had a long Alpine rope between us; I don't like tumbling in, if I can avoid it by such simple means. We set out to the east—the direction that had brought us out of the same broken ground before—and we had not gone more than a few paces when we were quite out of it. It was now clear enough to look about us. Our tent stood at the north-eastern corner of a tract that was full of hummocks; we could decide beyond a doubt that this was the dreaded trap. We continued a little way to the east until we saw our course clearly, and then returned to camp. We did not waste much time in getting things ready and leaving the place. It was a genuine relief to find ourselves once more on good ground, and we resumed our journey southward at a brisk pace.

That we were not quite out of the dangerous zone was shown by a number of small hummocks to the south of us. They extended across our course at right angles. We could also see from some long but narrow crevasses we crossed that we must keep a good look-out. When we came into the vicinity of the line of hummocks that lay in our course, we stopped and discussed our prospects. " We shall save a lot of time by going straight on through here instead of going round," said Hanssen. I had to admit this; but, on the other hand, the risk was much greater. " Oh, let's try it," he went on; "if we can't do it, we can't." I was weak, and allowed myself to be persuaded, and away we went among the haycocks. I could see how Hanssen was enjoying himself; this was just what he wanted. We went faster and faster. Curiously enough, we passed several of these formations without noticing anything, and began to hope that we should get through. Then suddenly Hanssen's three leading dogs disappeared, and the others stopped abruptly. He got them hauled up without much trouble and came over. We others, who were following, crossed without accident, but our further progress seemed doubtful, for after a few more paces the same three dogs fell in again. We were now in exactly the same kind of place as before; crevasses ran in every direction, like a broken pane of glass. I had had enough, and would take no more part in this death-ride. I announced decisively that we must turn back, follow our tracks, and go round it all. Hanssen looked quite disappointed. "Well," he said, "but we shall be over it directly." "I dare say we shall," I replied; "but we must go back first." This was evidently hard on him; there was one formation in particular that attracted him, and he wanted to try his strength with it. It was a pressure-mass that, as far as appearance went, might just as well have been formed out in the drift-ice. It looked as if it was formed of four huge lumps of ice raised on end against each other. We knew what it contained without examination—a yawning chasm. Hanssen cast a last regretful glance upon it, and then turned back.

We could now see all our surroundings clearly. This place lay, as we had remarked before, in a hollow; we followed it round, and came up the rise on the south without accident. Here we caught sight of one of our flags; it stood to the east of us, and thus confirmed our suspicion that we had been going too far to the west. We had one more contact with the broken ground, having to cross some crevasses and pass a big hole; but then it was done, and we could once more rejoice in having solid ice beneath us. Hanssen, however, was not satisfied till he had been to look into the hole. In the evening we reached the two snow-huts we had built on the last trip, and we camped there, twenty-six miles from the depot. The huts were drifted up with snow, so we left them in peace, and as the weather was now so mild and fine, we preferred the tent.

It had been an eventful day, and we had reason to be satisfied that we had come off so easily. The going had been good, and it had all gone like a game. When we started the next morning it was overcast and thick, and before we had gone very far we were in the midst of a south-wester, with snow so thick that we could hardly see ten sledge-lengths ahead of us. We had intended to reach the depot that day, but if this continued, it was more than doubtful whether we should find it. Meanwhile we put on the pace. It was a long

way on, so there was no danger of driving past it.
During this while it had remained clear in the zenith,
and we had been hoping that the wind and snow would
cease; but we had no such luck—it increased rather
than dropped.   Our best sledge-meter—one we knew
we could depend on—was on Wisting's sledge; therefore
he had to check the distance.   At 1.30 p.m. he turned
round to me, and pointed out that we had gone the exact
distance; I called out to Hanssen to use his eyes well.
Then, at that very moment, the depot showed up a few
sledge-lengths to the left of us, looking like a regular
palace of snow in the thick air.   This was a good test
both for the sledge-meter and the compass.   We drove
up to it and halted.   There were three important points
to be picked up on our way south, and one of them was
found; we were all glad and in good spirits.

The ninety-nine miles from Framheim to this point
had been covered in four marches, and we could now
rest our dogs, and give them as much seal's flesh as they
were capable of eating.   Thus far the trip had been a
good one for the animals; with one exception, they were
all in the best condition.   This exception was Uranus.
We had never been able to get any fat on his bones; he
remained thin and scraggy, and awaited his death at the
depot, a little later, in 82° S.   If Uranus was lanky to
look at, the same could not be said of Jaala, poor beast!
In spite of her condition, she struggled to keep up; she
did her utmost, but unless her dimensions were reduced

before we left 82° S., she would have to accompany Uranus to another world.

The cases of provisions and outfit that we had left here on the last trip were almost entirely snowed under, but it did not take long to dig them out. The first thing to be done was to cut up the seals for the dogs. These grand pieces of meat, with the blubber attached, did not have to be thrown at the dogs ; they just helped themselves as long as there was any meat cut up, and when that was finished, they did not hesitate to attack the " joint." It was a pleasure to see them, as they lay all over the place, enjoying their food ; it was all so delightfully calm and peaceful, to begin with. They were all hungry, and thought of nothing but satisfying their immediate cravings ; but when this was done there was an end of the truce. Although Hai had only half finished his share, he must needs go up to Rap and take away the piece he was eating. Of course, this could not happen without a great row, which resulted in the appearance of Hanssen ; then Hai made himself scarce. He was a fine dog, but fearfully obstinate ; if he had once taken a thing into his head, it was not easy to make him give it up. On one of our depot journeys it happened that I was feeding Hanssen's dogs. Hai had made short work of his pemmican, and looked round for more. Ah ! there was Rap enjoying his—that would just do for him. In a flash Hai was upon him, forced him to give up his dinner, and was about to convert it

to his own use.   Meanwhile I had witnessed the whole
scene, and before Hai knew anything about it, I was
upon him in turn.   I hit him over the nose with the
whip-handle, and tried to take the pemmican from him,
but it was not so easy.   Neither of us would give in,
and soon we were both rolling over and over in the
snow struggling for the mastery.   I came off victorious
after a pretty hot fight, and Rap got his dinner again.
Any other dog would have dropped it at once on being
hit over the nose, but not Hai.

It was a treat to get into the tent ; the day had been
a bitter one.   During the night the wind went round
to the north, and all the snow that had been blown
northward by the wind of the previous day had nothing
to do but to come back again ; the road was free.   And
it made the utmost use of its opportunity ; nothing
could be seen for driving snow when we turned out
next morning.   We could only stay where we were,
and console ourselves with the thought that it made no
difference, as it had been decided that we were to remain
here two days.   But staying in a tent all day is never
very amusing, especially when one is compelled to keep
to one's sleeping-bag the whole time.   You soon get
tired of talking, and you can't write all day long, either.
Eating is a good way of passing the time, if you can
afford it, and so is reading, if you have anything to
read ; but as the menu is limited, and the library as
a rule somewhat deficient on a sledging trip, these two

expedients fall to the ground. There is, however, one form of entertainment that may be indulged in under these circumstances without scruple, and that is a good nap. Happy the man who can sleep the clock round on days like these; but that is a gift that is not vouchsafed to all, and those who have it will not own up to it. I have heard men snore till I was really afraid they would choke, but as for acknowledging that they had been asleep—never! Some of them even have the coolness to assert that they suffer from sleeplessness, but it was not so bad as that with any of us.

In the course of the day the wind dropped, and we went out to do some work. We transferred the old depot to the new one. We now had here three complete sledge-loads, for which there would be little use, and which, therefore, were left behind. The eastern party availed themselves of part of these supplies on their journey, but not much. This depot is a fairly large one, and might come in useful if anyone should think of exploring the region from King Edward Land southward. As things were, we had no need of it. At the same time the sledges were packed, and when evening came everything was ready for our departure. There had really been no hurry about this, as we were going to stay here on the following day as well; but one soon learns in these regions that it is best to take advantage of good weather when you have it—you never know how long it will last. There was, however, nothing to be said

about the day that followed; we could doze and doze as
much as we liked. The work went on regularly, nevertheless. The dogs gnawed and gnawed, storing up
strength with every hour that went by.

We will now take a trip out to our loaded sledges,
and see what they contain. Hanssen's stands first, bow
to the south; behind it come Wisting's, Bjaaland's and
Hassel's. They all look pretty much alike, and as
regards provisions their loads are precisely similar.

Case No. 1 contains about 5,300 biscuits, and weighs
111 pounds.

Case No. 2: 112 rations of dogs' pemmican; 11 bags
of dried milk, chocolate, and biscuits. Total gross
weight, 177 pounds.

Case No. 3: 124 rations of dogs' pemmican; 10 bags
of dried milk and biscuits. Gross weight, 161 pounds.

Case No. 4: 39 rations of dogs' pemmican; 86 rations
of men's pemmican; 9 bags of dried milk and biscuits.
Gross weight, 165 pounds.

Case No. 5: 96 rations of dogs' pemmican. Weight,
122 pounds.

Total net weight of provisions per sledge, 668
pounds.

With the outfit and the weight of the sledge itself,
the total came to pretty nearly 880 pounds.

Hanssen's sledge differed from the others, in that it
had aluminium fittings instead of steel and no sledge-
meter, as it had to be free from iron on account of the

steering-compass he carried. Each of the other three sledges had a sledge-meter and compass. We were thus equipped with three sledge-meters and four compasses. The instruments we carried were two sextants and three artificial horizons—two glass and one mercury —a hypsometer for measuring heights, and one aneroid. For meteorological observations, four thermometers. Also two pairs of binoculars. We took a little travelling case of medicines from Burroughs Wellcome and Co. Our surgical instruments were not many: a dental forceps and—a beard-clipper. Our sewing outfit was extensive. We carried a small, very light tent in reserve; it would have to be used if any of us were obliged to turn back. We also carried two Primus lamps. Of paraffin we had a good supply: twenty-two and a half gallons divided among three sledges. We kept it in the usual cans, but they proved too weak; not that we lost any paraffin, but Bjaaland had to be constantly soldering to keep them tight. We had a good soldering outfit. Every man carried his own personal bag, in which he kept reserve clothing, diaries and observation books. We took a quantity of loose straps for spare ski-bindings. We had double sleeping-bags for the first part of the time; that is to say, an inner and an outer one. There were five watches among us, of which three were chronometer watches.

We had decided to cover the distance between 80° and 82° S. in daily marches of seventeen miles. We could easily have done twice this, but as it was more important to arrive than to show great speed, we limited the distance; besides which, here between the depots we had sufficient food to allow us to take our time. We were interested in seeing how the dogs would manage the loaded sledges. We expected them to do well, but not so well as they did.

On October 25 we left 80° S. with a light north-westerly breeze, clear and mild. I was now to take up my position in advance of the sledges, and placed myself a few paces in front of Hanssen's, with my ski pointing in the right direction. A last look behind me: "All ready?" and away I went. I thought—no; I didn't have time to think. Before I knew anything about it, I was sent flying by the dogs. In the confusion that ensued they stopped, luckily, so that I escaped without damage, as far as that went. To tell the truth, I was angry, but as I had sense enough to see that the situation, already sufficiently comic, would be doubly ridiculous if I allowed my annoyance to show itself, I wisely kept quiet. And, after all, whose fault was it? I was really the only one to blame; why in the world had I not got away faster? I now changed my plan entirely—there is nothing to be ashamed of in that, I hope—and fell in with the awkward squad; there I was more successful. "All ready? Go!" And go they did. First Hanssen went off like a meteor; close behind him came Wisting, and then Bjaaland and Hassel. They all had ski on, and were driving with a line. I had made up my mind to follow in the rear, as I thought the dogs would not keep this up for long, but I soon had enough of it. We did the first six and a quarter miles in an hour. I thought that would do for me, so I went up to Wisting, made a rope fast to his sledge, and there I stood till we reached 85° 5′ S.—three hundred and forty miles. Yes; that was a pleasant surprise. We had never dreamed of anything of the sort—driving on ski to the Pole! Thanks to Hanssen's brilliant talents as a dog-driver, we could easily do this. He had his dogs well in hand, and they knew their master. They knew that the moment they failed to do their duty they would be pulled up, and a hiding all round would follow. Of course, as always happens, Nature occasionally got the better of discipline; but the " confirmation " that resulted checked any repetition of such conduct for a long while. The day's march was soon completed in this way, and we camped early.

On the following day we were already in sight of the large pressure-ridges on the east, which we had seen for the first time on the second depot journey between 81° and 82° S., and this showed that the atmosphere must be very clear. We could not see any greater number than the first time, however. From our experience of beacons built of snow, we could see that if we built such beacons now, on our way south, they would be splendid marks for our return journey ; we therefore decided to adopt this system of landmarks to the greatest possible extent. We built in all 150 beacons, 6 feet high, and used in their construction 9,000 blocks, cut out of the snow with specially large snow-knives. In each of them was deposited a paper, giving the number and position of the beacon, and indicating the distance and the direction to be taken to reach the next beacon to the north. It may appear that my prudence was exaggerated, but it always seemed to me that one could not be too careful on this endless, uniform surface. If we lost our way here, it would be difficult enough to reach home. Besides which, the building of these beacons had other advantages, which we could all see and appreciate. Every time we stopped to build one, the dogs had a rest, and they wanted this, if they were to keep up the pace.

We erected the first beacon in 80° 23′ S. To begin with, we contented ourselves with putting them up at every thirteenth or fifteenth kilometre. On the 29th we shot the first dog, Hanssen's Bone. He was too old to keep up, and was only a hindrance. He was placed in depot under a beacon, and was a great joy to us—or rather to the dogs—later on.

On the same day we reached the second important point—the depot in 81° S. Our course took us very slightly to the east of it. The small pieces of packing-case that had been used as marks on each side of the depot could be seen a long way off. On a subsequent

examination they showed no sign of snowfall; they
stood just as they had been put in. In the neighbourhood of the depot we crossed two quite respectable
crevasses; they were apparently filled up, and caused us
no trouble. We reached the depot at 2 p.m.; everything was in the best of order. The flag was flying, and
hardly looked as if it had been up a day, although it had
now been waving there for nearly eight months. The
drifts round the depot were about $1\frac{1}{2}$ feet high.

The next day was brilliant—calm and clear. The
sun really baked the skin of one's face. We put all
our skin clothing out to dry; a little rime will always
form at the bottom of a sleeping-bag. We also availed
ourselves of this good opportunity to determine our
position and check our compasses; they proved to be
correct. We replaced the provisions we had consumed
on the way, and resumed our journey on October 31.

There was a thick fog next morning, and very disagreeable weather; perhaps we felt it more after the
previous fine day. When we passed this way for the
first time going south, Hanssen's dogs had fallen into
a crevasse, but it was nothing to speak of; otherwise
we had no trouble. Nor did we expect any this time;
but in these regions what one least expects frequently
happens. The snow was loose and the going heavy;
from time to time we crossed a narrow crevasse. Once
we saw through the fog a large open hole; we could not
have been very far from it, or we should not have seen

it, the weather was so thick. But all went well till we had
come thirteen and a half miles.   Then Hanssen had to
cross a crevasse a yard wide, and in doing it he was unlucky enough to catch the point of his ski in the traces
of the hindmost dogs, and fall right across the crevasse.
This looked unpleasant.   The dogs were across, and a
foot or two on the other side, but the sledge was right
over the crevasse, and had twisted as Hanssen fell, so that
a little more would bring it into line with the crevasse,
and then, of course, down it would go.   The dogs had
quickly scented the fact that their lord and master was
for the moment incapable of administering a " confirmation," and they did not let slip the golden opportunity.
Like a lot of roaring tigers, the whole team set upon each
other and fought till the hair flew.   This naturally produced short, sharp jerks at the traces, so that the sledge
worked round more and more, and at the same time the
dogs, in the heat of the combat, were coming nearer
and nearer to the brink.   If this went on, all was
irretrievably lost.   One of us jumped the crevasse,
went into the middle of the struggling team, and,
fortunately, got them to stop.   At the same time,
Wisting threw a line to Hanssen and hauled him out
of his unpleasant position—although, I thought to
myself, as we went on : I wonder whether Hanssen
did not enjoy the situation ? Stretched across a giddy
abyss, with the prospect of slipping down it at any
moment—that was just what he would like.   We

secured the sledge, completed our seventeen miles, and camped.

From 81° S. we began to erect beacons at every nine kilometres. The next day we observed the lowest temperature of the whole of this journey: —30·1° F The wind was south-south-east, but not very strong. It did not feel like summer, all the same. We now adopted the habit which we kept up all the way to the south—of taking our lunch while building the beacon that lay half-way in our day's march. It was nothing very luxurious—three or four dry oatmeal biscuits, that was all. If one wanted a drink, one could mix snow with the biscuit—"bread and water." It is a diet that is not much sought after in our native latitudes, but latitude makes a very great difference in this world. If anybody had offered us more "bread and water," we should gladly have accepted it.

That day we crossed the last crevasse for a long time to come, and it was only a few inches wide. The surface looked grand ahead of us; it went in very long, almost imperceptible undulations. We could only notice them by the way in which the beacons we put up often disappeared rather rapidly.

On November 2 we had a gale from the south, with heavy snow. The going was very stiff, but the dogs got the sledges along better than we expected. The temperature rose, as usual, with a wind from this quarter: +14° F. It was a pleasure to be out in such a temperature, although it did blow a little. The day after we had a light breeze from the north. The heavy going of the day before had completely disappeared; instead of it we had the best surface one could desire, and it made our dogs break into a brisk gallop. That was the day we were to reach the depot in 82° S., but as it was extremely thick, our chances of doing so were small. In the course of the afternoon the distance was accomplished, but no depot was visible. However, our range of vision was nothing to boast of—ten sledge-lengths; not more. The most sensible thing to do, under the circumstances, was to camp and wait till it cleared.

At four o'clock next morning the sun broke through. We let it get warm and disperse the fog, and then went out. What a morning it was—radiantly clear and mild. So still, so still lay the mighty desert before us, level and white on every side. But, no; there in the distance the level was broken: there was a touch of colour on the white. The third important point was reached, the extreme outpost of civilization. Our last depot lay before us; that was an unspeakable relief. The victory now seemed half won. In the fog we had come about three and a half miles too far to the west; but we now saw that if we had continued our march the day before, we should have come right into our line of flags. There they stood, flag after flag, and the little strip of black cloth seemed to wave quite proudly, as though it claimed credit for the way in which it had discharged its duty. Here, as at the depot in 81° S., there was hardly a sign of snowfall. The drift round the depot had reached the same height as there—1½ feet. Clearly the same conditions of weather had prevailed all over this region. The depot stood as we had made it, and the sledge as we had left it. Falling snow and drift had not been sufficient to cover even this. The little drift that there was offered an excellent place for the tent, being hard and firm. We at once set about the work that had to be done. First, Uranus was sent into the next world, and although he had always given us the impression of being thin and bony, it was now seen that there were masses of fat along his back; he would be much appreciated when we reached here on the return. Jaala did not look as if she would fulfil the conditions, but we gave her another night. The dogs' pemmican in the depot was just enough to give the dogs a good feed and load up the sledges again. We were so well supplied with all other provisions that we were able to leave a considerable quantity behind for the return journey.

Next day we stayed here to give the dogs a thorough rest for the last time. We took advantage of the fine weather to dry our outfit and check our instruments. When evening came we were all ready, and now we could look back with satisfaction to the good work of the autumn; we had fully accomplished what we aimed at—namely, transferring our base from 78° 38' to 82° S. Jaala had to follow Uranus; they were both laid on the top of the depot, beside eight little ones that never saw the light of day. During our stay here we decided to build beacons at every fifth kilometre, and to lay down depots at every degree of latitude. Although the dogs were drawing the sledges easily at present, we knew well enough that in the long-run they would find it hard work if they were always to have heavy weights to pull. The more we could get rid of, and the sooner we could begin to do so, the better.

On November 6, at 8 a.m., we left 82° S. Now the unknown lay before us; now our work began in earnest. The appearance of the Barrier was the same everywhere—flat, with a splendid surface. At the first beacon we put up we had to shoot Lucy. We were sorry to put an end to this beautiful creature, but there was nothing else to be done. Her friends—Karenius, Sauen, and Schwartz—scowled up at the beacon where she lay as they passed, but duty called, and the whip sang dangerously near them, though they did not seem to hear it. We had now extended our daily march to twenty-three miles; in this way we should do a degree in three days.

On the 7th we decided to stop for a day's rest. The dogs had been picking up wonderfully every day, and were now at the top of their condition, as far as health and training went. With the greatest ease they covered

DEPOT IN 83° S.

DEPOT IN 82° S.

the day's march at a pace of seven and a half kilometres (four miles and two-thirds) an hour. As for ourselves, we never had to move a foot; all we had to do was to let ourselves be towed. The same evening we had to put an end to the last of our ladies—Else. She was Hassel's pride and the ornament of his team; but there was no help for it. She was also placed at the top of a beacon.

When we halted that evening in 82° 20′ S., we saw on the south-western horizon several heavy masses of drab-coloured cloud, such as are usually to be seen over land. We could make out no land that evening, however; but when we came out next morning and directed our glasses to that quarter, the land lay there, lofty and clear in the morning sun. We were now able to distinguish several summits, and to determine that this was the land extending south-eastward from Beardmore Glacier in South Victoria Land. Our course had been true south all the time; at this spot we were about 250 miles to the east of Beardmore Glacier. Our course would continue to be true south.

The same evening—November 8—we reached 83° S. by dead reckoning. The noon altitude next day gave 83° 1′ S. The depot we built here contained provisions for five men and twelve dogs for four days; it was made square—6 feet each way—of hard, solid blocks of snow. A large flag was placed on the top. That evening a strange thing happened—three dogs deserted, going northward on our old tracks. They were Lucy's favourites, and had probably taken it into their heads that they ought to go back and look after their friend. It was a great loss to us all, but especially to Bjaaland; they were all three first-rate animals, and among the best we had. He had to borrow a dog from Hanssen's team, and if he did not go quite so smoothly as before, he was still able to keep up.

On the 10th we got a bearing of the mountain chain right down in south by west true. Each day we drew considerably nearer the land, and could see more and more of its details: mighty peaks, each loftier and wilder than the last, rose to heights of 15,000 feet. What struck us all were the bare sides that many of these mountains showed; we had expected to see them far more covered with snow. Mount Fridtjof Nansen, for example, had quite a blue-black look. Only quite at the summit was it crowned by a mighty hood of ice that raised its shining top to some 15,000 feet. Farther to the south rose Mount Don Pedro Christophersen; it was more covered with snow, but the long, gabled summit was to a great extent bare. Still farther south Mounts Alice Wedel Jarlsberg, Alice Gade, and Ruth Gade, came in sight; all snow-clad from peak to base. I do not think I have ever seen a more beautiful or wilder landscape. Even from where we were, we seemed to be able to see a way up from several places. There lay Liv's Glacier,* for instance, which would

* Named after Dr. Nansen's daughter.—Tr.

undoubtedly afford a good and even ascent, but it lay too far to the north. It is of enormous extent, and would prove interesting to explore. Crown Prince Olav's Mountains looked less promising, but they also lay too far to the north. A little to the west of south lay an apparently good way up. The mountains nearest to the Barrier did not seem to offer any great obstruction. What one might find later, between Mounts Pedro Christophersen and Fridtjof Nansen, was not easy to say.

On the 12th we reached 84° S. On that day we made the interesting discovery of a chain of mountains running to the east; this, as it appeared from the spot where we were, formed a semicircle, where it joined the mountains of South Victoria Land. This semicircle lay true south, and our course was directed straight towards it.

In the depot in 84° S. we left, besides the usual quantity of provisions for five men and twelve dogs for four days, a can of paraffin, holding 17 litres (about 3¾ gallons). We had abundance of matches, and could therefore distribute them over all the depots. The Barrier continued as flat as before, and the going was as good as it could possibly be. We had thought that a day's rest would be needed by the dogs for every degree of latitude, but this proved superfluous; it looked as if they could no longer be tired. One or two had shown signs of bad feet, but were now perfectly well; instead of losing strength, the dogs seemed to become stronger and more

active every day.   Now they, too, had sighted the land,
and the black mass of Mount Fridtjof Nansen seemed
specially to appeal to them; Hanssen often had hard
work to keep them in the right course.   Without any
longer stay, then, we left 84° S. the next day, and steered
for the bay ahead.

That day we went twenty-three miles in thick fog,
and saw nothing of the land.   It was hard to have to
travel thus blindly off an unknown coast, but we could
only hope for better weather.   During the previous
night we had heard, for a change, a noise in the ice.   It
was nothing very great, and sounded like scattered
infantry fire—a few rifle-shots here and there underneath
our tent; the artillery had not come up yet.   We took
no notice of it, though I heard one man say in the
morning: "Blest if I didn't think I got a whack on the
ear last night."   I could witness that it had not cost
him his sleep, as that night he had very nearly snored us
all out of the tent.   During the forenoon we crossed
a number of apparently newly-formed crevasses; most
of them only about an inch wide.   There had thus
been a small local disturbance occasioned by one of the
numerous small glaciers on land.   On the following
night all was quiet again, and we never afterwards heard
the slightest sound.

On November 14 we reached 84° 40' S.   We were
now rapidly approaching land; the mountain range on
the east appeared to turn north-eastward.   Our line of

ascent, which we had chosen long ago and now had our eyes fixed upon as we went, would take us a trifle to the west of south, but so little that the digression was of no account. The semicircle we saw to the south made a more disquieting impression, and looked as if it would offer great irregularities. On the following day the character of the surface began to change ; great wave-like formations seemed to roll higher and higher as they approached the land, and in one of the troughs of these we found the surface greatly disturbed. At some bygone time immense fissures and chasms would have rendered its passage practically impossible, but now they were all drifted up, and we had no difficulty in crossing.

That day—November 15—we reached 85° S., and camped at the top of one of these swelling waves. The valley we were to cross next day was fairly broad, and rose considerably on the other side. On the west, in the direction of the nearest land, the undulation rose to such a height that it concealed a great part of the land from us. During the afternoon we built the usual depot, and continued our journey on the following day. As we had seen from our camping-ground, it was an immense undulation that we had to traverse ; the ascent on the other side felt uncomfortably warm in the powerful sun, but it was no higher than 300 feet by the aneroid. From the top of this wave the Barrier stretched away before us, flat at first, but we could see disturbances of the surface in the distance. Now we are going to have some fun in getting to land, I thought, for it seemed very natural that the Barrier, hemmed in as it was here, would be much broken up. The disturbances we had seen consisted of some big, old crevasses, which were partly filled up; we avoided them easily. Now there was another deep depression before us, with a correspondingly high rise on the other side. We went over it capitally; the surface was absolutely smooth, without a sign of fissure or hole anywhere. Then we shall get them when we are on the top, I thought. It was rather stiff work uphill, unaccustomed as we were to slopes. I stretched my neck more and more to get a view. At last we were up; and what a sight it was that met us! Not an irregularity, not a sign of disturbance; quietly and evenly the ascent continued. I believe that we were then already above land; the large crevasses that we had avoided down below probably formed the boundary. The hypsometer gave 930 feet above the sea.

We were now immediately below the ascent, and made the final decision of trying it here. This being settled, we pitched our camp. It was still early in the day, but we had a great deal to arrange before the morrow. Here we should have to overhaul our whole supply of provisions, take with us what was absolutely necessary for the remainder of the trip, and leave the rest behind in depot. First, then, we camped,

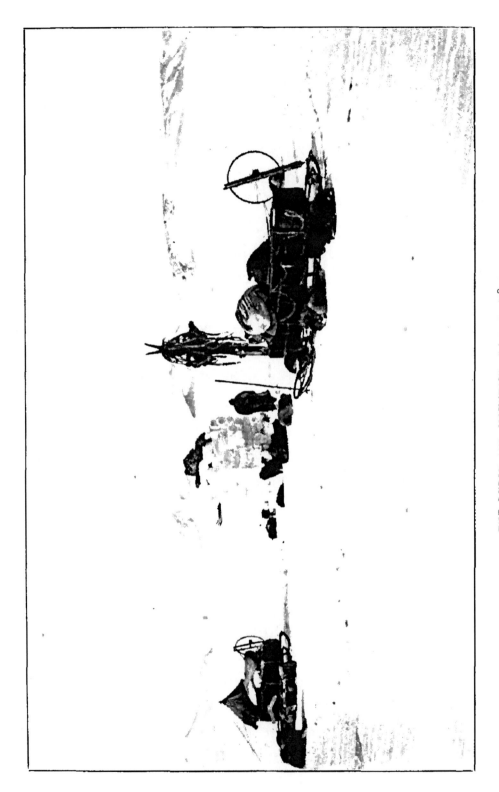

THE DEPOT AND MOUNTAINS IN LAT. 85° S.

worked out our position, fed the dogs and let them
loose again, and then went into our tent to have
something to eat and go through the provision
books.

We had now reached one of the most critical points
of our journey. Our plan had now to be laid so that
we might not only make the ascent as easily as possible,
but also get through to the end. Our calculations had
to be made carefully, and every possibility taken into
account. As with every decision of importance, we
discussed the matter jointly. The distance we had
before us, from this spot to the Pole and back, was
683 miles. Reckoning with the ascent that we saw
before us, with other unforeseen obstructions, and finally
with the certain factor that the strength of our dogs
would be gradually reduced to a fraction of what it now
was, we decided to take provisions and equipment for
sixty days on the sledges, and to leave the remaining
supplies—enough for thirty days—and outfit in depot.
We calculated, from the experience we had had, that
we ought to be able to reach this point again with
twelve dogs left. We now had forty-two dogs. Our
plan was to take all the forty-two up to the plateau;
there twenty-four of them were to be slaughtered, and
the journey continued with three sledges and eighteen
dogs. Of these last eighteen, it would be necessary, in
our opinion, to slaughter six in order to bring the other
twelve back to this point. As the number of dogs grew

less, the sledges would become lighter and lighter, and when the time came for reducing their number to twelve, we should only have two sledges left. This time again our calculations came out approximately right; it was only in reckoning the number of days that we made a little mistake—we took eight days less than the time allowed. The number of dogs agreed exactly; we reached this point again with twelve.

After the question had been well discussed and each had given his opinion, we went out to get the repacking done. It was lucky the weather was so fine, otherwise this taking stock of provisions might have been a bitter piece of work. All our supplies were in such a form that we could count them instead of weighing them. Our pemmican was in rations of $\frac{1}{2}$ kilogram (1 pound $1\frac{1}{2}$ ounces). The chocolate was divided into small pieces, as chocolate always is, so that we knew what each piece weighed. Our milk-powder was put up in bags of $10\frac{1}{2}$ ounces—just enough for a meal. Our biscuits possessed the same property—they could be counted, but this was a tedious business, as they were rather small. On this occasion we had to count 6,000 biscuits. Our provisions consisted only of these four kinds, and the combination turned out right enough. We did not suffer from a craving either for fat or sugar, though the want of these substances is very commonly felt on such journeys as ours. In our biscuits we had an excellent product, consisting of oatmeal, sugar, and dried milk. Sweetmeats, jam, fruit, cheese, etc., we had left behind at Framheim.

We took our reindeer-skin clothing, for which we had had no use as yet, on the sledges. We were now coming on to the high ground, and it might easily happen that it would be a good thing to have. We did not forget the temperature of $-40°$ F. that Shackleton had experienced in $88°$ S., and if we met with the same, we could hold out a long while if we had the skin clothing. Otherwise, we had not very much in our bags. The only change we had with us was put on here, and the old clothes hung out to air. We reckoned that by the time we came back, in a couple of months, they would be sufficiently aired, and we could put them on again. As far as I remember, the calculation proved correct. We took more foot-gear than anything else: if one's feet are well shod, one can hold out a long time.

When all this was finished, three of us put on our ski and made for the nearest visible land. This was a little peak, a mile and three-quarters away—Mount Betty. It did not look lofty or imposing, but was, nevertheless, 1,000 feet above the sea. Small as it was, it became important to us, as it was there we got all our geological specimens. Running on ski felt quite strange, although I had now covered 385 miles on them; but we had driven the whole way, and were somewhat out of training. We could feel this, too, as we went up the slope

that afternoon.   After Mount Betty the ascent became
rather steep, but the surface was even, and the going
splendid, so we got on fast.   First we came up a smooth
mountain-side, about 1,200 feet above the sea, then
over a little plateau ; after that another smooth slope like
the first, and then down a rather long, flat stretch, which
after a time began to rise very gradually, until it finally
passed into small glacier formations.   Our reconnaissance extended to these small glaciers.   We had ascertained that the way was practicable, as far as we were
able to see ; we had gone about five and a half miles
from the tent, and ascended 2,000 feet.   On the way
back we went gloriously ; the last two slopes down to
the Barrier gave us all the speed we wanted.   Bjaaland
and I had decided to take a turn round by Mount Betty
for the sake of having real bare ground under our feet ;
we had not felt it since Madeira in September, 1910,
and now we were in November, 1911.   No sooner said
than done.   Bjaaland prepared for an elegant " Telemark swing," and executed it in fine style.   What I
prepared to do, I am still not quite sure.   What I did
was to roll over, and I did it with great effect.   I was
very soon on my feet again, and glanced at Bjaaland ;
whether he had seen my tumble, I am not certain.
However, I pulled myself together after this unfor-
tunate performance, and remarked casually that it is
not so easy to forget what one has once learnt.   No
doubt he thought that I had managed the " Telemark

ASCENDING MOUNT BETTY.

swing "; at any rate, he was polite enough to let me think so.

Mount Betty offered no perpendicular crags or deep precipices to stimulate our desire for climbing ; we only had to take off our ski, and then we arrived at the top. It consisted of loose screes, and was not an ideal promenade for people who had to be careful of their boots. It was a pleasure to set one's foot on bare ground again, and we sat down on the rocks to enjoy the scene. The rocks very soon made themselves felt, however, and brought us to our feet again. We photographed each other in "picturesque attitudes," took a few stones for those who had not yet set foot on bare earth, and strapped on our ski. The dogs, after having been so eager to make for bare land when they first saw it, were now not the least interested in it ; they lay on the snow, and did not go near the top. Between the bare ground and the snow surface there was bright, blue-green ice, showing that at times there was running water here. The dogs did what they could to keep up with us on the way down, but they were soon left behind. On our return, we surprised our comrades with presents from the country, but I fear they were not greatly appreciated. I could hear such words as, " Norway—stones —heaps of them," and I was able to put them together and understand what was meant. The " presents " were put in depot, as not absolutely indispensable on the southern journey.

By this time the dogs had already begun to be very voracious. Everything that came in their way disappeared ; whips, ski-bindings, lashings, etc., were regarded as delicacies. If one put down anything for a moment, it vanished. With some of them this voracity went so far that we had to chain them.

CHAPTER XI

THROUGH THE MOUNTAINS

ON the following day—November 17—we began the ascent. To provide for any contingency, I left in the depot a paper with information of the way we intended to take through the mountains, together with our plan for the future, our outfit, provisions, etc. The weather was fine, as usual, and the going good. The dogs exceeded our expectations ; they negotiated the two fairly steep slopes at a jog-trot. We began to think there was no difficulty they could not surmount ; the five miles or so that we had gone the day before, and imagined would be more than enough for this day's journey, were now covered with full loads in shorter time. The small glaciers higher up turned out fairly steep, and in some places we had to take two sledges at a time with double teams. These glaciers had an appearance of being very old, and of having entirely ceased to move. There were no new crevasses to be seen ; those that there were, were large and wide, but their edges were rounded off everywhere, and the crevasses themselves were almost entirely filled with snow. So as not to fall into these on the return, we erected our beacons in such a way that the line between any two of them would take us clear of any danger. It was no use working in Polar clothing among these hills; the sun, which stood high and clear, was uncomfortably warm, and we were obliged to take off most of our things. We passed several summits from 3,000 to 7,000 feet high ; the snow on one of them had quite a reddish-brown tint.

Our distance this first day was eleven and a half miles, with a rise of 2,000 feet. Our camp that evening lay on a little glacier among huge crevasses ; on three sides of us were towering summits. When we had set our tent, two parties went out to explore the way in advance. One party—Wisting and Hanssen—took the way that looked easiest from the tent—namely, the course of the glacier; it here rose rapidly to 4,000 feet, and disappeared in a south-westerly direction between two peaks. Bjaaland formed the other party. He evidently looked upon this ascent as too tame, and started up the steepest part of the mountain-side. I saw him disappear up aloft like a fly. Hassel and I attended to the necessary work round about and in the tent.

We were sitting inside chatting, when we suddenly heard someone come swishing down towards the tent. We looked at each other; that fellow had some pace on. We had no doubt as to who it was—Bjaaland, of course.

He must have gone off to refresh old memories. He had a lot to tell us; amongst other things, he had found "the finest descent" on the other side. What he meant by "fine" I was not certain. If it was as fine as the ascent he had made, then I asked to be excused. We now heard the others coming, and these we could hear a long way off. They had also seen a great deal, not to mention "the finest descent." But both parties agreed in the mournful intelligence that we should have to go down again. They had both observed the immense glacier that stretched beneath us running east and west. A lengthy discussion took place between the two parties, who mutually scorned each other's "discoveries." "Yes; but look here, Bjaaland, we could see that from where you were standing there's a sheer drop——"—"You couldn't see me at all. I tell you I was to the west of the peak that lies to the south of the peak that——" I gave up trying to follow the discussion any longer. The way in which the different parties had disappeared and come in sight again gave me every reason to decide in favour of the route the last arrivals had taken. I thanked these keen gentlemen for their strenuous ramble in the interests of the expedition, and went straight off to sleep. I dreamed of mountains and precipices all night, and woke up with Bjaaland whizzing down from the sky. I announced once more that I had made up my mind for the other course, and went to sleep again.

We debated next morning whether it would not be better to take the sledges two by two to begin with; the glacier before us looked quite steep enough to require double teams. It had a rise of 2,000 feet in quite a short distance. But we would try first with the single teams. The dogs had shown that their capabilities were far above our expectation; perhaps they would be able to do even this. We crept off. The ascent began at once—good exercise after a quart of chocolate. We did not get on fast, but we won our way. It often looked as if the sledge would stop, but a shout from the driver and a sharp crack of the whip kept the dogs on the move. It was a fine beginning to the day, and we gave them a well-deserved rest when we got up. We then drove in through the narrow pass and out on the other side. It was a magnificent panorama that opened before us. From the pass we had come out on to a very small flat terrace, which a few yards farther on began to drop steeply to a long valley. Round about us lay summit after summit on every side. We had now come behind the scenes, and could get our bearings better. We now saw the southern side of the immense Mount Nansen; Don Pedro Christophersen we could see in his full length. Between these two mountains we could follow the course of a glacier that rose in terraces along their sides. It looked fearfully broken and disturbed, but we could follow a little connected line among the many crevasses; we saw that we could go a long way, but we also saw that the glacier forbade us to use it in its full extent. Between the first and second terraces the ice was evidently impassable. But we could see that there was an unbroken ledge up on the side of the mountain; *Don Pedro would help us out.* On the north along the Nansen Mountain there was nothing but chaos, perfectly impossible to get through. We put up a big beacon where we were standing, and took bearings from it all round the compass.

I went back to the pass to look out over the Barrier for the last time. The new mountain chain lay there sharp and clear; we could see how it turned from the east up to east-north-east, and finally disappeared in the north-east—as we judged, about 84° S. From the look of the sky, it appeared that the chain was continued farther. According to the aneroid, the height of the terrace on which we stood was 4,000 feet above the sea. From here there was only one way down, and we began to go. In making these descents with loaded sledges, one has to use the greatest care, lest the speed increase to such a degree that one loses command over the sledge. If this happens, there is a danger, not only of running over the dogs, but of colliding with the sledge in front and smashing it. This was all the more important in our case, as the sledges carried sledge-meters. We therefore put brakes of rope under our runners when we were to go downhill. This was done very simply by taking a few turns with a thin piece of rope round each runner; the more of these turns one took, the more powerful, of course, was the brake. The art consisted in choosing the right number of turns, or the right brake; this was not always attained, and the consequence was that, before we had come to the end of these descents, there were several collisions. One of the drivers, in particular, seemed to have a supreme contempt for a proper brake; he would rush down like a flash of lightning, and carry the man in front with him. With practice we avoided this, but several times things had an ugly look.

The first drop took us down 800 feet; then we had to cross a wide, stiff piece of valley before the ascent began again. The snow between the mountains was loose and deep, and gave the dogs hard work. The next ascent was up very steep glaciers, the last of which was the steepest bit of climbing we had on the whole journey—stiff work even for double teams. Going in front of the dogs up these slopes was, I could see, a business that Bjaaland would accomplish far more satisfactorily than I, and I gave up the place to him. The first glacier was steep, but the second was like the side of a house. It was a pleasure to watch Bjaaland use his ski up there; one could see that he had been up a hill before. Nor was it less interesting to see the dogs and the drivers go up. Hanssen drove one sledge alone; Wisting and Hassel the other. They went by jerks, foot by foot, and ended by reaching the top. The second relay went somewhat more easily in the tracks made by the first.

Our height here was 4,550 feet, the last ascent having brought us up 1,250 feet ; we had arrived on a plateau, and after the dogs had rested we continued our march. Now, as we advanced, we had a better view of the way we were going ; before this the nearest mountains had shut us in. The mighty glacier opened out before us, stretching, as we could now see, right up from the Barrier between the lofty mountains running east and west. It was by this glacier that we should have to gain the plateau ; we could see that. We had one more descent to make before reaching it, and from above we could distinguish the edges of some big gaps in this descent, and found it prudent to examine it first. As we thought, there was a side-glacier coming down into it, with large, ugly crevasses in many places ; but it was not so bad as to prevent our finally reaching, with caution and using good brakes, the great main ice-field—Axel Heiberg Glacier. The plan we had proposed to ourselves was to work our way up to the place where the glacier rose in abrupt masses between the two mountains. The task we had undertaken was greater than we thought. In the first place, the distance was three times as great as any of us had believed ; and, in the second place, the snow was so loose and deep that it was hard work for the dogs after all their previous efforts. We set our course along the

white line that we had been able to follow among the
numerous crevasses right up to the first terrace.   Here
tributary glaciers came down on all sides from the
mountains and joined the main one; it was one of
these many small arms that we reached that evening,
directly under Don Pedro Christophersen.

The mountain below which we had our camp was
covered with a chaos of immense blocks of ice.   The
glacier on which we were was much broken up, but, as
with all the others, the fissures were of old date, and,
to a large extent, drifted up.   The snow was so loose
that we had to trample a place for the tent, and we
could push the tent-pole right down without meeting
resistance; probably it would be better higher up.   In
the evening Hanssen and Bjaaland went out to reconnoitre, and found the conditions as we had seen them
from a distance.   The way up to the first terrace was
easily accessible; what the conditions would be like
between this and the second terrace we had still to
discover.

It was stiff work next day getting up to the first
terrace.   The arm of the glacier that led up was not
very long, but extremely steep and full of big crevasses;
it had to be taken in relays, two sledges at a time.
The state of the going was, fortunately, better than on
the previous day, and the surface of the glacier was
fine and hard, so that the dogs got a splendid hold.
Bjaaland went in advance up through this steep glacier,

and had his work cut out to keep ahead of the eager
animals. One would never have thought we were
between 85° and 86° S.; the heat was positively disagreeable, and, although lightly clad, we sweated as if we
were running races in the tropics. We were ascending
rapidly, but, in spite of the sudden change of pressure,
we did not yet experience any difficulty of breathing,
headache, or other unpleasant results. That these
sensations would make their appearance in due course
was, however, a matter of which we could be certain.
Shackleton's description of his march on the plateau,
when headache of the most violent and unpleasant kind
was the order of the day, was fresh in the memory of
all of us.

In a comparatively short time we reached the ledge
in the glacier that we had noticed a long way off; it
was not quite flat, but sloped slightly towards the edge.
When we came to the place to which Hanssen and
Bjaaland had carried their reconnaissance on the previous
evening, we had a very fine prospect of the further
course of the glacier. To continue along it was an
impossibility; it consisted here—between the two vast
mountains—of nothing but crevasse after crevasse, so
huge and ugly that we were forced to conclude that
our further advance that way was barred. Over by
Fridtjof Nansen we could not go; this mountain
here rose perpendicularly, in parts quite bare, and
formed with the glacier a surface so wild and cut up

that all thoughts of crossing the ice-field in that direction had to be instantly abandoned. Our only chance lay in the direction of Don Pedro Christophersen; here, so far as we could see, the connection of the glacier and the land offered possibilities of further progress. Without interruption the glacier was merged in the snow-clad mountain-side, which rose rapidly towards the partially bare summit. Our view, however, did not extend very far. The first part of the mountain-side was soon bounded by a lofty ridge running east and west, in which we could see huge gaps here and there. From the place where we were standing, we had the impression that we should be able to continue our course up there under the ridge between these gaps, and thus come out beyond the disturbed tract of glacier. We might possibly succeed in this, but we could not be certain until we were up on the ridge itself.

We took a little rest—it was not a long one—and then started. We were impatient to see whether we could get forward up above. There could be no question of reaching the height without double teams; first we had to get Hanssen's and Wisting's sledges up, and then the two others. We were not particularly keen on thus covering the ground twice, but the conditions made it imperative. We should have been pleased just then if we had known that this was to be the last ascent that would require double teams; but we did not know this, and it was more than any of us dared to hope. The

MOUNT FRIDTJOF NANSEN, 15,000 FEET ABOVE THE SEA.

To face page 50, Vol. II.

same hard work, and the same trouble to keep the dogs at an even pace, and then we were up under the ridge amongst the open chasms. To go farther without a careful examination of the ground was not to be thought of. Doubtless, our day's march had not been a particularly long one, but the piece we had covered had indeed been fatiguing enough. We therefore camped, and set our tent at an altitude of 5,650 feet above the sea.

We at once proceeded to reconnoitre, and the first thing to be examined was the way we had seen from below. This led in the right direction—that is, in the direction of the glacier, east and west—and was thus the shortest. But it is not always the shortest way that is the best ; here, in any case, it was to be hoped that another and longer one would offer better conditions. The shortest way was awful—possibly not altogether impracticable, if no better was to be found. First we had to work our way across a hard, smooth slope, which formed an angle of 45 degrees, and ended in a huge, bottomless chasm. It was no great pleasure to cross over here on ski, but with heavily-laden sledges the enjoyment would be still less. The prospect of seeing sledge, driver, and dogs slide down sideways and disappear into the abyss was a great one. We got across with whole skins on ski, and continued our exploration. The mountain-side along which we were advancing gradually narrowed between vast fissures above and vaster fissures below, and finally passed by a very narrow bridge—hardly broader than the sledges—into the glacier. On each side of the bridge, one looked down into a deep blue chasm. To cross here did not look very inviting ; no doubt we could take the dogs out and haul the sledges over, and thus manage it—presuming the bridge held— but our further progress, which would have to be made on the glacier, would apparently offer many surprises of an unpleasant kind. It was quite possible that, with time and patience, one would be able to tack through the apparently endless succession of deep crevasses ; but we should first have to see whether something better than this could not be found in another direction. We therefore returned to camp.

Here in the meantime everything had been put in order, the tent set up, and the dogs fed. Now came the great question : What was there on the other side of the ridge ? Was it the same desperate confusion, or would the ground offer better facilities ? Three of us went off to see. Excitement rose as we neared the saddle ; so much depended on finding a reasonable way. One more pull and we were up ; it was worth the trouble. The first glance showed us that this was the way we had to go. The mountain-side ran smooth and even under the lofty summit—like a gabled church tower — of Mount Don Pedro Christophersen, and followed the direction of the glacier. We could see the place where this long, even surface united with the glacier; to all appearance it was free from disturbance. We saw some crevasses, of course, but they were far apart, and did not give us the idea that they would be a hindrance. But we were still too far from the spot to be able to draw any certain conclusions as to the character of the ground; we therefore set off towards the bottom to examine the conditions more closely. The surface was loose up here, and the snow fairly deep; our ski slipped over it well, but it would be heavy for dogs. We advanced rapidly, and soon came to the huge crevasses. They were big enough and deep enough, but so scattered that, without much trouble, we could find a way between them. The hollow between the two mountains, which was filled by the Heiberg Glacier, grew narrower and narrower towards the end, and, although appearances were still very pleasant, I expected to find some disturbance when we arrived at the point where the mountain-side passed into the glacier. But my fears proved groundless; by keeping right under Don Pedro we went clear of all trouble, and in a short time, to our great joy, we found ourselves above and beyond that chaotic part of the Heiberg Glacier which had completely barred our progress.

Up here all was strangely peaceful; the mountain-side and the glacier united in a great flat terrace—a plain, one might call it—without disturbance of any kind. We could see depressions in the surface where the huge crevasses had formerly existed, but now they were entirely filled up, and formed one with the surrounding level. We could now see right to the end of this mighty glacier, and form some idea of its proportions. Mount Wilhelm Christophersen and Mount Ole Engelstad formed the end of it ; these two beehive-shaped summits, entirely covered with snow, towered high into the sky. We understood now that the last of the ascent was before us, and that what we saw in the distance between these two mountains was the great plateau itself. The question, then, was to find a way up, and to conquer this last obstruction in the easiest manner. In the radiantly clear air we could see the smallest details with our excellent prismatic glasses, and make our calculations with great confidence. It would be possible to clamber up Don Pedro himself; we had done things as difficult before. But here the side of the mountain was fairly steep, and full of big crevasses and a fearful quantity of gigantic blocks of ice. Between Don Pedro and Wilhelm Christophersen an arm of the glacier went up on to the plateau, but it was so disturbed and broken up that it could not be used. Between Wilhelm Christophersen and Ole Engelstad there was no means of getting through. Between Ole Engelstad and Fridtjof Nansen, on the other hand, it looked more promising, but as yet the first of these mountains obstructed our view so much that we could not decide with certainty. We were all three rather tired, but agreed to continue our excursion, and find out what was here concealed. Our work to-day would make our progress to-morrow so much the easier. We therefore went on, and laid our course straight over the topmost flat terrace of the Heiberg Glacier. As we advanced, the ground between Nansen and Engelstad opened out more and more, and without going any farther we were able to decide from the formations that here we should undoubtedly find the best way up. If the final ascent at the end of the glacier, which was only partly visible, should present difficulties, we could make out from where we stood that it would be possible, without any great trouble, to work our way over the upper end of the Nansen Mountain itself, which here passed into the plateau by a not too difficult glacier. Yes, now we were certain that it was indeed the great plateau and nothing else that we saw before us. In the pass between the two mountains, and some little distance within the plateau, Helland Hansen showed up, a very curious peak to look at. It seemed to stick its nose up through the plateau, and no more; its shape was long, and it reminded one of nothing so much as the ridge of a roof. Although this peak was thus only just visible, it stood 11,000 feet above the sea.

After we had examined the conditions here, and found out that on the following day—if the weather permitted—we should reach the plateau, we turned back, well satisfied with the result of our trip. We all agreed that we were tired, and longing to reach camp and get some food. The place where we turned was, according to the aneroid, 8,000 feet above the sea; we were therefore 2,500 feet higher than our tent down on the hill-side. Going down in our old tracks was easier work, though the return journey was somewhat monotonous. In many places the slope was rapid, and not a few fine runs were made. On approaching our camping-ground we had the sharpest descent, and here, reluctant as we might be, we found it wiser to put both our poles together and form a strong brake. We came down smartly enough, all the same. It was a grand and imposing sight we had when we came out on the ridge under which—far below—our tent stood. Surrounded on all sides by huge crevasses and gaping chasms, it could not be said that the site of our camp looked very inviting. The wildness of the landscape seen from this point is not to be described; chasm after chasm, crevasse after crevasse, with great blocks of ice scattered promiscuously about, gave one the impression that here Nature was too powerful for us. Here no progress was to be thought of.

It was not without a certain satisfaction that we stood there and contemplated the scene. The little dark speck down there—our tent—in the midst of this chaos, gave us a feeling of strength and power. We knew in our hearts that the ground would have to be ugly indeed if we were not to manœuvre our way across it and find a place for that little home of ours. Crash upon crash,

roar upon roar, met our ears. Now it was a shot from
Mount Nansen, now from one of the others; we could
see the clouds of snow rise high into the air. It was
evident that these mountains were throwing off their
winter mantles and putting on a more spring-like garb.

We came at a tearing pace down to the tent, where
our companions had everything in most perfect order.
The dogs lay snoring in the heat of the sun, and hardly
condescended to move when we came scudding in among
them. Inside the tent a regular tropical heat prevailed;
the sun was shining directly on to the red cloth and
warming it. The Primus hummed and hissed, and the
pemmican-pot bubbled and spurted. We desired nothing
better in the world than to get in, fling ourselves down,
eat, and drink. The news we brought was no trifling
matter—the plateau to-morrow. It sounded almost too
good to be true; we had reckoned that it would take us
ten days to get up, and now we should do it in four. In
this way we saved a great deal of dog food, as we should
be able to slaughter the superfluous animals six days
earlier than we had calculated. It was quite a little
feast that evening in the tent; not that we had any
more to eat than usual—we could not allow ourselves
that—but the thought of the fresh dog cutlets that
awaited us when we got to the top made our mouths
water. In course of time we had so habituated
ourselves to the idea of the approaching slaughter that
this event did not appear to us so horrible as it would

otherwise have done. Judgment had already been pronounced, and the selection made of those who were worthy of prolonged life and those who were to be sacrificed. This had been, I may add, a difficult problem to solve, so efficient were they all.

The rumblings continued all night, and one avalanche after another exposed parts of the mountain-sides that had been concealed from time immemorial. The following day, November 20, we were up and away at the usual time, about 8 a.m. The weather was splendid, calm and clear. Getting up over the saddle was a rough beginning of the day for our dogs, and they gave a good account of themselves, pulling the sledges up with single teams this time. The going was heavy, as on the preceding day, and our advance through the loose snow was not rapid. We did not follow our tracks of the day before, but laid our course directly for the place where we had decided to attempt the ascent. As we approached Mount Ole Engelstad, under which we had to pass in order to come into the arm of the glacier between it and Mount Nansen, our excitement began to rise. What does the end look like? Does the glacier go smoothly on into the plateau, or is it broken up and impassable? We rounded Mount Engelstad more and more ; wider and wider grew the opening. The surface looked extremely good as it gradually came into view, and it did not seem as though our assumption of the previous day would be put to shame. At last the whole landscape opened out, and without obstruction of any kind whatever the last part of the ascent lay before us. It was both long and steep from the look of it, and we agreed to take a little rest before beginning the final attack.

We stopped right under Mount Engelstad in a warm and sunny place, and allowed ourselves on this occasion a little lunch, an indulgence that had not hitherto been permitted. The cooking-case was taken out, and soon the Primus was humming in a way that told us it would not be long before the chocolate was ready. It was a heavenly treat, that drink. We had all walked ourselves warm, and our throats were as dry as tinder. The contents of the pot were served round by the cook— Hanssen. It was no use asking him to share alike; he could not be persuaded to take more than half of what was due to him—the rest he had to divide among his comrades. The drink he had prepared this time was what he called chocolate, but I had some difficulty in believing him. He was economical, was Hanssen, and permitted no extravagance; that could be seen very well by his chocolate. Well, after all, to people who were accustomed to regard "bread and water" as a luxury, it tasted, as I have said, heavenly. It was the liquid part of the lunch that was served extra; if any-one wanted something to eat, he had to provide it himself—nothing was offered him. Happy was he who had saved some biscuits from his breakfast!

Our halt was not a very long one. It is a queer thing that, when one only has on light underclothing and windproof overalls, one cannot stand still for long without feeling cold. Although the temperature was no lower than $-4°$ F., we were glad to be on the move again. The last ascent was fairly hard work, especially the first half of it. We never expected to do it with single teams, but tried it all the same. For this last pull up I must give the highest praise both to the dogs and their drivers; it was a brilliant performance on both sides. 1 can still see the situation clearly before me. The dogs seemed positively to understand that this was the last big effort that was asked of them; they lay flat down and hauled, dug their claws in and dragged themselves forward. But they had to stop and get breath pretty often, and then the driver's strength was put to the test. It is no child's play to set a heavily-laden sledge in motion time after time. How they toiled, men and beasts, up that slope! But they got on, inch by inch, until the steepest part was behind them. Before them lay the rest of the ascent in a gentle rise, up which they could drive without a stop. It was stiff, nevertheless, and it took a long time before we were all up on the plateau on the southern side of Mount Engelstad.

We were very curious and anxious to see what the plateau looked like. We had expected a great, level plain, extending boundlessly towards the south; but in this we were disappointed. Towards the south-west it looked very level and fine, but that was not the way we had to go. Towards the south the ground continued to rise in long ridges running east and west, probably a continuation of the mountain chain running to the south-east, or a connection between it and the plateau. We stubbornly continued our march; we would not give in until we had the plain itself before us. Our hope was that the ridge projecting from Mount Don Pedro Christophersen would be the last; we now had it before us. The going changed at once up here; the loose snow disappeared, and a few wind-waves (*sastrugi*) began to show themselves. These were specially unpleasant to deal with on this last ridge; they lay from south-east to north-west, and were as hard as flints and as sharp as knives. A fall among them might have had very serious consequences. One would have thought the dogs had had enough work that day to tire them, but this last ridge, with its unpleasant snow-waves, did not seem to trouble them in the least. We all drove up gaily, towed by the sledges, on to what looked to us like the final plateau, and halted at 8 p.m. The weather had held fine, and we could apparently see a very long way. In the far distance, extending to the north-west, rose peak after peak; this was the chain of mountains running to the south-east, which we now saw from the other side. In our own vicinity, on the other hand, we saw nothing but the backs of the

mountains so frequently mentioned. We afterwards
learned how deceptive the light can be. I consulted
the aneroid immediately on our arrival at the camping-
ground, and it showed 10,920 feet above the sea, which
the hypsometer afterwards confirmed. All the sledge-
meters gave seventeen geographical miles, or thirty-one
kilometres (nineteen and a quarter statute miles). This
day's work—nineteen and a quarter miles, with an ascent
of 5,750 feet—gives us some idea of what can be
performed by dogs in good training. Our sledges still
had what might be considered heavy loads; it seems
superfluous to give the animals any other testimonial
than the bare fact.

It was difficult to find a place for the tent, so hard
was the snow up here. We found one, however, and
set the tent. Sleeping-bags and kit-bags were handed
in to me, as usual, through the tent-door, and I arranged
everything inside. The cooking-case and the necessary
provisions for that evening and the next morning
were also passed in; but the part of my work that
went more quickly than usual that night was getting
the Primus started, and pumping it up to high-
pressure. I was hoping thereby to produce enough
noise to deaden the shots that I knew would soon
be heard—twenty-four of our brave companions and
faithful helpers were marked out for death. It was
hard—but it had to be so. We had agreed to shrink
from nothing in order to reach our goal. Each man

was to kill his own dogs to the number that had been fixed.

The pemmican was cooked remarkably quickly that evening, and I believe I was unusually industrious in stirring it. There went the first shot—I am not a nervous man, but I must admit that I gave a start. Shot now followed upon shot—they had an uncanny sound over the great plain. A trusty servant lost his life each time. It was long before the first man reported that he had finished; they were all to open their dogs, and take out the entrails to prevent the meat being contaminated. The entrails were for the most part devoured warm on the spot by the victims' comrades, so voracious were they all. Suggen, one of Wisting's dogs, was especially eager for warm entrails; after enjoying this luxury, he could be seen staggering about in a quite misshapen condition. Many of the dogs would not touch them at first, but their appetite came after a while.

The holiday humour that ought to have prevailed in the tent that evening—our first on the plateau—did not make its appearance; there was depression and sadness in the air—we had grown so fond of our dogs. The place was named the "Butcher's Shop." It had been arranged that we should stop here two days to rest and eat dog. There was more than one among us who at first would not hear of taking any part in this feast; but as time went by, and appetites became sharper, this view underwent a change, until, during the last few

days before reaching the Butcher's Shop, we all thought
and talked of nothing but dog cutlets, dog steaks, and
the like.   But on this first evening we put a restraint
on ourselves ; we thought we could not fall upon our
four-footed friends and devour them before they had
had time to grow cold.

We quickly found out that the Butcher's Shop was
not a hospitable locality.   During the night the temperature sank, and violent gusts of wind swept over the
plain ; they shook and tore at the tent, but it would
take more than that to get a hold of it.   The dogs
spent the night in eating ; we could hear the crunching
and grinding of their teeth whenever we were awake for
a moment.   The effect of the great and sudden change
of altitude made itself felt at once ; when I wanted to
turn round in my bag, I had to do it a bit at a time, so
as not to get out of breath.   That my comrades were
affected in the same way, I knew without asking them ;
my ears told me enough.

It was calm when we turned out, but the weather did
not look altogether promising ; it was overcast and
threatening.   We occupied the forenoon in flaying a
number of dogs.   As I have said, all the survivors were
not yet in a mood for dog's flesh, and it therefore had
to be served in the most enticing form.   When flayed
and cut up, it went down readily all along the line ;
even the most fastidious then overcame their scruples.
But with the skin on we should not have been able to

persuade them all to eat that morning; probably this distaste was due to the smell clinging to the skins, and I must admit that it was not appetizing. The meat itself, as it lay there cut up, looked well enough, in all conscience; no butcher's shop could have exhibited a finer sight than we showed after flaying and cutting up ten dogs. Great masses of beautiful fresh, red meat, with quantities of the most tempting fat, lay spread over the snow. The dogs went round and sniffed at it. Some helped themselves to a piece; others were digesting. We men had picked out what we thought was the youngest and tenderest one for ourselves. The whole arrangement was left to Wisting, both the selection and the preparation of the cutlets. His choice fell upon Rex, a beautiful little animal—one of his own dogs, by the way. With the skill of an expert, he hacked and cut away what he considered would be sufficient for a meal. I could not take my eyes off his work; the delicate little cutlets had an absolutely hypnotizing effect as they were spread out one by one over the snow. They recalled memories of old days, when no doubt a dog cutlet would have been less tempting than now—memories of dishes on which the cutlets were elegantly arranged side by side, with paper frills on the bones, and a neat pile of *petits pois* in the middle. Ah, my thoughts wandered still farther afield—but that does not concern us now, nor has it anything to do with the South Pole.

I was aroused from my musings by Wisting digging his axe into the snow as a sign that his work was done, after which he picked up the cutlets, and went into the tent. The clouds had dispersed somewhat, and from time to time the sun appeared, though not in its most genial aspect. We succeeded in catching it just in time to get our latitude determined—85° 36′ S. We were lucky, as not long after the wind got up from the east-south-east, and, before we knew what was happening, everything was in a cloud of snow. But now we snapped our fingers at the weather; what difference did it make to us if the wind howled in the guy-ropes and the snow drifted? We had, in any case, made up our minds to stay here for a while, and we had food in abundance. We knew the dogs thought much the same: so long as we have enough to eat, let the weather go hang.

Inside the tent Wisting was getting on well when we came in after making these observations. The pot was on, and, to judge by the savoury smell, the preparations were already far advanced. The cutlets were not fried; we had neither frying-pan nor butter. We could, no doubt, have got some lard out of the pemmican, and we might have contrived some sort of a pan, so that we could have fried them if it had been necessary; but we found it far easier and quicker to boil them, and in this way we got excellent soup into the bargain. Wisting knew his business surprisingly well; he had put into the soup all those parts of the pemmican that contained most vegetables, and now he served us the finest fresh meat soup with vegetables in it. The *clou* of the repast was the dish of cutlets. If we had entertained the slightest doubt of the quality of the meat, this vanished instantly on the first trial. The meat was excellent, quite excellent, and one cutlet after another disappeared with lightning-like rapidity. I must admit that they would have lost nothing by being a little more tender, but one must not expect too much of a dog. At this first meal I finished five cutlets myself, and looked in vain in the pot for more. Wisting appeared not to have reckoned on such a brisk demand.

We employed the afternoon in going through our stock of provisions, and dividing the whole of it among three sledges; the fourth—Hassel's—was to be left behind. The provisions were thus divided. Sledge No. 1 (Wisting's) contained:

Biscuits, 3,700 (daily ration, 40 biscuits per man).

Dogs' pemmican, $277\frac{3}{4}$ pounds ($\frac{1}{2}$ kilogram, or 1 pound $1\frac{1}{2}$ ounces per dog per day).

Men's pemmican, $59\frac{1}{2}$ pounds (350 grams, or 12·34 ounces per man per day).

Chocolate, $12\frac{3}{4}$ pounds (40 grams, or 1·4 ounces per man per day).

Milk-powder, $13\frac{1}{4}$ pounds (60 grams, or 2·1 ounces per man per day).

The other two sledges had approximately the same supplies, and thus permitted us on leaving this place to extend our march over a period of sixty days with full rations.   Our eighteen surviving dogs were divided into three teams, six in each.   According to our calculation, we ought to be able to reach the Pole from here with these eighteen, and to leave it again with sixteen. Hassel, who was to leave his sledge at this point, thus concluded his provision account, and the divided provisions were entered in the books of the three others.

All this, then, was done that day on paper.   It remained to make the actual transfer of provisions later, when the weather permitted.   To go out and do it that afternoon was not advisable.   Next day, November 23, the wind had gone round to the north-east, with comparatively manageable weather, so at seven in the morning we began to repack the sledges.   This was not an altogether pleasant task ; although the weather was what I have called " comparatively manageable," it was very far from being suitable for packing provisions.   The chocolate, which by this time consisted chiefly of very small pieces, had to be taken out, counted, and then divided among the three sledges. The same with the biscuits ; every single biscuit had to be taken out and counted, and as we had some thousands of them to deal with, it will readily be understood what it was to stand there in about $-4°$ F. and a gale of wind, most of the time with bare hands, fumbling over this troublesome occupation.   The wind increased while we were at work, and when at last we had finished, the

snow was so thick that we could scarcely see the
tent.

Our original intention of starting again as soon as
the sledges were ready was abandoned. We did not
lose very much by this; on the contrary, we gained on
the whole. The dogs—the most important factor of all
—had a thorough rest, and were well fed. They had
undergone a remarkable change since our arrival at the
Butcher's Shop; they now wandered about, fat, sleek,
and contented, and their former voracity had completely
disappeared. As regards ourselves, a day or two longer
made no difference; our most important article of diet,
the pemmican, was practically left untouched, as for the
time being dog had completely taken its place. There
was thus no great sign of depression to be noticed when
we came back into the tent after finishing our work,
and had to while away the time. As I went in, I could
descry Wisting a little way off kneeling on the ground,
and engaged in the manufacture of cutlets. The dogs
stood in a ring round him, and looked on with interest.
The north-east wind whistled and howled, the air was
thick with driving snow, and Wisting was not to be
envied. But he managed his work well, and we got
our dinner as usual. During the evening the wind
moderated a little, and went more to the east; we went
to sleep with the best hopes for the following day.

Saturday, November 25, came; it was a grand day in
many respects. I had already seen proofs on several

occasions of the kind of men my comrades were, but their conduct that day was such that I shall never forget it, to whatever age I may live. In the course of the night the wind had gone back to the north, and increased to a gale. It was blowing and snowing so that when we came out in the morning we could not see the sledges; they were half snowed under. The dogs had all crept together, and protected themselves as well as they could against the blizzard. The temperature was not so very low ($-16\cdot6°$ F.), but low enough to be disagreeably felt in a storm. We had all taken a turn outside to look at the weather, and were sitting on our sleeping-bags discussing the poor prospect. "It's the devil's own weather here at the Butcher's," said one; "it looks to me as if it would never get any better. This is the fifth day, and it's blowing worse than ever." We all agreed. "There's nothing so bad as lying weather-bound like this," continued another; "it takes more out of you than going from morning to night." Personally, I was of the same opinion. One day may be pleasant enough, but two, three, four, and, as it now seemed, five days—no, it was awful. "Shall we try it?" No sooner was the proposal submitted than it was accepted unanimously and with acclamation. When I think of my four friends of the southern journey, it is the memory of that morning that comes first to my mind. All the qualities that I most admire in a man were clearly shown at that

AT THE END OF A DAY'S MARCH : THE POLE EXPEDITION.

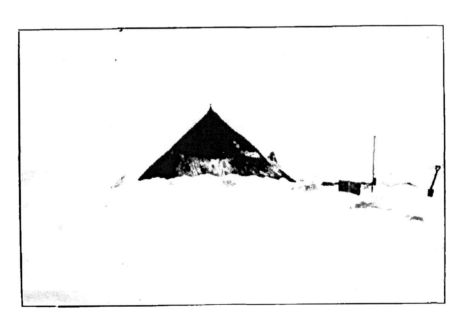

THE TENT AFTER A BLIZZARD.

To face page 70. Vol. II

juncture : courage and dauntlessness, without boasting
or big words. Amid joking and chaff, everything was
packed, and then—out into the blizzard.

It was practically impossible to keep one's eyes open ;
the fine drift-snow penetrated everywhere, and at times
one had a feeling of being blind. The tent was not
only drifted up, but covered with ice, and in taking
it down we had to handle it with care, so as not to
break it in pieces. The dogs were not much inclined
to start, and it took time to get them into their harness,
but at last we were ready. One more glance over the
camping-ground to see that nothing we ought to have
with us had been forgotten. The fourteen dogs' carcasses that were left were piled up in a heap, and
Hassel's sledge was set up against it as a mark. The
spare sets of dog-harness, some Alpine ropes, and all
our crampons for ice-work, which we now thought
would not be required, were left behind. The last
thing to be done was planting a broken ski upright
by the side of the depot. It was Wisting who did this,
thinking, presumably, that an extra mark would do no
harm. That it was a happy thought the future will
show.

And then we were off. It was a hard pull to begin
with, both for men and beasts, as the high *sastrugi*
continued towards the south, and made it extremely
difficult to advance. Those who had sledges to drive
had to be very attentive, and support them so that they

did not capsize on the big waves, and we who had no sledges found great difficulty in keeping our feet, as we had nothing to lean against. We went on like this, slowly enough, but the main thing was that we made progress. The ground at first gave one the impression of rising, though not much. The going was extremely heavy; it was like dragging oneself through sand. Meanwhile the *sastrugi* grew smaller and smaller, and finally they disappeared altogether, and the surface became quite flat. The going also improved by degrees, for what reason it is difficult to say, as the storm continued unabated, and the drift—now combined with falling snow—was thicker than ever. It was all the driver could do to see his own dogs. The surface, which had become perfectly level, had the appearance at times of sinking; in any case, one would have thought so from the pace of the sledges. Now and again the dogs would set off suddenly at a gallop. The wind aft, no doubt, helped the pace somewhat, but it alone could not account for the change.

I did not like this tendency of the ground to fall away. In my opinion, we ought to have done with anything of that sort after reaching the height at which we were; a slight slope upward, possibly, but down—no, that did not agree with my reckoning. So far the incline had not been so great as to cause uneasiness, but if it seriously began to go downhill, we should have to stop and camp. To run down at full gallop, blindly and in complete ignorance of the ground, would be madness. We might risk falling into some chasm before we had time to pull up.

Hanssen, as usual, was driving first. Strictly speaking, I should now have been going in advance, but the uneven surface at the start and the rapid pace afterwards had made it impossible to walk as fast the dogs could pull. I was therefore following by the side of Wisting's sledge, and chatting with him. Suddenly I saw Hanssen's dogs shoot ahead, and downhill they went at the wildest pace, Wisting after them. I shouted to Hanssen to stop, and he succeeded in doing so by twisting his sledge. The others, who were following, stopped when they came up to him. We were in the middle of a fairly steep descent; what there might be below was not easy to decide, nor would we try to find out in that weather. Was it possible that we were on our way down through the mountains again? It seemed more probable that we lay on one of the numerous ridges; but we could be sure of nothing before the weather cleared. We trampled down a place for the tent in the loose snow, and soon got it up. It was not a long day's march that we had done—eleven and three-quarter miles—but we had put an end to our stay at the Butcher's Shop, and that was a great thing. The boiling-point test that evening showed that we were 10,300 feet above the sea, and that we had thus gone down 620 feet from the Butcher's. We turned in and went to sleep. As soon as it brightened, we should have to be ready to jump out and look at the weather; one has to seize every opportunity in these regions. If one neglects to do so, it may mean a long wait and much may be lost. We therefore all slept with one eye open, and we knew well that nothing could happen without our noticing it.

At three in the morning the sun cut through the clouds and we through the tent-door. To take in the situation was more than the work of a moment. The sun showed as yet like a pat of butter, and had not succeeded in dispersing the thick mists; the wind had dropped somewhat, but was still fairly strong. This is, after all, the worst part of one's job—turning out of one's good, warm sleeping-bag, and standing outside for some time in thin clothes, watching the weather. We knew by experience that a gleam like this, a clearing in the weather, might come suddenly, and then one had to be on the spot. The gleam came; it did not last long, but long enough. We lay on the side of a ridge that fell away pretty steeply. The descent on the south was too abrupt, but on the south-east it was better and more gradual, and ended in a wide, level tract. We could see no crevasses or unpleasantness of any kind. It was not very far that we could see, though; only our nearest surroundings. Of the mountains we saw nothing, neither Fridtjof Nansen nor Don Pedro Christophersen. Well content with our morning's work, we turned in again and slept till 6 a.m., when we began our morning preparations. The weather, which had somewhat improved during the night, had now broken loose again, and the north-easter was doing all it could. However, it would take more than storm and snow to stop us now, since we had discovered the nature of our immediate surroundings ; if we once got down to the plain, we knew that we could always feel our way on.

After putting ample brakes on the sledge-runners, we started off downhill in a south-easterly direction. The slight idea of the position that we had been able to get in the morning proved correct. The descent was easy and smooth, and we reached the plain without any adventure. We could now once more set our faces to the south, and in thick driving snow we continued our way into the unknown, with good assistance from the howling north-easterly gale. We now recommenced the erection of beacons, which had not been necessary during the ascent. In the course of the forenoon we again passed over a little ridge, the last of them that we encountered. The surface was now fine enough, smooth as a floor and without a sign of *sastrugi*. If our progress was nevertheless slow and difficult, this was due to the wretched going, which was real torture to all of us. A sledge journey through the Sahara could not have offered a worse surface to move over. Now the forerunners came into their own, and from here to the Pole Hassel and I took it in turns to occupy the position.

The weather improved in the course of the day, and when we camped in the afternoon it looked quite smiling. The sun came through and gave a delightful warmth after the last few bitter days. It was not yet clear, so that we could see nothing of our surroundings. The distance according to our three sledge-meters was eighteen and a half miles; taking the bad going into consideration, we had reason to be well satisfied with it. Our altitude came out at 9,475 feet above the sea, or a drop of 825 feet in the course of the day. This surprised me greatly. What did it mean? Instead of rising gradually, we were going slowly down. Something extraordinary must await us farther on, but what? According to dead reckoning our latitude that evening was 86° S.

November 27 did not bring us the desired weather; the night was filled with sharp gusts from the north; the morning came with a slack wind, but accompanied by mist and snowfall. This was abominable; here we were, advancing over absolutely virgin ground, and able to see nothing. The surface remained about the same —possibly rather more undulating. That it had been blowing here at some time, and violently too, was shown by the under-surface, which was composed of *sastrugi* as hard as iron. Luckily for us, the snowfall of the last few days had filled these up, so as to present a level surface. It was heavy going, though better than on the previous day.

As we were advancing, still blindly, and fretting at the persistently thick weather, one of us suddenly called out: "Hullo, look there!" A wild, dark summit rose high out of the mass of fog to the east-south-east. It was not far away—on the contrary, it seemed threateningly near and right over us. We stopped and looked at the imposing sight, but Nature did not expose her objects of interest for long. The fog rolled over again, thick, heavy and dark, and blotted out the view. We knew now that we had to be prepared for surprises. After we had gone about ten miles the fog again lifted for a moment, and we saw quite near—a mile or so away—two long, narrow mountain ridges to the west of us, running north and south, and completely covered with snow. These—Helland Hansen's Mountains— were the only ones we saw on our right hand during the march on the plateau; they were between 9,000 and 10,000 feet high, and would probably serve as excellent landmarks on the return journey. There was no connection to be traced between these mountains and those lying to the east of them; they gave us the impression of being entirely isolated summits, as we could not make out any lofty ridge running east and west. We continued our course in the constant expectation of finding some surprise or other in our line of route. The air ahead of us was as black as pitch, as though it concealed something. It could not be a storm, or it would have been already upon us. But we went on and on, and nothing came. Our day's march was eighteen and a half miles.

I see that my diary for November 28 does not begin very promisingly: "Fog, fog—and again fog. Also fine falling snow, which makes the going impossible. Poor beasts, they have toiled hard to get the sledges forward to-day." But the day did not turn out so badly after all, as we worked our way out of this uncertainty and found out what was behind the pitch-dark clouds. During the forenoon the sun came through and thrust aside the fog for a while; and there, to the south-east, not many miles away, lay an immense mountain mass. From this mass, right across our course, ran a great, ancient glacier; the sun shone down upon it and showed us a surface full of huge irregularities. On the side nearest to the mountain these disturbances were such that a hasty glance was enough to show us the impossibility of advancing that way. But right in our line of route—straight on to the glacier —it looked, as far as we could see, as though we could get along. The fog came and went, and we had to take advantage of the clear intervals to get our bearings. It would, no doubt, have been better if we could have halted, set up our tent, and waited for decently clear weather, so that we might survey the ground at our ease and choose the best way. Going forward without an idea of what the ground was like, was not very pleasant. But how long should we have to wait for clear weather? That question was unanswerable; possibly a week, or even a fortnight, and we had no time for that. Better go straight on, then, and take what might come.

What we could see of the glacier appeared to be pretty steep; but it was only between the south and south-east, under the new land, that the fog now and again lifted sufficiently to enable us to see anything. From the south round to the west the fog lay as thick as gruel. We could see that the big crevasses lost themselves in it, and the question of what the glacier looked like on the west had to be put aside for the moment. It was to the south we had to go, and there it was possible to go forward a little way. We continued our march until the ground began to show signs of the glacier in the form of small crevasses, and then we halted. It was our intention to lighten our sledges before tackling the glacier; from the little we could see of it, it was plain enough that we should have stiff work. It was therefore important to have as little as possible on the sledges.

We set to work at once to build the depot; the snow here was excellent for this purpose—as hard as glass. In a short time an immense erection of adamantine blocks of snow rose into the air, containing provisions for five men for six days and for eighteen dogs for five days. A number of small articles were also left behind.

While we were thus occupied, the fog had been coming and going; some of the intervals had been quite clear, and had given me a good view of the nearest part of the range. It appeared to be quite isolated, and to consist of four mountains; one of these—Mount Helmer Hanssen—lay separated from the rest. The other three—Mounts Oscar Wisting, Sverre Hassel, and Olav Bjaaland—lay closer together. Behind this group the air had been heavy and black the whole time, showing that more land must be concealed there. Suddenly, in one of the brightest intervals, there came a rift in this curtain, and the summits of a colossal mountain mass appeared. Our first impression was that this mountain —Mount Thorvald Nilsen—must be something over 20,000 feet high; it positively took our breath away, so formidable did it appear. But it was only a glimpse that we had, and then the fog enclosed it once more. We had succeeded in taking a few meagre bearings of the different summits of the nearest group; they were not very grand, but better ones were not to be obtained. For that matter, the site of the depot was so well marked by its position under the foot of the glacier that we agreed it would be impossible to miss it.

Having finished the edifice, which rose at least 6 feet into the air, we put one of our black provision cases on the top of it, so as to be able to see it still more easily on the way back. An observation we had contrived to take while the work was in progress gave us our latitude as 86° 21′ S. This did not agree very well with the latitude of our dead reckoning—86° 23′ S. Meanwhile the fog had again enveloped everything, and a fine, light snow was falling. We had taken a bearing of the line of glacier that was most free of crevasses, and so we moved on again. It was some time before we felt our way up to the glacier. The crevasses at its foot were not large, but we had no sooner entered upon the ascent than the fun began. There was something uncanny about this perfectly blind advance among crevasses and chasms on all sides. We examined the compass from time to time, and went forward cautiously.

Hassel and I went in front on a rope ; but that, after all, was not much of a help to our drivers. We naturally glided lightly on our ski over places where the dogs would easily fall through. This lowest part of the glacier was not entirely free from danger, as the crevasses were often rendered quite invisible by a thin overlying layer of snow. In clear weather it is not so bad to have to cross such a surface, as the effect of light and shade is usually to show up the edges of these insidious pitfalls, but on a day like this, when everything looked alike, one's advance is doubtful. We kept it going, however, by using the utmost caution. Wisting came near to sounding the depth of one of these dangerous crevasses with sledge, dogs and all, as the bridge he was about to cross gave way. Thanks to his presence of mind and a lightning-like movement—some would call it luck—he managed to save himself. In this way we worked up about 200 feet, but then we came upon such a labyrinth of yawning chasms and open abysses that we could not move. There was nothing to be done but to find the least disturbed spot, and set the tent there.

As soon as this was done Hanssen and I set out to explore. We were roped, and therefore safe enough. It required some study to find a way out of the trap we had run ourselves into. Towards the group of mountains last described—which now lay to the east of us—it had cleared sufficiently to give us a fairly good view of the appearance of the glacier in that direction. What we had before seen at a distance, was now confirmed. The part extending to the mountains was so ground up and broken that there was positively not a spot where one could set one's foot. It looked as if a battle had been fought here, and the ammunition had been great blocks of ice. They lay pell-mell, one on the top of another, in all directions, and evoked a picture of violent confusion. Thank God we were not here while this was going on, I thought to myself, as I stood looking out over this battlefield; it must have been a spectacle like doomsday, and not on a small scale either. To advance in that direction, then, was hopeless, but that was no great matter, since our way was to the south. On the south we could see nothing; the fog lay thick and heavy there. All we could do was to try to make our way on, and we therefore crept southward.

On leaving our tent we had first to cross a comparatively narrow snow-bridge, and then go along a ridge or saddle, raised by pressure, with wide open crevasses on both sides. This ridge led us on to an ice-wave about 25 feet high—a formation which was due to the pressure having ceased before the wave had been forced to break and form hummocks. We saw well enough that this would be a difficult place to pass with sledges and dogs, but in default of anything better it would have to be done. From the top of this wave-formation we could see down on the other side, which had hitherto been hidden from us. The fog prevented our seeing far, but the immediate surroundings were enough to convince us that with caution we could beat up farther. From the height on which we stood, every precaution would be required to avoid going down on the other side; for there the wave ended in an open crevasse, specially adapted to receive any drivers, sledges or dogs that might make a slip.

This trip that Hanssen and I took to the south was made entirely at random, as we saw absolutely nothing; our object was to make tracks for the following day's journey. The language we used about the glacier as we went was not altogether complimentary; we had endless tacking and turning to get on. To go one yard forward, I am sure we had to go at least ten to one side. Can anyone be surprised that we called it the Devil's Glacier? At any rate, our companions acknowledged the justness of the name with ringing acclamations when we told them of it.

At Hell's Gate Hanssen and I halted. This was a very remarkable formation; the glacier had here formed a long ridge about 20 feet high; then, in the middle of this ridge, a fissure had opened, making a gateway about 6 feet wide. This formation—like everything else on the glacier—was obviously very old, and for the most part filled with snow. From this point the glacier, as far as our view extended to the south, looked better and better; we therefore turned round and followed our tracks in the comforting conviction that we should manage to get on.

Our companions were no less pleased with the news we brought of our prospects. Our altitude that evening was 8,650 feet above the sea—that is to say, at the foot of the glacier we had reached an altitude of 8,450 feet, or a drop from the Butcher's of 2,570 feet. We now knew very well that we should have this ascent to make again, perhaps even more; and this idea did not arouse any particular enthusiasm. In my diary I see that I conclude the day with the following words: "What will the next surprise be, I wonder?"

It was, in fact, an extraordinary journey that we were undertaking, through new regions, new mountains, glaciers, and so on, without being able to see. That

A LARGE FILLED CREVASSE ON THE DEVIL'S GLACIER.

we were prepared for surprises was perhaps quite natural. What I liked least about this feeling one's way forward in the dark was that it would be difficult—very difficult indeed—to recognize the ground again on the way back. But with this glacier lying straight across our line of route, and with the numerous beacons we had erected, we reassured ourselves on this score. It would take a good deal to make us miss them on the return. The point for us, of course, was to find our descent on to the Barrier again—a mistake there might be serious enough. And it will appear later in this narrative that my fear of our not being able to recognize the way was not entirely groundless. The beacons we had put up came to our aid, and for our final success we owe a deep debt of gratitude to our prudence and thoughtfulness in adopting this expedient.

Next morning, November 29, brought considerably clearer weather, and allowed us a very good survey of our position. We could now see that the two mountain ranges uniting in 86° S. were continued in a mighty chain running to the south-east, with summits from 10,000 to 15,000 feet. Mount Thorvald Nilsen was the most southerly we could see from this point. Mounts Hanssen, Wisting, Bjaaland, and Hassel formed, as we had thought the day before, a group by themselves, and lay separated from the main range.

The drivers had a warm morning's work. They had to drive with great circumspection and patience to grapple with the kind of ground we had before us; a slight mistake might be enough to send both sledge and dogs with lightning rapidity into the next world. It took, nevertheless, a remarkably short time to cover the bistance we had explored on the previous evening; defore we knew it, we were at Hell's Gate.

Bjaaland took an excellent photograph here, which gives a very good idea of the difficulties this part of the journey presented. In the foreground, below the high snow-ridge that forms one side of a very wide but partly filled-up crevasse, the marks of ski can be seen in the snow. This was the photographer, who, in passing over this snow-bridge, struck his ski into it to try the strength of the support. Close to the tracks can be seen an open piece of the crevasse; it is a pale blue at the top, but ends in the deepest black—in a bottomless abyss. The photographer got over the bridge and back with a whole skin, but there could be no question of risking sledges and dogs on it, and it can be seen in the photograph that the sledges have been turned right round to try another way. The two small black figures in the distance, on the right, are Hassel and I, who are reconnoitring ahead.

It was no very great distance that we put behind us that day—nine and a quarter miles in a straight line. But, taking into account all the turns and circuits we had been compelled to make, it was not so short after all. We set our tent on a good, solid foundation, and

HELL'S GATE ON THE DEVIL'S GLACIER.

To face page 86, Vol. II.

were well pleased with the day's work. The altitude
was 8,960 feet above the sea. The sun was now in the
west, and shining directly upon the huge mountain
masses. It was a fairy landscape in blue and white,
red and black, a play of colours that defies description.
Clear as it now appeared to be, one could understand
that the weather was not all that could be wished, for
the south-eastern end of Mount Thorvald Nilsen lost
itself in a dark, impenetrable cloud, which led one to
suspect a continuation in that direction, though one
could not be certain.

Mount Nilsen—ah! anything more beautiful, taking
it altogether, I have never seen. Peaks of the most
varied forms rose high into the air, partly covered with
driving clouds. Some were sharp, but most were long
and rounded. Here and there one saw bright, shining
glaciers plunging wildly down the steep sides, and
merging into the underlying ground in fearful confusion.
But the most remarkable of them all was Mount Helmer
Hanssen; its top was as round as the bottom of a bowl,
and covered by an extraordinary ice-sheet, which was
so broken up and disturbed that the blocks of ice bristled
in every direction like the quills of a porcupine. It
glittered and burned in the sunlight—a glorious spectacle. There could only be one such mountain in the
world, and as a landmark it was priceless. We knew
that we could not mistake that, however the surroundings might appear on the return journey, when

possibly the conditions of lighting might be altogether different.

After camping, two of us went out to explore farther. The prospect from the tent was not encouraging, but we might possibly find things better than we expected. We were lucky to find the going so fine as it was on the glacier; we had left our crampons behind at the Butcher's Shop, and if we had found smooth ice, instead of a good, firm snow surface, such as we now had, it would have caused us much trouble. Up—still up, among monsters of crevasses, some of them hundreds of feet wide and possibly thousands of feet deep. Our prospects of advancing were certainly not bright; as far as we could see in the line of our route one immense ridge towered above another, concealing on their farther sides huge, wide chasms, which all had to be avoided. We went forward—steadily forward—though the way round was both long and troublesome. We had no rope on this time, as the irregularities were so plain that it would have been difficult to go into them. It turned out, however, at several points, that the rope would not have been out of place. We were just going to cross over one of the numerous ridges—the surface here looked perfectly whole—when a great piece broke right under the back half of Hanssen's ski. We could not deny ourselves the pleasure of glancing down into the hole. The sight was not an inviting one, and we agreed to avoid this place when we came on with our dogs and sledges.

Every day we had occasion to bless our ski. We often used to ask each other where we should now have been without these excellent appliances. The usual answer was: Most probably at the bottom of some crevasse. When we first read the different accounts of the aspect and nature of the Barrier, it was clear to all of us, who were born and bred with ski on our feet, that these must be regarded as indispensable. This view was confirmed and strengthened every day, and I am not giving too much credit to our excellent ski when I say that they not only played a very important part, but possibly the most important of all, on our journey to the South Pole. Many a time we traversed stretches of surface so cleft and disturbed that it would have been an impossibility to get over them on foot. I need scarcely insist on the advantages of ski in deep, loose snow.

After advancing for two hours, we decided to return. From the raised ridge on which we were then standing, the surface ahead of us looked more promising than ever; but we had so often been deceived on the glacier that we had now become definitely sceptical. How often, for instance, had we thought that beyond this or that undulation our trials would be at an end, and that the way to the south would lie open and free; only to reach the place and find that the ground behind the ridge was, if possible, worse than what we had already been struggling with. But this time we seemed some-

how to feel victory in the air. The formations appeared
to promise it, and yet—had we been so often deceived
by these formations that we now refused to offer them
a thought? Was it possibly instinct that told us this?
I do not know, but certain it is that Hanssen and I
agreed, as we stood there discussing our prospects, that
behind the farthest ridge we saw, we should conquer
the glacier. We had a feverish desire to go and have
a look at it; but the way round the many crevasses
was long, and—I may as well admit it—we were
beginning to get tired. The return, downhill as it
was, did not take long, and soon we were able to tell
our comrades that the prospects for the morrow were
very promising.

While we had been away, Hassel had measured the
Nilsen Mountain, and found its height to be 15,500 feet
above the sea. How well I remember that evening,
when we stood contemplating the glorious sight that
Nature offered, and believing the air to be so clear that
anything within range of vision must have shown itself;
and how well, too, I remember our astonishment on the
return journey on finding the whole landscape completely transformed! If it had not been for Mount
Helmer Hanssen, it would have been difficult for us to
know where we were. The atmosphere in these regions
may play the most awkward tricks. Absolutely clear
as it seemed to us that evening, it nevertheless turned
out later that it had been anything but clear. One has,

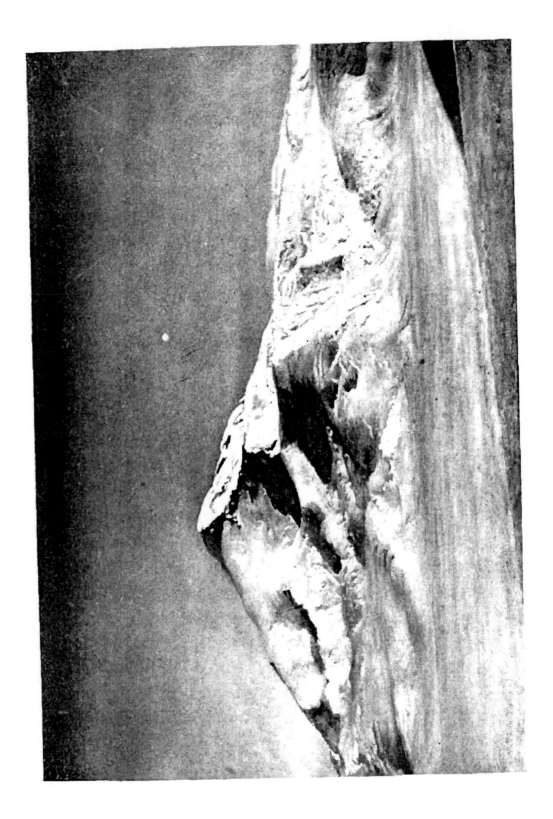

therefore, to be very careful about what one sees or does not see. In most cases it has proved that travellers in the Polar regions have been more apt to see too much than too little; if, however, we had charted this tract as we saw it the first time, a great part of the mountain ranges would have been omitted.

During the night a gale sprang up from the south-east, and blew so that it howled in the guy-ropes of the tent; it was well that the tent-pegs had a good hold. In the morning, while we were at breakfast, it was still blowing, and we had some thoughts of waiting for a time; but suddenly, without warning, the wind dropped to such an extent that all our hesitation vanished. What a change the south-east wind had produced! The splendid covering of snow that the day before had made ski-running a pleasure, was now swept away over great stretches of surface, exposing the hard substratum. Our thoughts flew back; the crampons we had left behind seemed to dance before my eyes, backwards and forwards, grinning and pointing fingers at me. It would be a nice little extra trip back to the Butcher's to fetch them.

Meanwhile, we packed and made everything ready. The tracks of the day before were not easy to follow; but if we lost them now and again on the smooth ice surface, we picked them up later on a snow-wave that had resisted the attack of the wind. It was hard and strenuous work for the drivers. The sledges were diffi-

cult to manage over the smooth, sloping ice; sometimes
they went straight, but just as often cross-wise, requiring
sharp attention to keep them from capsizing. And this
had to be prevented at all costs, as the thin provision
cases would not stand many bumps on the ice; besides
which, it was such hard work righting the sledges again
that for this reason alone the drivers exercised the
greatest care. The sledges were put to a severe test
that day, with the many great and hard irregularities
we encountered on the glacier; it is a wonder they survived it, and is a good testimonial for Bjaaland's work.

The glacier that day presented the worst confusion
we had yet had to deal with. Hassel and I went in
front, as usual, with the rope on. Up to the spot
Hanssen and I had reached the evening before our progress was comparatively easy; one gets on so much
quicker when one knows that the way is practicable.
After this point it became worse; indeed, it was often
so bad that we had to stop for a long time and try in
various directions, before finding a way. More than
once the axe had to be used to hack away obstructions.
At one time things looked really serious; chasm after
chasm, hummock after hummock, so high and steep
that they were like mountains. Here we went out and
explored in every direction to find a passage; at last we
found one, if, indeed, it deserved the name of a passage.
It was a bridge so narrow that it scarcely allowed room
for the width of the sledge; a fearful abyss on each

side. The crossing of this place reminded me of the tight-rope walker going over Niagara. It was a good thing none of us was subject to giddiness, and that the dogs did not know exactly what the result of a false step would be.

On the other side of this bridge we began to go downhill, and our course now lay in a long valley between lofty undulations on each side. It tried our patience severely to advance here, as the line of the hollow was fairly long and ran due west. We tried several times to lay our course towards the south and clamber up the side of the undulation, but these efforts did not pay us. We could always get up on to the ridge, but we could not come down again on the other side; there was nothing to be done but to follow the natural course of the valley until it took us into the tract lying to the south. It was especially the drivers whose patience was sorely tried, and I could see them now and then take a turn up to the top of the ridge, not satisfied with the exploration Hassel and I had made. But the result was always the same; they had to submit to Nature's caprices and follow in our tracks.

Our course along this natural line was not entirely free from obstruction; crevasses of various dimensions constantly crossed our path. The ridge or undulation, at the top of which we at last arrived, had quite an imposing effect. It terminated on the east in a steep drop to the underlying surface, and attained at this

point a height of over 100 feet.   On the west it sloped
gradually into the lower ground and allowed us to
advance that way.   In order to have a better view of
the surroundings we ascended the eastern and highest
part of the ridge, and from here we at once had a
confirmation of our supposition of the day before.   The
ridge we had then seen, behind which we hoped to find
better conditions, could now be seen a good way ahead.
And what we then saw made our hearts beat fast with
joy.   Could that great white, unbroken plain over
there be real, or was it only an illusion ?   Time would
show.

Meanwhile Hassel and I jogged on, and the others
followed.   We had to get through a good many
difficulties yet before we reached that point, but,
compared with all the breakneck places we had already
crossed, these were of a comparatively tame description.
It was with a sigh of relief that we arrived at the plain
that promised so well; its extent was not very great,
but we were not very exacting either in this respect,
after our last few days' march over the broken surface.
Farther to the south we could still see great masses
piled up by pressure, but the intervals between them
were very great and the surface was whole.   This
was, then, the first time since we tackled the Devil's
Glacier that we were able to steer true south for a few
minutes.

As we progressed, it could be seen that we had really

come upon another kind of ground; for once we had not been made fools of. Not that we had an unbroken, level surface to go upon—it would be a long time before we came to that—but we were able to keep our course for long stretches at a time. The huge crevasses became rarer, and so filled up at both ends that we were able to cross them without going a long way round. There was new life in all of us, both dogs and men, and we went rapidly southward. As we advanced, the conditions improved more and more. We could see in the distance some huge dome-shaped formations, that seemed to tower high into the air: these turned out to be the southernmost limit of the big crevasses and to form the transition to the third phase of the glacier.

It was a stiff climb to get up these domes, which were fairly high and swept smooth by the wind. They lay straight in our course, and from their tops we had a good view. The surface we were entering upon was quite different from that on the northern side of the domes. Here the big crevasses were entirely filled with snow and might be crossed anywhere. What specially attracted one's attention here was an immense number of small formations in the shape of haycocks. Great stretches of the surface were swept bare, exposing the smooth ice.

It was evident that these various formations or phases in the glacier were due to the underlying ground. The first tract we had passed, where the confusion was so extreme, must be the part that lay nearest the bare land; in proportion as the glacier left the land, it became less disturbed. In the haycock district the disturbance had not produced cracks in the surface to any extent, only upheaval here and there. How these haycocks were formed and what they looked like inside we were soon to find out. It was a pleasure to be able to advance all the time, instead of constantly turning and going round; only once or twice did we have to turn aside for the larger haycocks, otherwise we kept our course. The great, clean-swept stretches of surface that we came upon from time to time were split in every direction, but the cracks were very narrow—about half an inch wide.

We had difficulty in finding a place for the tent that evening; the surface was equally hard everywhere, and at last we had to set it on the bare ice. Luckily for our tent-pegs, this ice was not of the bright, steely variety; it was more milky in appearance and not so hard, and we were thus able to knock in the pegs with the axe. When the tent was up, Hassel went out as usual to fetch snow for the cooker. As a rule he performed this task with a big knife, specially made for snow; but this evening he went out armed with an axe. He was very pleased with the abundant and excellent material that lay to his hand; there was no need to go far. Just outside the tent door, two feet away, stood a fine little haycock, that looked as if it would serve the purpose well. Hassel raised his axe and gave a good sound blow; the axe met with no resistance, and went in up to the haft. The haycock was hollow. As the axe was pulled out the surrounding part gave way, and one could hear the pieces of ice falling down through the dark hole. It appeared, then, that two feet from our door we had a most convenient way down into the cellar. Hassel looked as if he enjoyed the situation. "Black as a sack," he smiled; "couldn't see any bottom." Hanssen was beaming; no doubt he would have liked the tent a little nearer. The material provided by the haycock was of the best quality, and well adapted for cooking purposes.

The next day, December 1, was a very fatiguing one for us all. From early morning a blinding blizzard raged from the south-east, with a heavy fall of snow. The going was of the very worst kind—polished ice. I stumbled forward on ski, and had comparatively easy work. The drivers had been obliged to take off their ski and put them on the loads, so as to walk by the side, support the sledges, and give the dogs help when they came to a difficult place; and that was pretty often, for on this smooth ice surface there were a number of small scattered *sastrugi*, and these consisted of a kind of snow that reminded one more of fish-glue than of anything else when the sledges came in contact with it. The dogs could get no hold with their claws on the smooth ice, and when the sledge came on to one of these tough little waves, they could not manage to haul it over, try as they might. The driver then had to put all his strength into it to prevent the sledge stopping. Thus in most cases the combined efforts of men and dogs carried the sledge on.

In the course of the afternoon the surface again began to be more disturbed, and great crevasses crossed our path time after time. These crevasses were really rather dangerous; they looked very innocent, as they were quite filled up with snow, but on a nearer acquaintance with them we came to understand that they were far more hazardous than we dreamed of at first. It turned out that between the loose snow-filling and the firm ice edges there was a fairly broad, open space, leading straight down into the depths. The layer of snow which covered it over was in most cases quite thin. In driving out into one of these snow-filled crevasses nothing happened as a rule; but it was in getting off on the other side that the critical moment arrived. For here the dogs came up on to the smooth ice surface, and could get no hold for their claws, with the result that it was left entirely to the driver to haul the the sledge up. The strong pull he then had to give sent him through the thin layer of snow. Under these circumstances he took a good, firm hold of the sledge-lashing, or of a special strap that had been made with a view to these accidents. But familiarity breeds contempt, even with the most cautious, and some of the drivers were often within an ace of going down into " the cellar."

If this part of the journey was trying for the dogs, it was certainly no less so for the men. If the weather had even been fine, so that we could have looked about us, we should not have minded it so much, but in this vile weather it was, indeed, no pleasure. Our time was also a good deal taken up with thawing noses and cheeks as they froze—not that we stopped; we had no time for that. We simply took off a mit, and laid the warm hand on the frozen spot as we went; when we thought we had restored sensation, we put the hand back into the mit. By this time it would want warming. One does not keep one's hands bare for long with the thermometer several degrees below zero and a storm blowing. In spite of the unfavourable conditions we had been working in, the sledge-meters that evening showed a distance of fifteen and a half miles. We were well satisfied with the day's work when we camped.

Let us cast a glance into the tent this evening. It looks cosy enough. The inner half of the tent is occupied by three sleeping-bags, whose respective owners have found it both comfortable and expedient to turn in, and may now be seen engaged with their diaries. The outer half—that nearest the door—has only two sleeping-bags, but the rest of the space is taken up with the whole cooking apparatus of the expedition. The owners of these two bags are still sitting up. Hanssen is cook, and will not turn in until the food is ready and served. Wisting is his sworn comrade and assistant, and is ready to lend him any aid that may be required. Hanssen appears to be a careful cook; he evidently does not like to burn the food, and his spoon stirs the contents of the pot incessantly. "Soup!" The effect of the word is instantaneous. Everyone sits up at once with a cup in one hand and a spoon in the other. Each one in his turn has his cup filled with what looks like the most tasty vegetable soup. Scalding hot it is, as one can see by the faces, but for all that it disappears with surprising rapidity. Again the cups are filled, this time with more solid stuff—pemmican. With praiseworthy despatch their contents are once more demolished, and they are filled for the third time. There is nothing the matter with these men's appetites. The cups are carefully scraped, and the enjoyment of bread and water begins. It is easy to see, too, that it is an enjoyment—greater, to judge by the pleasure on their faces, than the most skilfully devised menu could afford. They positively caress the biscuits before they eat them. And the water—ice-cold water they all call for—this also disappears in great quantities, and procures, I feel certain from their expression, a far greater pleasure and satisfaction than the finest wine that was ever produced.

The Primus hums softly during the whole meal, and the temperature in the tent is quite pleasant.

When the meal is over, one of them calls for scissors and looking-glass, and then one may see the Polar explorers dressing their hair for the approaching Sunday. The beard is cut quite short with the clipper every Saturday evening; this is done not so much from motives of vanity as from considerations of utility and comfort. The beard invites an accumulation of ice, which may often be very embarrassing. A beard in the Polar regions seems to me to be just as awkward and unpractical as—well, let us say, walking with a tall hat on each foot. As the beard-clipper and the mirror make their round, one after the other disappears into his bag, and with five " Good-nights," silence falls upon the tent. The regular breathing soon announces that the day's work demands its tribute. Meanwhile the south-easter howls, and the snow beats against the tent. The dogs have curled themselves up, and do not seem to trouble themselves about the weather.

The storm continued unabated on the following day, and on account of the dangerous nature of the ground we decided to wait awhile. In the course of the morning—towards noon, perhaps—the wind dropped a little, and out we went. The sun peeped through at times, and we took the welcome opportunity of getting an altitude—86° 47′ S. was the result.

At this camp we left behind all our delightful reindeer-skin clothing, as we could see that we should have no use for it, the temperature being far too high. We kept the hoods of our reindeer coats, however; we might be glad of them in going against the wind. Our day's march was not to be a long one; the little slackening of the wind about midday was only a joke. It soon came on again in earnest, with a sweeping blizzard from the same quarter—the south-east. If we had known the ground, we should possibly have gone on; but in this storm and driving snow, which prevented our keeping our eyes open, it was no use. A serious accident might happen and ruin all. Two and half miles was therefore our whole distance. The temperature when we camped was −5·8° F. Height above the sea, 9,780 feet.

In the course of the night the wind veered from south-east to north, falling light, and the weather cleared. This was a good chance for us, and we were not slow to avail ourselves of it. A gradually rising ice surface lay before us, bright as a mirror. As on the preceding days, I stumbled along in front on ski, while the others, without their ski, had to follow and support the sledges. The surface still offered filled crevasses, though perhaps less frequently than before. Meanwhile small patches of snow began to show themselves on the polished surface, and soon increased in number and size, until before very long they united and covered the unpleasant ice with a good and even layer of snow.

Then ski were put on again, and we continued our way to the south with satisfaction.

We were all rejoicing that we had now conquered this treacherous glacier, and congratulating ourselves on having at last arrived on the actual plateau. As we were going along, feeling pleased about this, a ridge suddenly appeared right ahead, telling us plainly that perhaps all our sorrows were not yet ended. The ground had begun to sink a little, and as we came nearer we could see that we had to cross a rather wide, but not deep, valley before we arrived under the ridge. Great lines of hummocks and haycock-shaped pieces of ice came in view on every side; we could see that we should have to keep our eyes open.

And now we came to the formation in the glacier that we called the Devil's Ballroom. Little by little the covering of snow that we had praised in such high terms disappeared, and before us lay this wide valley, bare and gleaming. At first it went well enough; as it was downhill, we were going at a good pace on the smooth ice. Suddenly Wisting's sledge cut into the surface, and turned over on its side. We all knew what had happened—one of the runners was in a crevasse. Wisting set to work, with the assistance of Hassel, to raise the sledge, and take it out of its dangerous position; meanwhile Bjaaland had got out his camera and was setting it up. Accustomed as we were to such incidents, Hanssen and I were watching the scene from a point a little way in advance, where we had arrived when it happened. As the photography took rather a long time, I assumed that the crevasse was one of the filled ones and presented no particular danger, but that Bjaaland wanted to have a souvenir among his photographs of the numerous crevasses and ticklish situations we had been exposed to. As to the crack being filled up, there was of course no need to inquire. I hailed them, and asked how they were getting on. "Oh, all right," was the answer; "we've just finished."—"What does the crevasse look like?"— "Oh, as usual," they shouted back; "no bottom." I mention this little incident just to show how one can grow accustomed to anything in this world. There were these two—Wisting and Hassel—lying over a yawning, bottomless abyss, and having their photograph taken; neither of them gave a thought to the serious side of the situation. To judge from the laughter and jokes we heard, one would have thought their position was something quite different.

When the photographer had quietly and leisurely finished his work—he got a remarkably good picture of the scene—the other two together raised the sledge, and the journey was continued. It was at this crevasse that we entered his Majesty's Ballroom. The surface did not really look bad. True, the snow was blown away, which made it difficult to advance, but we did not see many cracks. There were a good many pressure-

masses, as already mentioned, but even in the neighbourhood of these we could not see any marked
disturbance. The first sign that the surface was more
treacherous than it appeared to be was when Hanssen's
leading dogs went right through the apparently solid
floor. They remained hanging by their harness, and
were easily pulled up again. When we looked through
the hole they had made in the crust, it did not give us
the impression of being very dangerous, as, 2 or 3 feet
below the outer crust, there lay another surface, which
appeared to consist of pulverized ice. We assumed
that this lower surface was the solid one, and that
therefore there was no danger in falling through the
upper one. But Bjaaland was able to tell us a different
story. He had, in fact, fallen through the outer crust,
and was well on his way through the inner one as well,
when he got hold of a loop of rope on his sledge and
saved himself in the nick of time. Time after time the
dogs now fell through, and time after time the men went
in. The effect of the open space between the two
crusts was that the ground under our feet sounded
unpleasantly hollow as we went over it. The drivers
whipped up their dogs as much as they could, and with
shouts and brisk encouragement they went rapidly over
the treacherous floor. Fortunately this curious formation was not of great extent, and we soon began to
observe a change for the better as we came up the
ridge. It soon appeared that the Ballroom was the

glacier's last farewell to us. With it all irregularities ceased, and both surface and going improved by leaps and bounds, so that before very long we had the satisfaction of seeing that at last we had really conquered all these unpleasant difficulties. The surface at once became fine and even, with a splendid covering of snow everywhere, and we went rapidly on our way to the south with a feeling of security and safety.

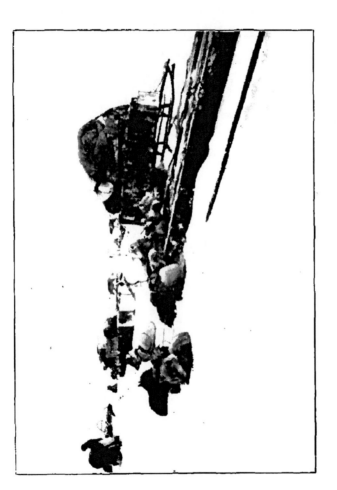

THE SLEDGES PACKED FOR THE FINAL MARCH.

To face page 106, Vol. II.

CHAPTER XII

AT THE POLE

In lat. 87° S.—according to dead reckoning—we saw the last of the land to the north-east. The atmosphere was then apparently as clear as could be, and we felt certain that our view covered all the land there was to be seen from that spot. We were deceived again on this occasion, as will be seen later. Our distance that day (December 4) was close upon twenty-five miles ; height above the sea, 10,100 feet.

The weather did not continue fine for long. Next day (December 5) there was a gale from the north, and once more the whole plain was a mass of drifting snow. In addition to this there was thick falling snow, which blinded us and made things worse, but a feeling of security had come over us and helped us to advance rapidly and without hesitation, although we could see nothing. That day we encountered new surface conditions—big, hard snow-waves (*sastrugi*). These were anything but pleasant to work among, especially when one could not see them. It was of no use for us "fore-runners" to think of going in advance under these

107

circumstances, as it was impossible to keep on one's feet. Three or four paces was often the most we managed to do before falling down. The *sastrugi* were very high, and often abrupt; if one came on them unexpectedly, one required to be more than an acrobat to keep on one's feet. The plan we found to work best in these conditions was to let Hanssen's dogs go first; this was an unpleasant job for Hanssen, and for his dogs too, but it succeeded, and succeeded well. An upset here and there was, of course, unavoidable, but with a little patience the sledge was always righted again. The drivers had as much as they could do to support their sledges among these *sastrugi*, but while supporting the sledges, they had at the same time a support for themselves. It was worse for us who had no sledges, but by keeping in the wake of them we could see where the irregularities lay, and thus get over them. Hanssen deserves a special word of praise for his driving on this surface in such weather. It is a difficult matter to drive Eskimo dogs forward when they cannot see; but Hanssen managed it well, both getting the dogs on and steering his course by compass. One would not think it possible to keep an approximately right course when the uneven ground gives such violent shocks that the needle flies several times round the compass, and is no sooner still again than it recommences the same dance; but when at last we got an observation, it turned out that Hanssen had steered to a hair, for the observations and dead reckoning agreed to a mile. In spite of all hindrances, and of being able to see nothing, the sledge-meters showed nearly twenty-five miles. The hypsometer showed 11,070 feet above the sea; we had therefore reached a greater altitude than the Butcher's.

December 6 brought the same weather : thick snow, sky and plain all one, nothing to be seen. Nevertheless we made splendid progress. The *sastrugi* gradually became levelled out, until the surface was perfectly smooth; it was a relief to have even ground to go upon once more. These irregularities that one was constantly falling over were a nuisance ; if we had met with them in our usual surroundings it would not have mattered so much ; but up here on the high ground, where we had to stand and gasp for breath every time we rolled over, it was certainly not pleasant.

That day we passed 88° S., and camped in 88° 9′ S. A great surprise awaited us in the tent that evening. I expected to find, as on the previous evening, that the boiling-point had fallen somewhat ; in other words, that it would show a continued rise of the ground, but to our astonishment this was not so. The water boiled at exactly the same temperature as on the preceding day. I tried it several times, to convince myself that there was nothing wrong, each time with the same result. There was great rejoicing among us all when I was able to announce that we had arrived on the top of the plateau.

December 7 began like the 6th, with absolutely thick weather, but, as they say, you never know what the day is like before sunset. Possibly I might have chosen a better expression than this last—one more in agreement with the natural conditions—but I will let it stand. Though for several weeks now the sun had not set, my readers will not be so critical as to reproach me with inaccuracy. With a light wind from the north-east, we now went southward at a good speed over the perfectly level plain, with excellent going. The uphill work had taken it out of our dogs, though not to any serious extent. They had turned greedy—there is no denying that—and the half kilo of pemmican they got each day was not enough to fill their stomachs. Early and late they were looking for something—no matter what—to devour. To begin with they contented themselves with such loose objects as ski-bindings, whips, boots, and the like; but as we came to know their proclivities, we took such care of everything that they found no extra meals lying about. But that was not the end of the matter. They then went for the fixed lashings of the sledges, and—if we had allowed it—would very quickly have resolved the various sledges into their component parts. But we found a way of stopping that: every evening, on halting, the sledges were buried in the snow, so as to hide all the lashings. That was successful; curiously enough, they never tried to force the "snow rampart."

I may mention as a curious thing that these ravenous

animals, that devoured everything they came across, even to the ebonite points of our ski-sticks, never made any attempt to break into the provision cases. They lay there and went about among the sledges with their noses just on a level with the split cases, seeing and scenting the pemmican, without once making a sign of taking any. But if one raised a lid, they were not long in showing themselves. Then they all came in a great hurry and flocked about the sledges in the hope of getting a little extra bit. I am at a loss to explain this behaviour; that bashfulness was not at the root of it, I am tolerably certain.

During the forenoon the thick, grey curtain of cloud began to grow thinner on the horizon, and for the first time for three days we could see a few miles about us. The feeling was something like that one has on waking from a good nap, rubbing one's eyes and looking around. We had become so accustomed to the grey twilight that this positively dazzled us. Meanwhile, the upper layer of air seemed obstinately to remain the same and to be doing its best to prevent the sun from showing itself. We badly wanted to get a meridian altitude, so that we could determine our latitude. Since 86° 47′ S. we had had no observation, and it was not easy to say when we should get one. Hitherto, the weather conditions on the high ground had not been particularly favourable. Although the prospects were not very promising, we halted at 11 a.m. and made ready to catch the sun if it should be kind enough to look out. Hassel and Wisting used one sextant and artificial horizon, Hanssen and I the other set.

I don't know that I have ever stood and absolutely pulled at the sun to get it out as I did that time. If we got an observation here which agreed with our reckoning, then it would be possible, if the worst came to the worst, to go to the Pole on dead reckoning; but if we got none now, it was a question whether our claim to the Pole would be admitted on the dead reckoning we should be able to produce. Whether my pulling helped or not, it is certain that the sun appeared. It was not very brilliant to begin with, but, practised as we now were in availing ourselves of even the poorest chances, it was good enough. Down it came, was checked by all, and the altitude written down. The curtain of cloud was rent more and more, and before we had finished our work—that is to say, caught the sun at its highest, and convinced ourselves that it was descending again—it was shining in all its glory. We had put away our instruments and were sitting on the sledges, engaged in the calculations. I can safely say that we were excited. What would the result be, after marching blindly for so long and over such impossible ground, as we had been doing? We added and subtracted, and at last there was the result. We looked at each other in sheer incredulity: the result was as astonishing as the most

TAKING AN OBSERVATION AT THE POLE.

consummate conjuring trick—88° 16′ S., precisely to a
minute the same as our reckoning, 88° 16′ S. If we
were forced to go to the Pole on dead reckoning, then
surely the most exacting would admit our right to
do so. We put away our observation books, ate one
or two biscuits, and went at it again.

We had a great piece of work before us that day:
nothing less than carrying our flag farther south than
the foot of man had trod. We had our silk flag
ready; it was made fast to two ski-sticks and laid
on Hanssen's sledge. I had given him orders that as
soon as we had covered the distance to 88° 23′ S., which
was Shackleton's farthest south, the flag was to be
hoisted on his sledge. It was my turn as forerunner,
and I pushed on. There was no longer any difficulty
in holding one's course; I had the grandest cloud-
formations to steer by, and everything now went like
a machine. First came the forerunner for the time
being, then Hanssen, then Wisting, and finally Bjaaland.
The forerunner who was not on duty went where he
liked; as a rule he accompanied one or other of the
sledges. I had long ago fallen into a reverie—far
removed from the scene in which I was moving; what
I thought about I do not remember now, but I was
so preoccupied that I had entirely forgotten my surroundings. Then suddenly I was roused from my
dreaming by a jubilant shout, followed by ringing
cheers. I turned round quickly to discover the reason

of this unwonted occurrence, and stood speechless and
overcome.

I find it impossible to express the feelings that
possessed me at this moment. All the sledges had
stopped, and from the foremost of them the Norwegian
flag was flying. It shook itself out, waved and flapped
so that the silk rustled; it looked wonderfully well
in the pure, clear air and the shining white surroundings. 88° 23′ was past; we were farther south than
any human being had been. No other moment of the
whole trip affected me like this. The tears forced
their way to my eyes; by no effort of will could I keep
them back. It was the flag yonder that conquered me
and my will. Luckily I was some way in advance of
the others, so that I had time to pull myself together
and master my feelings before reaching my comrades.
We all shook hands, with mutual congratulations; we
had won our way far by holding together, and we would
go farther yet—to the end.

We did not pass that spot without according our
highest tribute of admiration to the man, who—together
with his gallant companions—had planted his country's
flag so infinitely nearer to the goal than any of his
precursors. Sir Ernest Shackleton's name will always
be written in the annals of Antarctic exploration in
letters of fire. Pluck and grit can work wonders, and
I know of no better example of this than what that man
has accomplished.

The cameras of course had to come out, and we got an excellent photograph of the scene which none of us will ever forget. We went on a couple of miles more, to 88° 25′, and then camped. The weather had improved, and kept on improving all the time. It was now almost perfectly calm, radiantly clear, and, under the circumstances, quite summer-like: −0·4° F. Inside the tent it was quite sultry. This was more than we had expected.

After much consideration and discussion we had come to the conclusion that we ought to lay down a depot—the last one—at this spot. The advantages of lightening our sledges were so great that we should have to risk it. Nor would there be any great risk attached to it, after all, since we should adopt a system of marks that would lead even a blind man back to the place. We had determined to mark it not only at right angles to our course—that is, from east to west—but by snow beacons at every two geographical miles to the south.

We stayed here on the following day to arrange this depot. Hanssen's dogs were real marvels, all of them; nothing seemed to have any effect on them. They had grown rather thinner, of course, but they were still as strong as ever. It was therefore decided not to lighten Hanssen's sledge, but only the two others; both Wisting's and Bjaaland's teams had suffered, especially the latter's. The reduction in weight that was effected was considerable—nearly 110 pounds on each of the two sledges;

there was thus about 220 pounds in the depot.   The
snow here was ill-adapted for building, but we put up
quite a respectable monument all the same.   It was
dogs' pemmican and biscuits that were left behind; we
carried with us on the sledges provisions for about a
month.   If, therefore, contrary to expectation, we should
be so unlucky as to miss this depot, we should nevertheless be fairly sure of reaching our depot in 86° 21′
before supplies ran short.   The cross-marking of the
depot was done with sixty splinters of black packing-
case on each side, with 100 paces between each.   Every
other one had a shred of black cloth on the top.   The
splinters on the east side were all marked, so that on
seeing them we should know instantly that we were to
the east of the depot.   Those on the west had no marks.

The warmth of the past few days seemed to have
matured our frost-sores, and we presented an awful
appearance.   It was Wisting, Hanssen, and I who had
suffered the worst damage in the last south-east blizzard;
the left side of our faces was one mass of sore, bathed in
matter and serum.   We looked like the worst type of
tramps and ruffians, and would probably not have been
recognized by our nearest relations.   These sores were
a great trouble to us during the latter part of the journey.
The slightest gust of wind produced a sensation as if
one's face were being cut backwards and forwards with
a blunt knife.   They lasted a long time, too; I can
remember Hanssen removing the last scab when we

were coming into Hobart—three months later. We were very lucky in the weather during this depot work; the sun came out all at once, and we had an excellent opportunity of taking some good azimuth observations, the last of any use that we got on the journey.

December 9 arrived with the same fine weather and sunshine. True, we felt our frost-sores rather sharply that day, with —18·4° F. and a little breeze dead against us, but that could not be helped. We at once began to put up beacons—a work which was continued with great regularity right up to the Pole. These beacons were not so big as those we had built down on the Barrier; we could see that they would be quite large enough with a height of about 3 feet, as it was very easy to see the slightest irregularity on this perfectly flat surface. While thus engaged we had an opportunity of becoming thoroughly acquainted with the nature of the snow. Often—very often indeed—on this part of the plateau, to the south of 88° 25′, we had difficulty in getting snow good enough—that is, solid enough for cutting blocks. The snow up here seemed to have fallen very quietly, in light breezes or calms. We could thrust the tent-pole, which was 6 feet long, right down without meeting resistance, which showed that there was no hard layer of snow. The surface was also perfectly level; there was not a sign of *sastrugi* in any direction.

Every step we now took in advance brought us rapidly

nearer the goal; we could feel fairly certain of reaching it on the afternoon of the 14th. It was very natural that our conversation should be chiefly concerned with the time of arrival. None of us would admit that he was nervous, but I am inclined to think that we all had a little touch of that malady. What should we see when we got there? A vast, endless plain, that no eye had yet seen and no foot yet trodden; or—— No, it was an impossibility; with the speed at which we had travelled, we must reach the goal first, there could be no doubt about that. And yet—and yet—— Wherever there is the smallest loophole, doubt creeps in and gnaws and gnaws and never leaves a poor wretch in peace. "What on earth is Uroa scenting?" It was Bjaaland who made this remark, on one of these last days, when I was going by the side of his sledge and talking to him. "And the strange thing is that he's scenting to the south. It can never be——" Mylius, Ring, and Suggen, showed the same interest in the southerly direction; it was quite extraordinary to see how they raised their heads, with every sign of curiosity, put their noses in the air, and sniffed due south. One would really have thought there was something remarkable to be found there.

From 88° 25' S. the barometer and hypsometer indicated slowly but surely that the plateau was beginning to descend towards the other side. This was a pleasant surprise to us; we had thus not only found the very summit of the plateau, but also the slope down on the far side. This would have a very important bearing for obtaining an idea of the construction of the whole plateau. On December 9 observations and dead reckoning agreed within a mile. The same result again on the 10th : observation 2 kilometres behind reckoning. The weather and going remained about the same as on the preceding days : light south-easterly breeze, temperature —18·4° F. The snow surface was loose, but ski and sledges glided over it well. On the 11th, the same weather conditions. Temperature —13° F. Observation and reckoning again agreed exactly. Our latitude was 89° 15′ S. On the 12th we reached 89° 30′, reckoning 1 kilometre behind observation. Going and surface as good as ever. Weather splendid—calm with sunshine. The noon observation on the 13th gave 89° 37′ S. Reckoning 89° 38·5′ S. We halted in the afternoon, after going eight geographical miles, and camped in 89° 45′, according to reckoning.

The weather during the forenoon had been just as fine as before; in the afternoon we had some snow-showers from the south-east. It was like the eve of some great festival that night in the tent. One could feel that a great event was at hand. Our flag was taken out again and lashed to the same two ski-sticks as before. Then it was rolled up and laid aside, to be ready when the time came. I was awake several times during the night, and had the same feeling that I can remember as a little boy on the night before Christmas Eve—an intense expectation of what was going to happen. Otherwise I think we slept just as well that night as any other.

On the morning of December 14 the weather was of the finest, just as if it had been made for arriving at the Pole. I am not quite sure, but I believe we despatched our breakfast rather more quickly than usual and were out of the tent sooner, though I must admit that we always accomplished this with all reasonable haste. We went in the usual order—the forerunner, Hanssen, Wisting, Bjaaland, and the reserve forerunner. By noon we had reached 89° 53′ by dead reckoning, and made ready to take the rest in one stage. At 10 a.m. a light breeze had sprung up from the south-east, and it had clouded over, so that we got no noon altitude; but the clouds were not thick, and from time to time we had a glimpse of the sun through them. The going on that day was rather different from what it had been; sometimes the ski went over it well, but at others it was pretty bad. We advanced that day in the same mechanical way as before; not much was said, but eyes were used all the more. Hanssen's neck grew twice as long as before in his endeavour to see a few inches farther. I had asked him before we started to spy out ahead for all he was worth, and he did so with a vengeance. But, however keenly he stared, he could not descry anything but the endless flat plain ahead of us. The dogs had dropped

CHART OF THE
IMMEDIATE SURROUNDINGS
OF THE
SOUTH POLE

Scale

0   2   4   6   8 KILOMETRES.
0   1   2   3   4   5 MILES.

KING

FRAM

Polheim 17. XII. 1911.

SOUTH POLE

HAAKON VII'S

Sledge
89° 53' S. Lat.
14. XII. 1911.

PLATEAU

Course from Framheim to the Pole

Long. West 180 Long. East of Greenwich

Copyright 1912 Roald Amundsen.

their scenting, and appeared to have lost their interest in the regions about the earth's axis.

At three in the afternoon a simultaneous "Halt!" rang out from the drivers. They had carefully examined their sledge-meters, and they all showed the full distance—our Pole by reckoning. The goal was reached, the journey ended. I cannot say—though I know it would sound much more effective—that the object of my life was attained. That would be romancing rather too barefacedly. I had better be honest and admit straight out that I have never known any man to be placed in such a diametrically opposite position to the goal of his desires as I was at that moment. The regions around the North Pole—well, yes, the North Pole itself—had attracted me from childhood, and here I was at the South Pole. Can anything more topsy-turvy be imagined?

We reckoned now that we were at the Pole. Of course, every one of us knew that we were not standing on the absolute spot; it would be an impossibility with the time and the instruments at our disposal to ascertain that exact spot. But we were so near it that the few miles which possibly separated us from it could not be of the slightest importance. It was our intention to make a circle round this camp, with a radius of twelve and a half miles (20 kilometres), and to be satisfied with that. After we had halted we collected and congratulated each other. We had good grounds for

mutual respect in what had been achieved, and I
think that was just the feeling that was expressed in
the firm and powerful grasps of the fist that were
exchanged.   After this we proceeded to the greatest
and most solemn act of the whole journey—the planting
of our flag.   Pride and affection shone in the five pairs
of eyes that gazed upon the flag, as it unfurled itself with
a sharp crack, and waved over the Pole.   I had determined that the act of planting it—the historic event—
should be equally divided among us all.   It was not for
one man to do this ; it was for *all* who had staked their
lives in the struggle, and held together through thick
and thin.   This was the only way in which I could
show my gratitude to my comrades in this desolate spot.
I could see that they understood and accepted it in the
spirit in which it was offered.   Five weather-beaten,
frost-bitten fists they were that grasped the pole, raised
the waving flag in the air, and planted it as the first at
the geographical South Pole.   " Thus we plant thee,
beloved flag, at the South Pole, and give to the plain
on which it lies the name of King Haakon VII.'s
Plateau."   That moment will certainly be remembered
by all of us who stood there.

One gets out of the way of protracted ceremonies in
those regions—the shorter they are the better.   Everyday
life began again at once.   When we had got the tent up,
Hanssen set about slaughtering Helge, and it was hard
for him to have to part from his best friend.   Helge

had been an uncommonly useful and good-natured dog; without making any fuss he had pulled from morning to night, and had been a shining example to the team. But during the last week he had quite fallen away, and on our arrival at the Pole there was only a shadow of the old Helge left. He was only a drag on the others, and did absolutely no work. One blow on the skull, and Helge had ceased to live. " What is death to one is food to another," is a saying that can scarcely find a better application than these dog meals. Helge was portioned out on the spot, and within a couple of hours there was nothing left of him but his teeth and the tuft at the end of his tail. This was the second of our eighteen dogs that we had lost. The Major, one of Wisting's fine dogs, left us in 88° 25′ S., and never returned. He was fearfully worn out, and must have gone away to die. We now had sixteen dogs left, and these we intended to divide into two equal teams, leaving Bjaaland's sledge behind.

Of course, there was a festivity in the tent that evening—not that champagne corks were popping and wine flowing—no, we contented ourselves with a little piece of seal meat each, and it tasted well and did us good. There was no other sign of festival indoors. Outside we heard the flag flapping in the breeze. Conversation was lively in the tent that evening, and we talked of many things. Perhaps, too, our thoughts sent messages home of what we had done.

Everything we had with us had now to be marked with the words " South Pole " and the date, to serve afterwards as souvenirs. Wisting proved to be a first-class engraver, and many were the articles he had to mark. Tobacco—in the form of smoke—had hitherto never made its appearance in the tent. From time to time I had seen one or two of the others take a quid, but now these things were to be altered. I had brought with me an old briar pipe, which bore inscriptions from many places in the Arctic regions, and now I wanted it marked " South Pole." When I produced my pipe and was about to mark it, I received an unexpected gift: Wisting offered me tobacco for the rest of the journey. He had some cakes of plug in his kit-bag, which he would prefer to see me smoke. Can anyone grasp what such an offer meant at such a spot, made to a man who, to tell the truth, is very fond of a smoke after meals? There are not many who can understand it fully. I accepted the offer, jumping with joy, and on the way home I had a pipe of fresh, fine-cut plug every evening. Ah! that Wisting, he spoiled me entirely. Not only did he give me tobacco, but every evening—and I must confess I yielded to the temptation after a while, and had a morning smoke as well—he undertook the disagreeable work of cutting the plug and filling my pipe in all kinds of weather.

But we did not let our talk make us forget other

things. As we had got no noon altitude, we should have to try and take one at midnight. The weather had brightened again, and it looked as if midnight would be a good time for the observation. We therefore crept into our bags to get a little nap in the intervening hours. In good time—soon after 11 p.m.—we were out again, and ready to catch the sun; the weather was of the best, and the opportunity excellent. We four navigators all had a share in it, as usual, and stood watching the course of the sun. This was a labour of patience, as the difference of altitude was now very slight. The result at which we finally arrived was of great interest, as it clearly shows how unreliable and valueless a single observation like this is in these regions. At 12.30 a.m. we put our instruments away, well satisfied with our work, and quite convinced that it was the midnight altitude that we had observed. The calculations which were carried out immediately afterwards gave us 89° 56′ S. We were all well pleased with this result.

The arrangement now was that we should encircle this camp with a radius of about twelve and a half miles. By encircling I do not, of course, mean that we should go round in a circle with this radius; that would have taken us days, and was not to be thought of. The encircling was accomplished in this way: Three men went out in three different directions, two at right angles to the course we had been steering, and one in

continuation of that course. To carry out this work
I had chosen Wisting, Hassel, and Bjaaland. Having
concluded our observations, we put the kettle on to
give ourselves a drop of chocolate; the pleasure of
standing out there in rather light attire had not exactly
put warmth into our bodies. As we were engaged in
swallowing the scalding drink, Bjaaland suddenly observed : " I'd like to tackle this encircling straight
away. We shall have lots of time to sleep when we
get back." Hassel and Wisting were quite of the same
opinion, and it was agreed that they should start the
work immediately. Here we have yet another example
of the good spirit that prevailed in our little community.
We had only lately come in from our day's work—
a march of about eighteen and a half miles—and now
they were asking to be allowed to go on another
twenty-five miles. It seemed as if these fellows could
never be tired. We therefore turned this meal into
a little breakfast—that is to say, each man ate what he
wanted of his bread ration, and then they began to get
ready for the work. First, three small bags of light
windproof stuff were made, and in each of these was
placed a paper, giving the position of our camp. In
addition, each of them carried a large square flag of the
same dark brown material, which could be easily seen
at a distance. As flag-poles we elected to use our spare
sledge-runners, which were both long—12 feet—and
strong, and which we were going to take off here in any

case, to lighten the sledges as much as possible for the return journey.

Thus equipped, and with thirty biscuits as an extra ration, the three men started off in the directions laid down. Their march was by no means free from danger, and does great honour to those who undertook it, not merely without raising the smallest objection, but with the greatest keenness. Let us consider for a moment the risk they ran. Our tent on the boundless plain, without marks of any kind, may very well be compared with a needle in a haystack. From this the three men were to steer out for a distance of twelve and a half miles. Compasses would have been good things to take on such a walk, but our sledge-compasses were too heavy and unsuitable for carrying. They therefore had to go without. They had the sun to go by, certainly, when they started, but who could say how long it would last? The weather was then fine enough, but it was impossible to guarantee that no sudden change would take place. If by bad luck the sun should be hidden, then their own tracks might help them. But to trust to tracks in these regions is a dangerous thing. Before you know where you are the whole plain may be one mass of driving snow, obliterating all tracks as soon as they are made. With the rapid changes of weather we had so often experienced, such a thing was not impossible. That these three risked their lives that morning, when they left the tent at 2.30, there can be no doubt at all, and they all three knew it very well. But if anyone thinks that on this account they took a solemn farewell of us who stayed behind, he is much mistaken. Not a bit; they all vanished in their different directions amid laughter and chaff.

The first thing we did—Hanssen and I—was to set about arranging a lot of trifling matters; there was something to be done here, something there, and above all we had to be ready for the series of observations we were to carry out together, so as to get as accurate a determination of our position as possible. The first observation told us at once how necessary this was. For it turned out that this, instead of giving us a greater altitude than the midnight observation, gave us a smaller one, and it was then clear that we had gone out of the meridian we thought we were following. Now the first thing to be done was to get our north and south line and latitude determined, so that we could find our position once more. Luckily for us, the weather looked as if it would hold. We measured the sun's altitude at every hour from 6 a.m. to 7 p.m., and from these observations found, with some degree of certainty, our latitude and the direction of the meridian.

By nine in the morning we began to expect the return of our comrades; according to our calculation they should then have covered the distance—twenty-five miles. It was not till ten o'clock that Hanssen made out the first black dot on the horizon, and not long after the second and third appeared. We both gave a sigh of relief as they came on; almost simultaneously the three arrived at the tent. We told them the result of our observations up to that time; it looked as if our camp was in about 89° 54′ 30″ S., and that with our encircling we had therefore included the actual Pole. With this result we might very well have been content, but as the weather was so good and gave the impression that it would continue so, and our store of provisions proved on examination to be very ample, we decided to go on for the remaining ten kilometres (five and a half geographical miles), and get our position determined as near to the Pole as possible. Meanwhile the three wanderers turned in—not so much because they were tired, as because it was the right thing to do—and Hanssen and I continued the series of observations.

In the afternoon we again went very carefully through our provision supply before discussing the future. The result was that we had food enough for ourselves and the dogs for eighteen days. The surviving sixteen dogs were divided into two teams of eight each, and the contents of Bjaaland's sledge were shared between Hanssen's and Wisting's. The abandoned sledge was set upright in the snow, and proved to be a splendid mark. The sledge-meter was screwed to the sledge, and we left it there; our other two were quite sufficient for the return journey; they had all shown themselves very accurate. A couple of empty provision cases were

also left behind.   I wrote in pencil on a piece of case
the information that our tent—" Polheim "—would be
found five and a half geographical miles north-west
quarter west by compass from the sledge.   Having put
all these things in order the same day, we turned in,
very well satisfied.

Early next morning, December 16, we were on our
feet again.   Bjaaland, who had now left the company
of the drivers and been received with jubilation into
that of the forerunners, was immediately entrusted with
the honourable task of leading the expedition forward
to the Pole itself.   I assigned this duty, which we all
regarded as a distinction, to him as a mark of gratitude
to the gallant Telemarkers for their pre-eminent work
in the advancement of ski sport.   The leader that day
had to keep as straight as a line, and if possible to follow
the direction of our meridian.   A little way after
Bjaaland came Hassel, then Hanssen, then Wisting, and
I followed a good way behind.   I could thus check the
direction of the march very accurately, and see that no
great deviation was made.   Bjaaland on this occasion
showed himself a matchless forerunner ; he went perfectly straight the whole time.   Not once did he incline
to one side or the other, and when we arrived at the
end of the distance, we could still clearly see the sledge
we had set up and take its bearing.   This showed it to
be absolutely in the right direction.

It was 11 a.m. when we reached our destination.

Kl 4ƒ ⊙ N t V ¾ V 46° 9' 00"
„ 5. ⊙ N V ¾ N 46° 9' 00"
„ 6. ⊙ N V ½ V 46° 8' 00"
„ 7. ⊙ V t N ½ N 46° 8' 00"
„ 8. ⊙ V ¼ N 46° 6' 20"
„ 9. ⊙ V t S 46° 6' 20"
„ 10. ⊙ V S V. 46° 6' 20"
„ 11. ⊙ S V ½ V 46° 8' 30"
„ 12. ⊙ S V t S 46° 10' 00"
„ 12. Sex l = lqf. 1.1 46° 8' 00"

R. Amundsen. *H. Hanssen*
O. Wisting *Hassel.*

A PAGE FROM THE OBSERVATION BOOK, DECEMBER 17, 1911.

While some of us were putting up the tent, others began to get everything ready for the coming observations. A solid snow pedestal was put up, on which the artificial horizon was to be placed, and a smaller one to rest the sextant on when it was not in use. At 11.30 a.m. the first observation was taken. We divided ourselves into two parties—Hanssen and I in one, Hassel and Wisting in the other. While one party slept, the other took the observations, and the watches were of six hours each. The weather was altogether grand, though the sky was not perfectly bright the whole time. A very light, fine, vaporous curtain would spread across the sky from time to time, and then quickly disappear again. This film of cloud was not thick enough to hide the sun, which we could see the whole time, but the atmosphere seemed to be disturbed. The effect of this was that the sun appeared not to change its altitude for several hours, until it suddenly made a jump.

Observations were now taken every hour through the whole twenty-four. It was very strange to turn in at 6 p.m., and then on turning out again at midnight to find the sun apparently still at the same altitude, and then once more at 6 a.m. to see it still no higher. The altitude had changed, of course, but so slightly that it was imperceptible with the naked eye. To us it appeared as though the sun made the circuit of the heavens at exactly the same altitude. The times of day that I have given here are calculated according to the meridian of Framheim ; we continued to reckon our time from this. The observations soon told us that we were not on the absolute Pole, but as close to it as we could hope to get with our instruments. The observations, which have been submitted to Mr. Anton Alexander, will be published, and the result given later in this book.

On December 17 at noon we had completed our observations, and it is certain that we had done all that could be done. In order if possible to come a few inches nearer to the actual Pole, Hanssen and Bjaaland went out four geographical miles (seven kilometres) in the direction of the newly found meridian.

Bjaaland astonished me at dinner that day. Speeches had not hitherto been a feature of this journey, but now Bjaaland evidently thought the time had come, and surprised us all with a really fine oration. My amazement reached its culmination when, at the conclusion of his speech, he produced a cigar-case full of cigars and offered it round. A cigar at the Pole ! What do you say to that ? But it did not end there. When the cigars had gone round, there were still four left. I was quite touched when he handed the case and cigars to me with the words : " Keep this to remind you of the Pole." I have taken good care of the case, and shall preserve it as one of the many happy signs of my comrades' devotion on this journey. The cigars I shared out afterwards, on Christmas Eve, and they gave us a visible mark of that occasion.

When this festival dinner at the Pole was ended, we began our preparations for departure. First we set up the little tent we had brought with us in case we should be compelled to divide into two parties. It had been made by our able sailmaker, Rönne, and was of very thin windproof gabardine. Its drab colour made it easily visible against the white surface. Another pole was lashed to the tent-pole, making its total height about 13 feet. On the top of this a little Norwegian flag was lashed fast, and underneath it a pennant, on which "Fram" was painted. The tent was well secured with guy-ropes on all sides. Inside the tent, in a little bag, I left a letter, addressed to H.M. the King, giving information of what we had accomplished. The way home was a long one, and so many things might happen to make it impossible for us to give an account of our expedition. Besides this letter, I wrote a short epistle to Captain Scott, who, I assumed, would be the first to find the tent. Other things we left there were a sextant with a glass horizon, a hypsometer case, three reindeer-skin foot-bags, some kamiks and mits.

When everything had been laid inside, we went into the tent, one by one, to write our names on a tablet we had fastened to the tent-pole. On this occasion we received the congratulations of our companions on the successful result, for the following messages were written on a couple of strips of leather, sewed to the tent: "Good luck," and "Welcome to 90°." These good wishes, which we suddenly discovered, put us in very good spirits. They were signed by Beck and Rönne. They had good faith in us. When we had finished this we came out, and the tent-door was securely laced together, so that there was no danger of the wind getting a hold on that side.

And so good-bye to Polheim. It was a solemn moment when we bared our heads and bade farewell to our home and our flag. And then the travelling tent was taken down and the sledges packed. Now the homeward journey was to begin—homeward, step by step, mile after mile, until the whole distance was accomplished. We drove at once into our old tracks and followed them. Many were the times we turned to send a last look to Polheim. The vaporous, white air set in again, and it was not long before the last of Polheim, our little flag, disappeared from view.

AT THE SOUTH POLE, DECEMBER 16, 17, 1911.

CHAPTER XIII

THE RETURN TO FRAMHEIM

THE going was splendid and all were in good spirits, so we went along at a great pace. One would almost have thought the dogs knew they were homeward bound. A mild, summer-like wind, with a temperature of $-2 \cdot 2°$ F., was our last greeting from the Pole.

When we came to our last camp, where the sledge was left, we stopped and took a few things with us. From this point we came into the line of beacons. Our tracks had already become very indistinct, but, thanks to his excellent sight, Bjaaland kept in them quite well. The beacons, however, served their purpose so satisfactorily that the tracks were almost superfluous. Although these beacons were not more than about 3 feet high, they were extremely conspicuous on the level surface. When the sun was on them, they shone like electric lighthouses; and when the sun was on the other side, they looked so dark in the shadow that one would have taken them for black rocks. We intended in future to travel at night; the advantages of this were many and great. In the first place, we should have the sun behind us, which meant a good deal to our eyes. Going against the sun on a snow surface like this tells fearfully on the eyes, even if one has good snow-goggles; but with the sun at one's back it is only play. Another great advantage—which we did not reap till later—was that it gave us the warmest part of the twenty-four hours in the tent, during which time we had an opportunity of drying wet clothes, and so on. This last advantage was, however, a doubtful one, as we shall see in due course.

It was a great comfort to turn our backs to the south. The wind, which had nearly always been in this quarter, had often been very painful to our cracked faces; now we should always have it at our backs, and it would help us on our way, besides giving our faces time to heal. Another thing we were longing for was to come down to the Barrier again, so that we could breathe freely. Up here we were seldom able to draw a good long breath; if we only had to say " Yes," we had to do it in two instalments. The asthmatic condition in which we found ourselves during our six weeks' stay on the plateau was anything but pleasant. We had fixed fifteen geographical miles (seventeen and three-eighths statute miles) as a suitable day's march on the homeward journey. We had, of course, many advantages now as compared with the southward journey, which would have enabled us to do longer marches than this; but we were afraid of overworking the dogs, and possibly using them up before we had gone very far, if we attempted too great a distance daily. It soon proved, however, that we had underestimated our dogs' powers; it only took us five hours to cover the appointed distance, and our rest was therefore a long one.

On December 19 we killed the first dog on the homeward trip. This was Lasse, my own favourite dog. He had worn himself out completely, and was no longer worth anything. He was divided into fifteen portions, as nearly equal as possible, and given to his companions. They had now learnt to set great store by fresh meat, and it is certain that the extra feeds, like this one, that took place from time to time on the way home, had no small share in the remarkably successful result. They seemed to benefit by these meals of fresh meat for several days afterwards, and worked much more easily.

December 20 began with bitter weather, a breeze from the south-east, grey and thick. We lost the trail, and for some time had to go by compass. But as usual it suddenly cleared, and once more the plain lay before us, light and warm. Yes, too warm it was. We had to take off everything—nearly—and still the sweat poured off us. It was not for long that we were uncertain of the way: our excellent beacons did us brilliant service, and one after another they came up on the horizon, flashed and shone, and drew us on to our all-important depot in 88° 25′ S. We were now going slightly uphill, but so slightly that it was unnoticeable. The hypsometer and barometer, however, were not to be deceived, and both fell in precisely the same degree as they had risen before. Even if we had not exactly noticed the rise, the feeling of it was present. It may perhaps be called imagination, but I certainly thought I could notice the rise by my breathing.

Our appetite had increased alarmingly during the last few days. It appeared that we ski-runners evinced a far greater voracity than the drivers. There were days —only a few days, be it said—when I believe any of us three—Bjaaland, Hassel, and myself—would have swallowed pebbles without winking. The drivers never showed such signs of starvation. It has occurred to me that this may possibly have been due to their being able to lean on the sledges as they went along, and thus have a rest and support which we had to do without. It seems little enough simply to rest one's hand on a sledge on the march, but in the long run, day after day, it may perhaps make itself felt. Fortunately we were so well supplied that when this sensation of hunger came over us, we could increase our daily rations. On leaving the Pole we added to our pemmican ration, with the result that our wild-beast appetites soon gave way and shrank to an ordinary good, everyday twist. Our daily programme on entering upon the return journey was so arranged that we began to get breakfast ready at 6 p.m., and by 8 p.m. we were usually quite ready to start the day's march. An hour or so after midnight the fifteen geographical miles were accomplished, and we could once more put up our tent, cook our food, and seek our rest. But this rest soon became so insufferably long. And then there was the fearful heat—considering the circumstances—which often made us get out of our sleeping-bags and lie with nothing over us. These rests of twelve, fourteen, sometimes as much as sixteen hours, were what most tried our patience during the early part of the return journey. We could see so well that all this rest was unnecessary, but still we kept it up as long as we were on the high ground. Our conversation at this time used to turn very often on the best way of filling up these long, unnecessary waits.

That day—December 20—Per—good, faithful, conscientious Per—broke down utterly and had to be taken on the sledge the last part of the way. On arrival at the camping-ground he had his reward. A little blow of the back of the axe was enough for him; without making a sound the worn-out animal collapsed. In him Wisting lost one of his best dogs. He was a curious animal—always went about quietly and peaceably, and never took part in the others' battles; from his looks and behaviour one would have judged him, quite mistakenly, to be a queer sort of beast who was good for nothing. But when he was in harness he showed what he could do. Without needing any shouts or cuts of the whip, he put himself into it from morning to night, and was priceless as a draught dog.

But, like others of the same character, he could not keep it going any longer; he collapsed, was killed and eaten.

Christmas Eve was rapidly approaching. For us it could not be particularly festive, but we should have to try to make as much of it as circumstances would permit. We ought, therefore, to reach our depot that evening, so as to keep Christmas with a dish of porridge. The night before Christmas Eve we slaughtered Svart-flekken. There was no mourning on this occasion: Svartflekken was one of Hassel's dogs, and had always been a reprobate. I find the following in my diary, written the same evening: "Slaughtered Svartflekken this evening. He would not do any more, although there was not much wrong with his looks. Bad character. If a man, he would have ended in penal servitude." He was comparatively fat, and was consumed with evident satisfaction.

Christmas Eve came; the weather was rather change-able—now overcast, now clear—when we set out at 8 p.m. the night before. We had not far to go before reaching our depot. At 12 midnight we arrived there in the most glorious weather, calm and warm. Now we had the whole of Christmas Eve before us, and could enjoy it at our ease. Our depot was at once taken down and divided between the two sledges. All crumbs of biscuit were carefully collected by Wisting, the cook for the day, and put into a bag. This was taken into the tent and vigorously beaten and kneaded;

the result was pulverized biscuit. With this product
and a sausage of dried milk, Wisting succeeded in
making a capital dish of Christmas porridge. I doubt
whether anyone at home enjoyed his Christmas dinner
so much as we did that morning in the tent. One of
Bjaaland's cigars to follow brought a festival spirit over
the whole camp.

Another thing we had to rejoice about that day was
that we had again reached the summit of the plateau,
and after two or three more days' march would begin to
go downhill, finally reaching the Barrier and our old
haunts. Our daily march had hitherto been interrupted
by one or two halts; we stopped to rest both the dogs
and ourselves. On Christmas Eve we instituted a new
order of things, and did the whole distance—fifteen
geographical miles—without a stop. We liked this
arrangement best, after all, and it seemed as if the
dogs did the same. As a rule it was hard to begin the
march again after the rest; one got rather stiff—lazy,
too, perhaps—and had to become supple again.

On the 26th we passed 88° S., going well. The
surface appeared to have been exposed to powerful
sunshine since we left it, as it had become quite
polished. Going over these polished levels was like
crossing smooth ice, but with the important difference
that here the dogs had a good foothold. This time we
sighted high land even in 88°, and it had great surprises
in store for us. It was clear that this was the same

mighty range running to the south-east as we had seen
before, but this time it stretched considerably farther to
the south. The weather was radiantly clear, and we
could see by the land that the range of vision was very
great. Summit after summit the range extended to
the south-east, until it gradually disappeared ; but to
judge from the atmosphere, it was continued beyond
our range of vision in the same direction. That this
chain traverses the Antarctic continent I therefore
consider beyond a doubt. Here we had a very good
example of how deceptive the atmosphere is in these
regions. On a day that appeared perfectly clear we
had lost sight of the mountains in 87°, and now we saw
them as far as the eye could reach in 88°. That we were
astonished is a mild expression. We looked and looked,
entirely unable to recognize our position ; little did we
guess that the huge mountain-mass that stood up so
high and clear on the horizon was Mount Thorvald
Nilsen. How utterly different it had looked in the
misty air when we said good-bye to it. It is amusing
to read my diary of this time and see how persistently
we took the bearings of land every day, and thought it
was new. We did not recognize that vast mountain
until Mount Helmer Hanssen began to stick up out of
the plain.

On December 28 we left the summit of the plateau,
and began the descent. Although the incline was not
perceptible to the naked eye, its effect could easily be

seen in the dogs. Wisting now used a sail on his sledge, and was thus able to keep up with Hanssen. If anyone had seen the procession that came marching over the plateau at that time, he would hardly have thought we had been out for seventy days at a stretch, for we came at a swinging pace. We always had the wind at our backs, with sunshine and warmth the whole time. There was never a thought of using the whip now; the dogs were bursting with health, and tugged at their harness to get away. It was a hard time for our worthy forerunner; he often had to spurt as much as he could to keep clear of Hanssen's dogs. Wisting in full sail, with his dogs howling for joy, came close behind. Hassel had his work cut out to follow, and, indeed, I had the same. The surface was absolutely polished, and for long stretches at a time we could push ourselves along with our sticks. The dogs were completely changed since we had left the Pole; strange as it may sound, it is nevertheless true that they were putting on flesh day by day, and getting quite fat. I believe it must have been feeding them on fresh meat and pemmican together that did this. We were again able to increase our ration of pemmican from December 28; the daily ration was 1 pound (450 grams) per man, and we could not manage more —at least, I think not.

On December 29 we went downhill more and more, and it was indeed tough work being a ski-runner. The drivers stood so jauntily by the side of their sledges, letting themselves be carried over the plain at a phenomenal pace. The surface consisted of *sastrugi*, alternating with smooth stretches like ice. Heaven help me, how we ski-runners had to struggle to keep up! It was all very well for Bjaaland; he had flown faster on even worse ground. But for Hassel and me it was different. I saw Hassel put out, now an arm, now a leg, and make the most desperate efforts to keep on his feet. Fortunately I could not see myself; if I had been able to, I am sure I should have been in fits of laughter. Early that day Mount Helmer Hanssen appeared. The ground now went in great undulations —a thing we had not noticed in the mist when we were going south. So high were these undulations that they suddenly hid the view from us. The first we saw of Mount Hanssen was from the top of one of these big waves; it then looked like the top of a pressure hummock that was just sticking up above the surface. At first we did not understand at all what it was; it was not till the next day that we really grasped it, when the pointed blocks of ice covering the top of the mountain came into view. As I have said, it was only then that we made sure of being on the right course; all the rest of the land that we saw was so entirely strange to us. We recognized absolutely nothing.

On the 30th we passed 87° S., and were thus rapidly

nearing the Devil's Ballroom and Glacier. The next day was brilliantly fine—temperature −2·2° F.—with a good breeze right aft. To our great joy, we got sight of the land around the Butcher's Shop. It was still a long way off, of course, but was miraged up in the warm, sunny air. We were extraordinarily lucky on our homeward trip; we escaped the Devil's Ballroom altogether.

On January 1 we ought, according to our reckoning, to reach the Devil's Glacier, and this held good. We could see it at a great distance; huge hummocks and ice-waves towered into the sky. But what astonished us was that between these disturbances and on the far side of them, we seemed to see an even, unbroken plain, entirely unaffected by the broken surface. Mounts Hassel, Wisting, and Bjaaland, lay as we had left them; they were easy to recognize when we came a little nearer to them. Now Mount Helmer Hanssen again towered high into the air; it flashed and sparkled like diamonds as it lay bathed in the rays of the morning sun. We assumed that we had come nearer to this range than when we were going south, and that this was the reason of our finding the ground so changed. When we were going south, it certainly looked impassable between us and the mountains; but who could tell? Perhaps in the middle of all the broken ground that we then saw there was a good even stretch, and that we had now been lucky enough to stumble upon it. But it was once more the atmosphere that deceived us, as we found out on the following day, for instead of being nearer the range we had come farther out from it, and this was the reason of our only getting a little strip of this undesirable glacier.

We had our camp that evening in the middle of a big, filled-up crevasse. We were a trifle anxious as to what kind of surface we should find farther on; that these few hummocks and old crevasses were all the glacier had to offer us this time, was more than we dared to hope. But the 2nd came, and brought— thank God!—no disappointment. With incredible luck we had slipped past all those ugly and dangerous places, and now, before we knew where we were, we found ourselves safe and sound on the plain below the glacier. The weather was not first-rate when we started at seven in the evening. It was fairly thick, and we could only just distinguish the top of Mount Bjaaland. This was bad, as we were now in the neighbourhood of our depot, and would have liked clear weather to find out where it lay; but instead of clearing, as we hoped, it grew thicker and thicker, and when we had gone about six and three-quarter miles, it was so bad that we thought it best to stop and wait for a while. We had all the time been going on the erroneous assumption that we had come too far to the east—that is, too near the mountains —and under the circumstances—in the short gleams that had come from time to time—we had not been able to

recognize the ground below the glacier. According to
our idea, we were on the east of the depot. The
bearings, which had been taken in thick air, and were
now to guide us in this heavy mist, gave no result
whatever. There was no depot to be seen.

We had just swallowed the grateful warm pemmican
when the sun suddenly showed itself. I don't think
the camp was ever broken and the sledges packed in
such a short time. From the moment we jumped out
of our bags till the sledges were ready, it only took us
fifteen minutes, which is incredibly quick. "What on
earth is that shining over there through the fog?" The
question came from one of the lads. The mist had
divided, and was rolling away on both sides; in the
western bank something big and white peeped through
—a long ridge running north and south. Hurrah! it's
Helland Hansen. Can't possibly be anything else.
Our only landmark on the west. We all shouted with
joy on meeting this old acquaintance. But in the
direction of the depot the fog hung thick. We held
a brief consultation, and agreed to let it go, to steer for
the Butcher's and put on the pace. We had food enough,
anyhow. No sooner said than done, and we started off.
It rapidly cleared, and then, on our way towards Helland
Hansen, we found out that we had come, not too far to
the east, but too far to the west. But to turn round
and begin to search for our depot was not to our liking.
Below Mount Helland Hansen we came up on a fairly

high ridge.   We had now gone our fixed distance, and
so halted.

Behind us, in the brightest, clearest weather, lay the
glacier, as we had seen it for the first time on our way
to the south: break after break, crevasse after crevasse.
But in among all this nastiness there ran a white, unbroken line, the very path we had stood and looked at
a few weeks back.   And directly below that white stripe
we knew, as sure as anything could be, that our depot
lay.   We stood there expressing our annoyance rather
forcibly at the depot having escaped us so easily, and
talking of how jolly it would have been to have picked
up all our depots from the plain we had strewed them
over.   Dead tired as I felt that evening, I had not the
least desire to go back the fifteen miles that separated
us from it.   " If anybody would like to make the trip,
he shall have many thanks."   They all wanted to make
it—all as one man.   There was no lack of volunteers in
that company.   I chose Hanssen and Bjaaland.   They
took nearly everything off the sledge, and went away
with it empty.

It was then five in the morning.   At three in the
afternoon they came back to the tent, Bjaaland running
in front, Hanssen driving the sledge.   That was a notable
feat, both for men and dogs.   Hanssen, Bjaaland, and
that team had covered about fifty miles that day, at an
average rate of three to three and a half miles an hour.
They had found the depot without much search.   Their

greatest difficulty had been in the undulating surface;
for long stretches at a time they were in the hollows
between the waves, which shut in their view entirely.
Ridge succeeded ridge, endlessly.   We had taken care
that everything was ready for their return—above all
great quantities of water.   Water, water was the first
thing, and generally the last, that was in request.   When
their thirst was a little quenched, great interest was
shown in the pemmican.   While these two were being
well looked after, the depot they had brought in was
divided between the two sledges, and in a short time all
was ready for our departure.   Meanwhile, the weather
had been getting finer and finer, and before us lay the
mountains, sharp and clear.   We thought we recognized
Fridtjof Nansen and Don Pedro Christophersen, and
took good bearings of them in case the fog should
return.   With most of us the ideas of day and night
began to get rather mixed. "Six o'clock," someone
would answer, when asked the time. "Yes, in the
morning," remarks the other.   "No; what are you
talking about?" answers the first one again; "it's evening, of course."   The date was hopeless; it was a good
thing if we remembered the year.   Only when writing
in our diaries and observation books did we come across
such things as dates; while at work we had not the
remotest idea of them.

Splendid weather it was when we turned out on the
morning of January 3.   We had now agreed to go as

it suited us, and take no notice of day or night ; for some time past we had all been sick of the long hours of rest, and wanted to break them up at any price. As I have said, the weather could not have been finer : brilliantly clear and a dead calm. The temperature of $-2 \cdot 2°$ F. felt altogether like summer in this bright, still air. Before we began our march all unnecessary clothes were taken off and put on the sledges. It almost looked as if everything would be considered superfluous, and the costume in which we finally started would no doubt have been regarded as somewhat unseemly in our latitudes. We smiled and congratulated ourselves that at present no ladies had reached the Antarctic regions, or they might have objected to our extremely comfortable and serviceable costume. The high land now stood out still more sharply. It was very interesting to see in these conditions the country we had gone through on the southward trip in the thickest blizzard. We had then been going along the foot of this immense mountain chain without a suspicion of how near we were to it, or how colossal it was. The ground was fortunately quite undisturbed in this part. I say fortunately, as Heaven knows what would have happened to us if we had been obliged to cross a crevassed surface in such weather as we then had. Perhaps we should have managed it—perhaps not.

The journey before us was a stiff one, as the Butcher's lay 2,680 feet higher than the place where we were.

We had been expecting to stumble upon one of our beacons before long, but this did not happen until we had gone twelve and a half miles. Then one of them suddenly came in sight, and was greeted with joy. We knew well enough that we were on the right track, but an old acquaintance like this was very welcome all the same. The sun had evidently been at work up here while we were in the south, as some of the beacons were quite bent over, and great icicles told us clearly enough how powerful the sunshine had been. After a march of about twenty-five miles we halted at the beacon we had built right under the hill, where we had been forced to stop by thick weather on November 25.

January 4 was one of the days to which we looked forward with anxiety, as we were then due at our depot at the Butcher's, and had to find it. This depot, which consisted of the finest, fresh dogs' flesh, was of immense importance to us. Not only had our animals got into the way of preferring this food to pemmican, but, what was of still greater importance, it had an extremely good effect on the dogs' state of health. No doubt our pemmican was good enough—indeed, it could not have been better—but a variation of diet is a great consideration, and seems, according to my experience, to mean even more to the dogs than to the men on a long journey like this. On former occasions I have seen dogs refuse pemmican, presumably because they were tired of it, having no variety; the result was that the dogs grew thin and weak, although we had food enough. The pemmican I am referring to on that occasion was made for human use, so that their distaste cannot have been due to the quality.

It was 1.15 a.m. when we set out. We had not had a long sleep, but it was very important to avail ourselves of this fine, clear weather while it lasted; we knew by experience that up here in the neighbourhood of the Butcher's the weather was not to be depended upon. From the outward journey we knew that the distance from the beacon where our camp was to the depot at the Butcher's was thirteen and a half miles. We had not put up more than two beacons on this stretch, but the ground was of such a nature that we thought we could not go wrong. That it was not so easy to find the way, in spite of the beacons, we were soon to discover. In the fine, clear weather, and with Hanssen's sharp eyes, we picked up both our beacons. Meanwhile we were astonished at the appearance of the mountains. As I have already mentioned, we thought the weather was perfectly clear when we reached the Butcher's for the first time, on November 20. I then took a bearing from the tent of the way we had come up on to the plateau between the mountains, and carefully recorded it. After passing our last beacon, when we were beginning to approach the Butcher's—as we reckoned— we were greatly surprised at the aspect of our surround- ings. Last time—on November 20—we had seen

mountains on the west and north, but a long way off.
Now the whole of that part of the horizon seemed to be
filled with colossal mountain masses, which were right
over us. What in the world was the meaning of this?
Was it witchcraft? I am sure I began to think so for
a moment. I would readily have taken my most solemn
oath that I had never seen that landscape before in my
life. We had now gone the full distance, and according
to the beacons we had passed, we ought to be on the
spot. This was very strange; in the direction in which
I had taken the bearing of our ascent, we now only saw
the side of a perfectly unknown mountain, sticking up
from the plain. There could be absolutely no way down
in that precipitous wall. Only on the north-west did
the ground give the impression of allowing a descent;
there a natural depression seemed to be formed, running
down towards the Barrier, which we could see far, far
away.

We halted and discussed the situation. "Hullo!"
Hanssen suddenly exclaimed, "somebody has been
here before."—"Yes," broke in Wisting; "I'm hanged
if that isn't my broken ski that I stuck up by the depot."
So it was Wisting's broken ski that brought us out
of this unpleasant situation. It was a good thing he
put it there—very thoughtful, in any case. I now
examined the place with the glasses, and by the side of
a snow mound, which proved to be our depot, but
might easily have escaped our notice, we could see the

ski sticking up out of the snow.   We cheerfully set our course for the spot, but did not reach it until we had gone three miles.

There was rejoicing in our little band when we arrived and saw that what we had considered the most important point of our homeward journey had been reached.   It was not so much for the sake of the food it contained that we considered it so necessary to find this spot, as for discovering the way down to the Barrier again.   And now that we stood there, we recognized this necessity more than ever.   For although we now knew, from our bearings, exactly where the descent lay, we could see nothing of it at all.   The plateau there seemed to go right up to the mountain, without any opening towards the lower ground beyond; and yet the compass told us that such an opening must exist, and would take us down.   The mountain, on which we had thus walked all day on the outward journey, without knowing anything of it, was Mount Fridtjof Nansen.   Yes, the difference in the light made a surprising alteration in the appearance of things.

The first thing we did on reaching the depot was to take out the dogs' carcasses that lay there and cut them into big lumps, that were divided among the dogs. They looked rather surprised; they had not been accustomed to such rations.   We threw three carcasses on to the sledges, so as to have a little extra food for them on the way down.   The Butcher's was not a very friendly spot this time, either. True, it was not the same awful weather as on our first visit, but it was blowing a fresh breeze with a temperature of −9·4° F., which, after the heat of the last few days, seemed to go to one's marrow, and did not invite us to stay longer than was absolutely necessary. Therefore, as soon as we had finished feeding the dogs and putting our sledges in order, we set out.

Although the ground had not given us the impression of sloping, we soon found out that it did so when we got under way. It was not only downhill, but the pace became so great that we had to stop and put brakes under the sledges. As we advanced, the apparently unbroken wall opened more and more, and showed us at last our old familiar ascent. There lay Mount Ole Engelstad, snowclad and cold, as we saw it the first time. As we rounded it we came on to the severe, steep slope, where, on the way south, I had so much admired the work done by my companions and the dogs that day. But now I had an even better opportunity of seeing how steep this ascent really had been. Many were the brakes we had to put on before we could reduce the speed to a moderate pace, but even so we came down rapidly, and soon the first part of the descent lay behind us. So as not to be exposed to possible gusts from the plain, we went round Mount Engelstad and camped under the lee of it, well content with the day's work. The snow lay here as on our first visit, deep and loose, and it was difficult to find anything like a good place for the tent. We could soon feel that we had descended a couple of thousand feet and come down among the mountains. It was still, absolutely still, and the sun broiled us as on a day of high summer at home. I thought, too, that I could notice a difference in my breathing; it seemed to work much more easily and pleasantly—perhaps it was only imagination.

At one o'clock on the following morning we were out again. The sight that met our eyes that morning, when we came out of the tent, was one of those that will always live in our memories. The tent stood in the narrow gap between Fridtjof Nansen and Ole Engelstad. The sun, which now stood in the south, was completely hidden by the latter mountain, and our camp was thus in the deepest shadow; but right against us on the other side the Nansen mountain raised its splendid ice-clad summit high towards heaven, gleaming and sparkling in the rays of the midnight sun. The shining white passed gradually, very gradually, into pale blue, then deeper and deeper blue, until the shadow swallowed it up. But down below, right on the Heiberg Glacier, its ice-covered side was exposed—dark and solemn the mountain mass stood out. Mount Engelstad lay in shadow, but on its summit rested a beautiful light little cirrus cloud, red with an edge of gold. Down over its side the blocks of ice lay scattered pell-mell. And farther down on the east rose Don Pedro Christophersen, partly

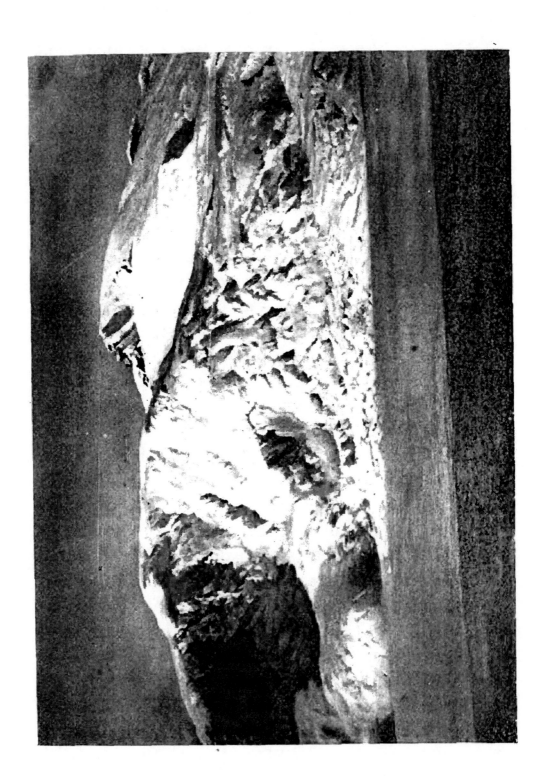

in shadow, partly gleaming in the sun—a marvellously beautiful sight. And all was so still; one almost feared to disturb the incomparable splendour of the scene.

We now knew the ground well enough to be able to go straight ahead without any detours. The huge avalanches were more frequent than on the outward journey. One mass of snow after another plunged down; Don Pedro was getting rid of his winter coat. The going was precisely the same—loose, fairly deep snow. We went quite easily over it, however, and it was all downhill. On the ridge where the descent to the glacier began we halted to make our preparations. Brakes were put under the sledges, and our two ski-sticks were fastened together to make one strong one; we should have to be able to stop instantly if surprised by a crevasse as we were going. We ski-runners went in front. The going was ideal here on the steep slope, just enough loose snow to give one good steering on ski. We went whizzing down, and it was not many minutes before we were on the Heiberg Glacier. For the drivers it was not quite such plain sailing: they followed our tracks, but had to be extremely careful on the steep fall.

We camped that evening on the selfsame spot where we had had our tent on November 18, at about 3,100 feet above the sea. From here one could see the course of the Axel Heiberg Glacier right down to its junction with the Barrier. It looked fine and even, and we decided to follow it instead of climbing over the mountain, as we had done on the way south. Perhaps the distance would be somewhat longer, but probably we should make a considerable saving of time. We had now agreed upon a new arrangement of our time ; the long spells of rest were becoming almost unbearable. Another very important side of the question was that, by a reasonable arrangement, we should be able to save a lot of time, and reach home several days sooner than we had reckoned. After a great deal of talk on one side and on the other, we agreed to arrange matters thus : we were to do our fifteen geographical miles, or twenty-eight kilometres, and then have a sleep of six hours, turn out again and do fifteen miles more, and so on. In this way we should accomplish a very good average distance on our day's march. We kept to this arrangement for the rest of the journey, and thus saved a good many days.

Our progress down the Heiberg Glacier did not encounter any obstructions ; only at the transition from the glacier to the Barrier were there a few crevasses that had to be circumvented. At 7 a.m. on January 6 we halted at the angle of land that forms the entrance to the Heiberg Glacier, and thence extends northward. We had not yet recognized any of the land we lay under, but that was quite natural, as we now saw it from the opposite side. We knew, though, that we were not far away from our main depot in 85° 5′ S. On the afternoon of the same day we were off again.

From a little ridge we crossed immediately after starting, Bjaaland thought he could see the depot down on
the Barrier, and it was not very long before we came in
sight of Mount Betty and our way up. And now we
could make sure with the glasses that it really was our
depot that we saw—the same that Bjaaland thought he
had seen before. We therefore set our course straight
for it, and in a few minutes we were once more on the
Barrier—January 6, 11 p.m.—after a stay of fifty-one
days on land. It was on November 17 that we had
begun the ascent.

We reached the depot, and found everything in
order. The heat here must have been very powerful;
our lofty, solid depot was melted by the sun into a
rather low mound of snow. The pemmican rations
that had been exposed to the direct action of the sun's
rays had assumed the strangest forms, and, of course,
they had become rancid. We got the sledges ready at
once, taking all the provisions out of the depot and
loading them. We left behind some of the old clothes
we had been wearing all the way from here to the Pole
and back. When we had completed all this repacking
and had everything ready, two of us went over to
Mount Betty, and collected as many different specimens of rock as we could lay our hands on. At the
same time we built a great cairn, and left there a can
of 17 litres of paraffin, two packets of matches—contain
ing twenty boxes—and an account of our expedition.

Possibly someone may find a use for these things in the future.

We had to kill Frithjof, one of Bjaaland's dogs, at this camp. He had latterly been showing marked signs of shortness of breath, and finally this became so painful to the animal that we decided to put an end to him. Thus brave Frithjof ended his career. On cutting him open it appeared that his lungs were quite shrivelled up; nevertheless, the remains disappeared pretty quickly into his companions' stomachs. What they had lost in quantity did not apparently affect their quality. Nigger, one of Hassel's dogs, had been destroyed on the way down from the plateau. We thus reached this point again with twelve dogs, as we had reckoned on doing, and left it with eleven. I see in my diary the following remark: "The dogs look just as well as when we left Framheim." On leaving the place a few hours later we had provisions for thirty-five days on the sledges. Besides this, of course, we had a depot at every degree of latitude up to 80°.

It looked as though we had found our depot at the right moment, for when we came out to continue our journey the whole Barrier was in a blizzard. A gale was blowing from the south, with a sky completely clouded over; falling snow and drift united in a delightful dance, and made it difficult to see. The lucky thing was that now we had the wind with us, and thus escaped getting it all in our eyes, as we had been accustomed to. The big crevasse, which, as we knew, lay right across the line of our route, made us go very carefully. To avoid any risk, Bjaaland and Hassel, who went in advance, fastened an alpine rope between them. The snow was very deep and loose, and the going very heavy. Fortunately, we were warned in time of our approach to the expected cracks by the appearance of some bare ice ridges. These told us clearly enough that disturbances had taken place here, and that even greater ones might be expected, probably near at hand. At that moment the thick curtain of cloud was torn asunder, and the sun pierced the whirling mass of snow. Instantly Hanssen shouted: " Stop, Bjaaland !" He was just on the edge of the yawning crevasse. Bjaaland himself has splendid sight, but his excellent snow-goggles—his own patent—entirely prevented his seeing. Well, Bjaaland would not have been in any serious danger if he had fallen into the crevasse, as he was roped to Hassel, but it would have been confoundedly unpleasant all the same.

As I have said before, I assume that these great disturbances here mark the boundary between the Barrier and the land. This time, curiously enough, they seemed also to form a boundary between good and bad weather, for on the far side of them—to the north—the Barrier lay bathed in sunshine. On the south the blizzard raged worse than ever. Mount Betty was the last to send us its farewell. South Victoria Land had gone into hiding, and did not show itself again. As soon as we came into the sunshine, we ran upon one of our beacons ; our course lay straight towards it. That was not bad steering in the dark. At 9 p.m. we reached the depot in 85° S. Now we could begin to be liberal with the dogs' food, too ; they had double pemmican rations, besides as many oatmeal biscuits as they would eat. We had such masses of biscuits now that we could positively throw them about. Of course, we might have left a large part of these provisions behind ; but there was a great satisfaction in being so well supplied with food, and the dogs did not seem to mind the little extra weight in the least. As long as things went so capitally as they were going—that is, with men and dogs exactly keeping pace with one another—we could ask for nothing better. But the weather that had cheered us was not of long duration. "Same beastly weather," my diary says of the next stage. The wind had shifted to the north-west, with overcast, thick weather, and very troublesome drifting snow. In spite of these unfavourable conditions, we passed beacon after beacon, and at the end of our march had picked up all the beacons we had erected on this distance of seventeen miles and three-eighths. But, as before, we owed this to Hanssen's good eyes.

On our way southward we had taken a good deal of seal meat and had divided it among the depots we built on the Barrier in such a way that we were now able to eat fresh meat every day. This had not been done without an object; if we should be visited with scurvy, this fresh meat would be invaluable. As we were—sound and healthy as we had never been before—the seal-beef was a pleasant distraction in our menu, nothing more. The temperature had risen greatly since we came down on to the Barrier, and kept steady at about +14° F. We were so warm in our sleeping-bags that we had to turn them with the hair out. That was better; we breathed more freely and felt happier. "Just like going into an ice-cellar," somebody remarked. The same feeling as when on a really warm summer day one comes out of the hot sun into cool shade.

January 9.—"Same beastly weather; snow, snow, snow, nothing but snow. Is there no end to it? Thick too, so that we have not been able to see ten yards ahead. Temperature +17·6° F. Thawing everywhere on the sledges. Everything getting wet. Have not found a single beacon in this blind man's weather. The snow was very deep to begin with and the going exceedingly heavy, but in spite of this the dogs managed their sledges very well." That evening the weather improved, fortunately, and became comparatively clear by the time we resumed our journey at 10 p.m. Not long after we sighted one of our beacons. It lay to the west, about 200 yards away. We were thus not far out of our course; we turned aside and went up to it, as it was interesting to see whether our reckoning was in order. The beacon was somewhat damaged by sunshine and storms, but we found the paper left in it, which told us that this beacon was erected on November 14, in 84° 26′ S. It also told us what course to steer by compass to reach the next beacon, which lay five kilometres from this one.

As we were leaving this old friend and setting our course as it advised, to our unspeakable astonishment two great birds—skua gulls—suddenly came flying straight towards us. They circled round us once or twice and then settled on the beacon. Can anyone who reads these lines form an idea of the effect this had upon us? It is hardly likely. They brought us a message from the living world into this realm of death—a message of all that was dear to us. I think the same thoughts filled us all. They did not allow themselves a long rest, these first messengers from another world; they sat still a while, no doubt wondering who we were, then rose aloft and flew on to the south. Mysterious creatures! they were now exactly half-way between Framheim and the Pole, and yet they were going farther inland. Were they going over to the other side?

Our march ended this time at one of our beacons, in 84° 15′. It felt so good and safe to lie beside one of these; it always gave us a sure starting-point for the following stage. We were up at 4 a.m. and left the place a few hours later, with the result that the day's

march brought us thirty-four miles nearer Framheim.
With our present arrangement, we had these long-day
marches every other day. Our dogs need no better
testimonial than this—one day seventeen miles, the next
day thirty-four, and fresh all the way home. The two
birds, agreeably as their first appearance had affected
me, led my thoughts after a while in another direction,
which was anything but agreeable. It occurred to me
that these two might only be representatives of a larger
collection of these voracious birds, and that the remainder
might now be occupied in consuming all the fresh meat
we had so laboriously transported with us and spread
all over the plain in our depots. It is incredible what
a flock of these birds of prey can get rid of ; it would
not matter if the meat were frozen as hard as iron, they
would have managed it, even if it had been a good deal
harder than iron. Of the seals' carcasses we had lying
in 80°, I saw in my thoughts nothing but the bones.
Of the various dogs we had killed on our way south
and laid on the tops of beacons I did not see even so
much as that. Well, it was possible that my thoughts
had begun to assume too dark a hue ; perhaps the reality
would be brighter.

Weather and going began by degrees to right themselves ; it looked as if things would improve in proportion to our distance from land. Finally, both became
perfect ; the sun shone from a cloudless sky, and the
sledges ran on the fine, even surface with all the ease

and speed that could be desired. Bjaaland, who had occupied the position of forerunner all the way from the Pole, performed his duties admirably; but the old saying that nobody is perfect applied even to him. None of us—no matter who it may be—can keep in a straight line, when he has no marks to follow. All the more difficult is this when, as so often happened with us, one has to go blindly. Most of us, I suppose, would swerve now to one side, now to the other, and possibly end, after all this groping, by keeping pretty well to the line. Not so with Bjaaland; he was a right-hand man. I can see him now; Hanssen has given him the direction by compass, and Bjaaland turns round, points his ski in the line indicated and sets off with decision. His movements clearly show that he has made up his mind, cost what it may, to keep in the right direction. He sends his ski firmly along, so that the snow spurts from them, and looks straight before him. But the result is the same; if Hanssen had let Bjaaland go on without any correction, in the course of an hour or so the latter would probably have described a beautiful circle and brought himself back to the spot from which he had started. Perhaps, after all, this was not a fault to complain of, since we always knew with absolute certainty that, when we had got out of the line of beacons, we were to the right of it and had to search for the beacons to the west. This conclusion proved very useful to us more than once, and we gradually became so familiar with Bjaaland's right-handed tendencies that we actually counted on them.

On January 13, according to our reckoning, we ought to reach the depot in 83° S. This was the last of our depots that was not marked at right angles to the route, and therefore the last critical point. The day was not altogether suited for finding the needle in the haystack. It was calm with a thick fog, so thick that we could only see a few yards in front of us. We did not see a single beacon on the whole march. At 4 p.m. we had completed the distance, according to the sledge-meters, and reckoned that we ought to be in 83° S., by the depot; but there was nothing to be seen. We decided, therefore, to set our tent and wait till it cleared. While we were at work with this, there was a rift in the thick mass of fog, and there, not many yards away—to the west, of course—lay our depot. We quickly took the tent down again, packed it on the sledge, and drove up to our food mound, which proved to be quite in order. There was no sign of the birds having paid it a visit. But what was that? Fresh, well-marked dog-tracks in the newly-fallen snow. We soon saw that they must be the tracks of the runaways that we had lost here on the way south. Judging by appearances, they must have lain under the lee of the depot for a considerable time; two deep hollows in the snow told us that plainly. And evidently they must have had enough food, but where on earth had they got it from? The depot was absolutely untouched, in spite of the fact that the lumps of pemmican lay exposed to the light of day and were very easy to get at; besides which, the snow on the depot was not so hard as to prevent the dogs pulling it down and eating up all the food. Meanwhile the dogs had left the place again, as shown by the fresh trail, which pointed to the north. We examined the tracks very closely, and agreed that they were not more than two days old. They went northward, and we followed them from time to time on our next stage. At the beacon in 82° 45′, where we halted, we saw them still going to the north. In 82° 24′ the trail began to be much confused, and ended by pointing due west. That was the last we saw of the tracks; but we had not done with these dogs, or rather with their deeds. We stopped at the beacon in 82° 20′. Else, who had been laid on the top of it, had fallen down and lay by the side; the sun had thawed away the lower part of the beacon. So the roving dogs had not been here; so much was certain, for otherwise we should not have found Else as we did. We camped at the end of that stage by the beacon in 82° 15′, and shared out Else's body. Although she had been lying in the strong sunshine, the flesh was quite good, when we had scraped away a little mouldiness. It smelt rather old, perhaps, but our dogs were not fastidious when it was a question of meat.

On January 16 we arrived at the depot in 82° S. We could see from a long way off that the order in which we had left it no longer prevailed. When we came up to it, we saw at once what had happened. The innumerable dog-tracks that had trampled the snow quite hard round the depot declared plainly enough that the runaways had spent a good deal of time here. Several of the cases belonging to the depot had fallen down, presumably from the same cause as Else, and the rascals had succeeded in breaking into one of them. Of the biscuits and pemmican which it had contained, nothing, of course, was left; but that made no difference to us now, as we had food in abundance. The two dogs' carcasses that we had placed on the top of the depot—Uranus and Jaala—were gone, not even the teeth were to be seen. Yet they had left the teeth of Lucy, whom they had eaten in 82° 3'. Jaala's eight puppies were still lying on the top of a case; curiously enough, they had not fallen down. In addition to all the rest, the beasts had devoured some ski-bindings and things of that sort. It was no loss to us, as it happened; but who could tell which way these creatures had gone? If they had succeeded in finding the depot in 80° S., they would probably by this time have finished our supply of seal meat there. Of course it would be regrettable if this had happened, although it would entail no danger either to ourselves or our animals. If we got as far as 80°, we should come through all right. For the time being, we had to console ourselves with the fact that we could see no continuation of the trail northward.

We permitted ourselves a little feast here in 82°. The "chocolate pudding" that Wisting served as dessert is still fresh in my memory; we all agreed that it came nearer perfection than anything it had hitherto fallen to our lot to taste. I may disclose the receipt: biscuit-crumbs, dried milk and chocolate are put into a kettle of boiling water. What happens afterwards, I don't know; for further information apply to Wisting. Between 82° and 81° we came into our old marks of the second depot journey; on that trip we had marked this distance with splinters of packing-case at every geographical mile. That was in March, 1911, and now we were following these splinters in the second half of January, 1912. Apparently they stood exactly as they had been put in. This marking stopped in 81° 33′ S., with two pieces of case on a snow pedestal. The pedestal was still intact and good.

I shall let my diary describe what we saw on January 18: " Unusually fine weather to-day. Light south-south-west breeze, which in the course of our march cleared the whole sky. In 81° 20′ we came abreast of our old big pressure ridges. We now saw far more of them than ever before. They extended as far as the eye could see, running north-east to south-west, in ridges and peaks. Great was our surprise when, a short time after, we made out high, bare land in the same direction,

and not long after that two lofty, white summits to the
south-east, probably in about 82° S. It could be seen
by the look of the sky that the land extended from
north-east to south-west. This must be the same land
that we saw lose itself in the horizon in about 84° S.,
when we stood at a height of about 4,000 feet and
looked out over the Barrier, during our ascent. We
now have sufficient indications to enable us without
hesitation to draw this land as continuous—Carmen
Land. The surface against the land is violently disturbed—crevasses and pressure ridges, waves and valleys,
in all directions. We shall no doubt feel the effect of it
to-morrow." Although what we have seen apparently
justifies us in concluding that Carmen Land extends
from 86° S. to this position — about 81° 30′ S.—
and possibly farther to the north-east, I have not
ventured to lay it down thus on the map. I have contented myself with giving the name of Carmen Land to
the land between 86° and 84°, and have called the rest
" Appearance of Land." It will be a profitable task for
an explorer to investigate this district more closely.

As we had expected, on our next stage we were made
to feel the effect of the disturbances. Three times we
had now gone over this stretch of the Barrier without
having really clear weather. This time we had it, and
were able to see what it actually looked like. The
irregularities began in 81° 12′ S., and did not extend
very far from north to south—possibly about five kilo-

metres (three and a quarter miles). How far they extended from east to west it is difficult to say, but at any rate as far as the eye could reach. Immense pieces of the surface had fallen away and opened up the most horrible yawning gulfs, big enough to swallow many caravans of the size of ours. From these open holes, ugly wide cracks ran out in all directions; besides which, mounds and haycocks were everywhere to be seen. Perhaps the most remarkable thing of all was that we had passed over here unharmed. We went across as light-footedly as possible, and at top speed. Hanssen went halfway into a crevasse, but luckily got out of it again without difficulty.

The depot in 81° S. was in perfect order; no dog-tracks to be seen there. Our hopes that the depot in 80° S. would be intact rose considerably. In 80° 45′ S. lay the first dog we had killed—Bone. He was particularly fat, and was immensely appreciated. The dogs no longer cared very much for pemmican. On January 21 we passed our last beacon, which stood in 80° 23′ S. Glad as we were to leave it behind, I cannot deny that it was with a certain feeling of melancholy that we saw it vanish. We had grown so fond of our beacons, and whenever we met them we greeted them as old friends. Many and great were the services these silent watchers did us on our long and lonely way.

On the same day we reached our big depot in 80° S., and now we considered that we were back. We could see at once that others had been at the depot since we had left it, and we found a message from Lieutenant Prestrud, the leader of the eastern party, saying that he, with Stubberud and Johansen, had passed here on November 12, with two sledges, sixteen dogs, and supplies for thirty days. Everything thus appeared to be in the best of order. Immediately on arriving at the depot we let the dogs loose, and they made a dash for the heap of seal's flesh, which had been attacked neither by birds nor dogs in our absence. It was not so much for the sake of eating that our dogs made their way to the meat mound, as for the sake of fighting. Now they really had something to fight about. They went round the seals' carcasses a few times, looked askance at the food and at each other, and then flung themselves into the wildest scrimmage. When this had been duly brought to a conclusion, they went away and lay round their sledges. The depot in 80° S. is still large, well supplied and well marked, so it is not impossible that it may be found useful later.

The journey from 80° S. to Framheim has been so often described that there is nothing new to say about it. On January 25, at 4 a.m., we reached our good little house again, with two sledges and eleven dogs; men and animals all hale and hearty. We stood and waited for each other outside the door in the early morning; our appearance must be made all together. It was so still and quiet—they must be all asleep. We came in.

Stubberud started up in his bunk and glared at us; no doubt he took us for ghosts. One after another they woke up — not grasping what was happening. Then there was a hearty welcome home on all sides " Where's the *Fram*?" was of course our first question Our joy was great when we heard all was well. " And what about the Pole ? Have you been there ?"—" Yes, of course; otherwise you would hardly have seen us again." Then the coffee kettle was put on, and the perfume of " hot cakes " rose as in old days. We agreed that it was good outside, but still better at home. Ninety-nine days the trip had taken. Distance about 1,860 miles.

The *Fram* had come in to the Barrier on January 8, after a three months' voyage from Buenos Aires; all were well on board. Meanwhile, bad weather had forced her to put out again. On the following day the look-out man reported that the *Fram* was approaching There was life in the camp; on with furs and out with the dogs. They should see that our dogs were not worn out yet. We heard the engine panting and grunting, saw the crow's-nest appear over the edge of the Barrier, and at last she glided in, sure and steady. It was with a joyful heart I went on board and greeted all these gallant men, who had brought the *Fram* to her destination through so many fatigues and perils, and had accomplished so much excellent work on the way. They all looked pleased and happy, but nobody asked

FRAMHEIM, ON THE RETURN OF THE POLAR PARTY.

LINDSTRÖM IN THE KITCHEN.

To face page 174, Vol. II.

about the Pole. At last it slipped out of Gjertsen:
"Have you been there?" Joy is a poor name for the
feeling that beamed in my comrades' faces; it was
something more.

I shut myself up in the chart-house with Captain
Nilsen, who gave me my mail and all the news. Three
names stood high above the rest, when I was able to
understand all that had happened—the names of the
three who gave me their support when it was most
needed. I shall always remember them in respectful
gratitude—

H.M. THE KING,
PROFESSOR FRIDTJOF NANSEN,
DON PEDRO CHRISTOPHERSEN.

CHAPTER XIV

NORTHWARD

AFTER two days of bustle in getting on board the things we were to take with us, we managed to be ready for sea on the afternoon of January 30. There could scarcely have been anything at that moment that rejoiced us more than just that fact, that we were able at so early a date to set our course northward and thus take the first step on the way to that world which, as we knew, would soon begin to expect news from us, or of us. And yet, I wonder whether there was not a little feeling of melancholy in the midst of all our joy? It can hardly be doubted that such was really the case, although to many this may seem a flat contradiction. But it is not altogether so easy to part from a place that has been one's home for any length of time, even though this home lie in the 79th degree of latitude, more or less buried in snow and ice. We human beings are far too dependent on habit to be able to tear ourselves abruptly from the surroundings with which we have been obliged to be familiar for many months. That outsiders would perhaps pray all

176

the powers of goodness to preserve them from such
surroundings, does not counteract the full validity of
this rule. To an overwhelming majority of our fellow-
men Framheim will certainly appear as one of those
spots on our planet where they would least of all wish
to find themselves—a God-forsaken, out-of-the-way
hole that could offer nothing but the very climax of
desolation, discomfort, and boredom. To us nine,
who stood on the gangway ready to leave this place,
things appeared somewhat differently. That strong
little house, that now lay entirely hidden beneath
the snow behind Mount Nelson, had for a whole year
been our home, and a thoroughly good and comfortable
home it was, where after so many a hard day's work
we had found all the rest and quiet we wanted. Through
the whole Antarctic winter—and it is a winter—those
four walls had protected us so well that many a poor
wretch in milder latitudes would have envied us with
all his heart, if he could have seen us. In conditions
so hard that every form of life flies headlong from
them, we had lived on at Framheim undisturbed and
untroubled, and lived, be it said, not as animals, but
as civilized human beings, who had always within their
reach most of the good things that are found in a well-
ordered home. Darkness and cold reigned outside,
and the blizzards no doubt did their best to blot out
most traces of our activity, but these enemies never
came within the door of our excellent dwelling; there

we shared quarters with light and warmth and comfort.
What wonder was it that this spot exercised a strong
attraction upon each of us at the moment when we
were to turn our backs upon it for good ?   Outside the
great world beckoned to us, that is true ; and it might
have much to offer us that we had had to forego for a
long time ; but in what awaited us there was certainly
a great deal that we would gladly have put off for as
long as possible.   When everyday life came with its
cares and worries, it might well happen that we should
look back with regret to our peaceful and untroubled
existence at Framheim.

However, this feeling of melancholy was hardly so
strong that we could not all get over it comparatively
quickly.   Judging by the faces, at any rate, one would
have thought that joy was the most predominant mood.
And why not ?   It was no use dwelling on the past,
however attractive it might seem just then, and as to
the future, we had every right to expect the best of
it.   Who cared to think of coming troubles ?   No one
Therefore the *Fram* was dressed with flags from stem to
stern, and therefore faces beamed at each other as we said
good-bye to our home on the Barrier.   We could leave
it with the consciousness that the object of our year's
stay had been attained, and, after all, this consciousness
was of considerably more weight than the thought that
we had been so happy there.   One thing that in the
course of our two years' association on this expedition

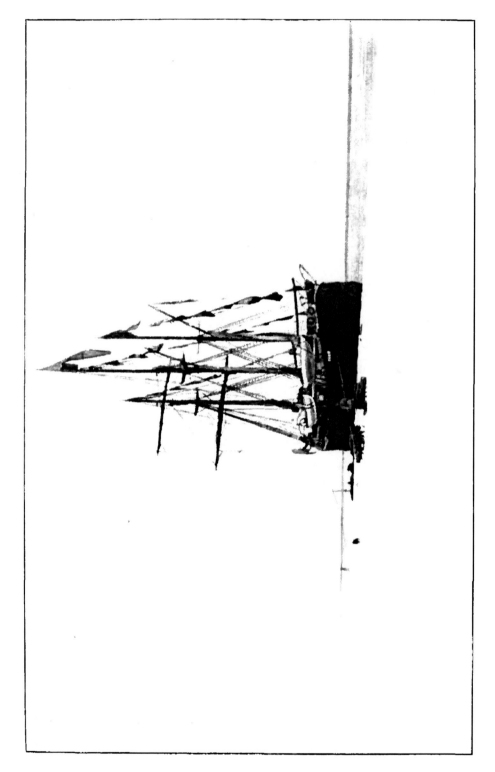

FAREWELL TO THE BARRIER.

contributed enormously to making time pass easily and
keeping each of us in full vigour was the entire absence
of what I may call " dead periods." As soon as one
problem was solved, another instantly appeared. No
sooner was one goal reached, than the next one beckoned
from afar. In this way we always had our hands full,
and when that is the case, as everyone knows, time
flies quickly. One often hears it asked, How is it
possible to make the time pass on such a trip ? My
good friends, I would answer, if anything caused us
worry, it was the thought of how we should find time
enough for all we had to do. Perhaps to many this
assertion will bear the stamp of improbability ; it is,
nevertheless, absolutely true. Those who have read
this narrative through will, in any case, have received
the impression that unemployment was an evil that was
utterly unknown in our little community.

At the stage where we now found ourselves, with the
main object of our enterprise achieved, there might have
been reason to expect a certain degree of relaxation of
interest. This, however, was not the case. The fact
was that what we had done would have no real value
until it was brought to the knowledge of mankind, and
this communication had to be made with as little loss of
time as possible. If anyone was interested in being first
in the market it was certainly ourselves. The probability was, no doubt, that we were out in good time ;
but, in spite of all, it was only a probability. On the

other hand, it was absolutely certain that we had a voyage of 2,400 nautical miles to Hobart, which had been selected as our first port of call; and it was almost equally certain that this voyage would be both slow and troublesome.   A year before our trip through Ross Sea had turned out almost like a pleasure cruise, but that was in the middle of summer.   Now we were in February, and autumn was at hand.   As regards the belt of drift-ice, Captain Nilsen thought that would cause us no delay in future.   He had discovered a patent and infallible way of getting through!   This sounded like a rather bold assertion, but, as will be seen later, he was as good as his word.   Our worst troubles would be up in the westerlies, where we should this time be exposed to the unpleasant possibility of having to beat.   The difference in longitude between the Bay of Whales and Hobart is nearly fifty degrees.   If we could have sailed off this difference in longitude in the latitudes where we then were, and where a degree of longitude is only about thirteen nautical miles, it would all have been done in a twinkling; but the mighty mountain ranges of North Victoria Land were a decisive obstacle.   We should first have to follow a northerly course until we had rounded the Antarctic Continent's northern outpost, Cape Adare, and the Balleny Islands to the north of it.   Not till then would the way be open for us to work to the west; but then we should be in a region where in all probability the

BJAALAND AS TINKER.

DOGS LANDED AT HOBART FOR DR. MAWSON'S EXPEDITION.

wind would be dead against us, and as to tacking with the *Fram*—no, thank you! Every single man on board knew enough of the conditions to be well aware of what awaited us, and it is equally certain that the thoughts of all were centred upon how we might conquer our coming difficulties in the best and quickest way. It was the one great, common object that still bound, and would continue to bind, us all together in our joint efforts.

Among the items of news that we had just received from the outer world was the message that the Australian Antarctic Expedition under Dr. Douglas Mawson would be glad to take over some of our dogs, if we had any to spare. The base of this expedition was Hobart, and as far as that went, this suited us very well. It chanced that we were able to do our esteemed colleague this small service. On leaving the Barrier we could show a pack of thirty-nine dogs, many of which had grown up during our year's stay there; about half had survived the whole trip from Norway, and eleven had been at the South Pole. It had been our intention only to keep a suitable number as the progenitors of a new pack for the approaching voyage in the Arctic Ocean, but Dr. Mawson's request caused us to take all the thirty-nine on board. Of these dogs, if nothing unforeseen happened, we should be able to make over twenty-one to him. When the last load was brought down, there was nothing to do but to pull

the dogs over the side, and then we were ready. It
was quite curious to see how several of the old veterans
seemed at home again on the *Fram's* deck. Wisting's
brave dog, the old Colonel, with his two adjutants,
Suggen and Arne, at once took possession of the places
where they had stood for so many a long day on the
voyage south—on the starboard side of the mainmast;
the two twins, Mylius and Ring, Helmer Hanssen's
special favourites, began their games away in the corner
of the fore-deck to port, as though nothing had happened. To look at those two merry rascals no one
would have thought they had trotted at the head of the
whole caravan both to and from the Pole. One solitary
dog could be seen stalking about, lonely and reserved,
in a continual uneasy search. This was the boss of
Bjaaland's team. He was unaffected by any advances;
no one could take the place of his fallen comrade and
friend, Frithjof, who had long ago found a grave in the
stomachs of his companions many hundreds of miles
across the Barrier.

No sooner was the last dog helped on board, and the
two ice-anchors released, than the engine-room telegraph
rang, and the engine was at once set going to keep us
from any closer contact with the ice-foot in the Bay of
Whales. Our farewell to this snug harbour took almost
the form of a leap from one world to another; the fog
hung over us as thick as gruel, concealing all the surrounding outlines behind its clammy curtain, as we

stood out. After a lapse of three or four hours, it lifted quite suddenly, but astern of us the bank of fog still stood like a wall; behind it the panorama, which we knew would have looked wonderful in clear weather, and which we should so gladly have let our eyes rest upon as long as we could, was entirely concealed.

The same course we had steered when coming in a year before could safely be taken in the opposite direction now we were going out. The outlines of the bay had remained absolutely unchanged during the year that had elapsed. Even the most projecting point of the wall on the west side of the bay, Cape Man's Head, stood serenely in its old place, and it looked as if it was in no particular hurry to remove itself. It will probably stay where it is for many a long day yet, for if any movement of the ice mass is taking place at the inner end of the bay, it is in any case very slight. Only in one respect did the condition of things differ somewhat this year from the preceding. Whereas in 1911 the greater part of the bay was free of sea-ice as early as January 14, in 1912 there was no opening until about fourteen days later. The ice-sheet had stubbornly held on until the fresh north-easterly breeze, that appeared on the very day the southern party returned, had rapidly provided a channel of open water. The breaking up of the ice could not possibly have taken place at a more convenient moment; the breeze in question saved us a great deal, both of time and trouble, as the way to the place where the *Fram* lay before the ice broke up was about five times as long as the distance we now had to go.   This difference of fourteen days in the time of the disappearance of the ice in two summers showed us how lucky we had been to choose that particular year—1911—for our landing here.   The work which we carried out in three weeks in 1911, thanks to the early breaking up of the ice, would certainly have taken us double the time in 1912, and would have caused us far more difficulty and trouble.

The thick fog that, as I have said, lay over the Bay of Whales when we left it, prevented us also from seeing what our friends the Japanese were doing.   The *Kainan Maru* had put to sea in company with the *Fram* during the gale of January 27, and since that time we had seen nothing of them.   Those members of the expedition who had been left behind in a tent on the edge of the Barrier to the north of Framheim had also been very retiring of late.   On the day we left the place, one of our own party had an interview with two of the foreigners.   Prestrud had gone to fetch the flag that had been set up on Cape Man's Head as a signal to the *Fram* that all had returned.   By the side of the flag a tent had been put up, which was intended as a shelter for a lookout man, in case the *Fram* had been delayed. When Prestrud came up, he was no doubt rather surprised to find himself face to face with two sons of Nippon, who were engaged in inspecting our tent and

its contents, which, however, only consisted of a sleeping-bag and a Primus. The Japanese had opened the conversation with enthusiastic phrases about "nice day" and "plenty ice"; when our man had expressed his absolute agreement on these indisputable facts, he tried to get information on matters of more special interest. The two strangers told him that for the moment they were the only inhabitants of the tent out on the edge of the Barrier. Two of their companions had gone on a tour into the Barrier to make meteorological observations, and were to be away about a week. The *Kainan Maru* had gone on another cruise in the direction of King Edward Land. As far as they knew, it was intended that the ship should be back before February 10, and that all the members of the expedition should then go on board and sail to the north. Prestrud had invited his two new acquaintances to visit us at Framheim, the sooner the better; they delayed their coming too long, however, for us to be able to wait for them. If they have since been at Framheim, they will at any rate be able to bear witness that we did our best to make things comfortable for any successors.

When the fog lifted, we found ourselves surrounded by open sea, practically free from ice, on all sides. A blue-black sea, with a heavy, dark sky above it, is not usually reckoned among the sights that delight the eye. To our organs of vision it was a real relief to come into surroundings where dark colours predominated. For months we had been staring at a dazzling sea of white, where artificial means had constantly to be employed to protect the eyes against the excessive flood of light. As a rule, it was even necessary to limit the exposure of the pupils to a minimum, and to draw the eyelids together. Now we could once more look on the world with open eyes, literally " without winking "; even such a commonplace thing as this is an experience in one's life. Ross Sea showed itself again on its most favourable side. A cat's paw of south-westerly wind enabled us to use the sails, so that after a lapse of two days we were already about two hundred miles from the Barrier. Modest as this distance may be in itself, when seen on the chart it looked quite imposing in our eyes. It must be remembered that, with the means of transport we had employed on land, it cost us many a hard day's march to cover a distance of two hundred geographical miles.

Nilsen had marked on the chart the limits of the belt of drift-ice during the three passages the *Fram* had already made. The supposition that an available opening is always to be found in the neighbourhood of the 150th meridian appears to be confirmed. The slight changes in the position of the channel were only caused, according to Nilsen's experiences, by variations in the direction of the wind. He had found that it always answered his purpose to turn and try to windward, if the pack showed signs of being close. This mode of procedure naturally had the effect of making the course somewhat crooked, but to make up for this it had always resulted in his finding open water. On this trip we reached the edge of the pack-ice belt three days after leaving the Barrier. The position of the belt proved to be very nearly the same as on previous passages. After we had held our course for some hours, however, the ice became so thick that it looked badly for our further progress. Now was the time to try Nilsen's method: the wind, which, by the way, was quite light, came about due west, and accordingly the helm was put to starboard and the bow turned to the west. For a good while we even steered true south, but it proved that this fairly long turn had not been made in vain; after we had worked our way to windward for a few hours, we found openings in numbers. If we had held our course as we began, it is not at all impossible that we should have been delayed for a long time, with a free passage a few miles away.

After having accomplished this first long turn, we escaped having to make any more in future. The ice continued slack, and on February 6 the rapidly increasing swell told us that we had done with the Antarctic drift-ice for good. I doubt if we saw a single seal during our passage through the ice-belt this time; and if we had seen any, we should scarcely have allowed the time for shooting them. There was plenty of good food both for men and dogs this time, without our having recourse to seal-beef. For the dogs we had brought all our remaining store of the excellent dogs' pemmican, and that was not a little. Besides this, we had a good lot of dried fish. They had fish and pemmican on alternate days. On this diet the animals kept in such splendid condition that, when on arrival at Hobart they had shed most of their rough winter coats, they looked as if they had been in clover for a year.

For the nine of us who had just joined the ship, our comrades on board had brought all the way from Buenos Aires several fat pigs, that were now living in luxury in their pen on the after-deck; in addition to these, three fine sheep's carcasses hung in the workroom. It need scarcely be said that we were fully capable of appreciating these unexpected luxuries. Seal-beef, no doubt, had done excellent service, but this did not prevent roast mutton and pork being a welcome change, especially as they came as a complete surprise. I hardly think one of us had counted on the possibility of getting fresh meat before we were back again in civilization.

On her arrival at the Bay of Whales there were eleven men on board the *Fram*, all included. Instead of Kutschin and Nödtvedt, who had gone home from Buenos Aires while the ship was there in the autumn of 1911, three new men were engaged—namely, Halvorsen, Olsen and Steller; the two first-named were from Bergen; Steller was a German, who had lived for several years in Norway, and talked Norwegian like a native.

All three were remarkably efficient and friendly men ; it was a pleasure to have any dealings with them. I venture to think that they, too, found themselves at home in our company ; they were really only engaged until the *Fram* called at the first port, but they stayed on board all the way to Buenos Aires, and will certainly go with us farther still.

When the shore party came on board, Lieutenant Prestrud took up his old position as first officer ; the others began duty at once. All told, we were now twenty men on board, and after the *Fram* had sailed for a year rather short-handed, she could now be said to have a full crew again. On this voyage we had no special work outside the usual sea routine, and so long as the weather was fair, we had thus a comparatively quiet life on board. But the hours of watch on deck passed quickly enough, I expect ; there was material in plenty for many a long chat now. If we, who came from land, showed a high degree of curiosity about what had been going on in the world, the sea-party were at least as eager to have full information of every detail of our year-long stay on the Barrier. One must almost have experienced something similar oneself to be able to form an idea of the hail of questions that is showered upon one on such an occasion What we land-lubbers had to relate has been given in outline in the preceding chapters. Of the news we heard from outside, perhaps nothing interested us so much as the story of how the change in the plan of the expedition had been received at home and abroad.

It must have been at least a week before there was any noticeable ebb in the flood of questions and answers. That week went by quickly; perhaps more quickly than we really cared for, since it proved that the *Fram* was not really able to keep pace with time. The weather remained quite well behaved, but not exactly in the way we wished. We had reckoned that the south-easterly and easterly winds, so frequent around Framheim, would also show themselves out in Ross Sea, but they entirely forgot to do so. We had little wind, and when there was any, it was, as a rule, a slant from the north, always enough to delay our honest old ship. It was impossible to take any observations for the first eight days, the sky was continuously overcast. If one occasionally asked the skipper about her position, he usually replied that the only thing that could be said for certain was that we were in Ross Sea. On February 7, however, according to a fairly good noon observation, we were well to the north of Cape Adare, and therefore beyond the limits of the Antarctic Continent. On the way northward we passed Cape Adare at a distance hardly greater than could have been covered with a good day's sailing; but our desire of making this detour had to give way to the chief consideration—northward, northward as quickly as possible.

There is usually plenty of wind in the neighbourhood

of bold promontories, and Cape Adare is no exception in this respect; it is well known as a centre of bad weather. Nor did we slip by without getting a taste of this; but it could not have been more welcome, as it happened that the wind was going the same way as ourselves. Two days of fresh south-east wind took us comparatively quickly past the Balleny Islands, and on February 9 we could congratulate ourselves on being well out of the south frigid zone. It was with joy that we had crossed the Antarctic Circle over a year ago, going south; perhaps we rejoiced no less at crossing it this time in the opposite direction.

In the bustle of getting away from our winter-quarters there had been no time for any celebration of the fortunate reunion of the land and sea parties. As this occasion for festivity had been let slip, we had to look out for another, and we agreed that the day of our passage from the frigid to the temperate zone afforded a very good excuse. The pre-arranged part of the programme was extremely simple: an extra cup of coffee, duly accompanied by punch and cigars, and some music on the gramophone. Our worthy gramophone could not offer anything that had the interest of novelty to us nine who had wintered at Framheim: we knew the whole repertoire pretty well by heart; but the well-known melodies awakened memories of many a pleasant Saturday evening around the toddy table in our cosy winter home down at the head of the Bay of

Whales—memories which we need not be ashamed of recalling. On board the *Fram* gramophone music had not been heard since Christmas Eve, 1910, and the members of the sea party were glad enough to encore more than one number.

Outside the limits of the programme we were treated to an extra number by a singer, who imitated the gramophone in utilizing a big megaphone, to make up for the deficiencies of his voice—according to his own statement. He hid behind the curtain of Captain Nilsen's cabin, and through the megaphone came a ditty intended to describe life on the Barrier from its humorous side. It was completely successful, and we again had a laugh that did us good. Performances of this kind, of course, only have a value to those who have taken part in or are acquainted with the events to which they refer. In case any outsider may be interested in seeing what our entertainment was like, a few of the verses are given here.

It must be remarked that the author composed his production in the supposition that we should be able to meet by Christmas, and he therefore proposed that for the moment we should imagine ourselves to be celebrating that festival. We made no difficulty about acceding to his request:

Well, here we are assembled to jollity once more,
Some from off the ocean and the rest from off the shore.
A year has passed since last we met and all are safe and sound,
Then let us banish all our cares and join our hands all round.

Christmas, happy Christmas! let us pass the flowing bowl,
Fill your glasses all, and let's make "Sails" a wee bit full.
For all I'll say is this—that it's in his country's cause ;
If he staggers just a little, it is in his country's cause.

Now you sailor boys shall hear about the time we have gone through :
The winter—well, it wasn't long, we had so much to do.
There was digging snow, and sleeping—you can bet we're good at
    that—
And eating, too—no wonder that we're all a little fat.
We had hot cakes for our breakfast and "hermetik" each day,
Mutton pies, ragouts and curries, for that is Lindström's way.
But all I'll say is this—that 'twas in our country's cause,
If we stuffed ourselves with dainties, it was in our country's cause.

September came and off we went—that trip was pretty tough ;
Our compasses all went on strike, they thought it cold enough.
The brandy in the Captain's flask froze to a lump of ice ;
We all agreed, both men and dogs, such weather wasn't nice.
So back we went to Framheim to thaw our heels and toes ;
It could not be quite healthy when our feet and fingers froze.
But all I say is this—that 'twas in our country's cause,
And we did not mind a frost-bite when 'twas in our country's cause.

The sun came up and warmed us then a little day by day ;
Five men went out again and toiled along the southern way.
This time they conquered snow and ice, and all the world may hear
That Norway's flag flies at the Pole. Now, boys, a ringing cheer
For him who led them forward through the mountains and the plain,
Up to the goal they aimed at, and safely back again.
But all I'll say is this—that 'twas in his country's cause ;
If he went through and won the Pole, 'twas in his country's cause.

It could soon be noticed, in one way and another, that we had reached latitudes where existence took a very different aspect from what we had been accustomed to south of the 66th parallel. One welcome change was the rise in temperature; the mercury now climbed well above freezing-point, and those individuals on board who were still more or less clad in skins, shed the last remnants of their Polar garb for a lighter and more convenient costume. Those who waited longest before making the change were the ones who belonged to the shore party. The numerous people who imagine that a long stay in the Polar regions makes a man less susceptible of cold than other mortals are completely mistaken. The direct opposite is more likely to be the case. A man who stays some time in a place where the everyday temperature is down in the fifties below zero, or more than that, will not trouble himself greatly about the cold, so long as he has good and serviceable skin clothing. Let the same man, rigged out in civilized clothes, be suddenly put down in the streets of Christiania on a winter day, with thirty or thirty-five degrees of frost, and the poor fellow's teeth will chatter till they fall out of his mouth. The fact is, that on a Polar trip one defends oneself effectively against the cold; when one comes back, and has to go about with the protection afforded by an overcoat, a stiff collar, and a hard hat— well, then one feels it.

A less welcome consequence of the difference in latitude was the darkening of the nights. It may be admitted that continual daylight would be unpleasant in the long run ashore, but aboard ship an everlasting day would certainly be preferred, if such a thing could be had. Even if we might now consider that we had done with the principal mass of Antarctic ice, we still had to reckon with its disagreeable outposts—the icebergs. It has already been remarked that a practised look-out man can see the blink of one of the larger bergs a long way off in the dark, but when it is a question of one of the smaller masses of ice, of which only an inconsiderable part rises above the surface, there is no such brightness, and therefore no warning. A little lump like this is just as dangerous as a big berg; you run the same risks in a possible collision of knocking a hole in the bows or carrying away the rigging. In these transitional regions, where the temperature of the water is always very low, the thermometer is a very doubtful guide.

The waters in which we were sailing are not yet so well known as to exclude the possibility of meeting with land. Captain Colbeck, who commanded one of the relief ships sent south during Scott's first expedition, came quite unexpectedly upon a little island to the east of Cape Adare; this island was afterwards named after Captain Scott. When Captain Colbeck made his discovery, he was about on the course that has usually been taken by ships whose destination was within the limits of Ross Sea. There is still a possibility that in going out of one's course, voluntarily or involuntarily, one may find more groups of islands in that part.

On the current charts of the South Pacific there are marked several archipelagoes and islands, the position of which is not a little doubtful. One of these—Emerald Island—is charted as lying almost directly in the course we had to follow to reach Hobart. Captain Davis, who took Shackleton's ship, the *Nimrod*, home to England in 1909, sailed, however, right over the point where Emerald Island should be found according to the chart without seeing anything of it. If it exists at all, it is, at any rate, incorrectly charted. In order to avoid its vicinity, and still more in order to get as far as possible to the west before we came into the westerly belt proper, we pressed on as much as we could for one hard week, or perhaps nearer two ; but a continual north-west wind seemed for a long time to leave us only two disagreeable possibilities, either of drifting to the eastward, or of finding ourselves down in the drift-ice to the north of Wilkes Land.

Those weeks were a very severe trial of patience to the many on board who were burning with eagerness to get ashore with our news, and perhaps to hear some in return. When the first three weeks of February were past, we were not much more than half-way ; with anything like favourable conditions we ought to have arrived by that time. The optimists always consoled us by saying that sooner or later there would be a change for the better, and at last it came. A good spell of favourable wind took us at a bound well to the windward both of the doubtful Emerald Island and of the authentic Macquarie group to the north of it. It may be mentioned in passing, that at the time we went by, the most southerly wireless telegraphy station in the world was located on one of the Macquarie Islands. The installation belonged to Dr. Mawson's Antarctic expedition. Dr. Mawson also took with him apparatus for installing a station on the Antarctic Continent itself, but, so far as is known, no connection was accomplished the first year.

During this fortunate run we had come so far to the west that our course to Hobart was rapidly approaching true north. On the other hand, we should have liked to be able to take advantage of the prevailing winds, —the westerlies. These vary little from one year to another, and we found them much the same as we had been accustomed to before : frequent, stiff breezes from the north-west, which generally held for about twelve hours, and then veered to west or south-west. So long as the north-wester was blowing, there was nothing to do but to lie to with shortened sail ; when the change of wind came, we made a few hours' progress in the right direction. In this way we crept step by step northward to our destination. It was slow enough, no doubt ; but every day the line of our course on the chart grew a little longer, and towards the end of February the distance between us and the southern point of Tasmania had shrunk to very modest dimensions.

With the constant heavy westerly swell, the *Fram*, light as she now was, surpassed herself in rolling, and that is indeed saying a great deal. This rolling brought us a little damage to the rigging, the gaff of the mainsail breaking; however, that affair did not stop us long. The broken spar was quickly replaced by a spare gaff.

Our hopes of arriving before the end of February came to naught, and a quarter of March went by before our voyage was at an end.

On the afternoon of March 4, we had our first glimpse of land; but, as the weather was by no means clear and we had not been able to determine our longitude with certainty for two days, we were uncertain which point of Tasmania we had before us. To explain the situation, a short description of the coast-line is necessary. The southern angle of Tasmania runs out in three promontories; off the easternmost of these, and only divided from it by a very narrow channel, lies a steep and apparently inaccessible island, called Tasman Island. It is, however, accessible, for on the top of it—900 feet above the sea—stands a lighthouse. The middle promontory is called Tasman Head, and between this and the eastern one we have Storm Bay, which forms the approach to Hobart; there, then, lay our course. The question was, which of the three heads we had sighted. This was difficult, or rather impossible, to decide, so indistinct was the outline of the land in the misty air; it was also entirely unknown to us, as not one of us had

ever before been in this corner of the world. When
darkness came on, a heavy rain set in, and without
being able to see anything at all, we lay there feeling
our way all night. With the appearance of daylight
a fresh south-west wind came and swept away most
of the rain, so that we could again make out the land.
We decided that what we saw was the middle promontory, Tasman Head, and gaily set our course into
Storm Bay — as we thought. With the rapidly
strengthening breeze we went spinningly, and the
possibility of reaching Hobart in a few hours began
to appear as a dead certainty. With this comfortable
feeling we had just sat down to the breakfast table
in the fore-saloon, when the door was pulled open with
what seemed unnecessary violence, and the face of the
officer of the watch appeared in the doorway. "We're
on the wrong side of the head," was the sinister message,
and the face disappeared. Good-bye to our pleasant
plans, good-bye to our breakfast! All hands went
on deck at once, and it was seen only too well that
the melancholy information was correct. We had
made a mistake in the thick rain. The wind, that
had now increased to a stiff breeze, had chased the
rain-clouds from the tops of the hills, and on the point
we had taken for Tasman Head, we now saw the
lighthouse. It was therefore Tasman Island, and
instead of being in Storm Bay, we were out in the
open Pacific, far to leeward of the infamous headland.

There was nothing to be done but to beat and attempt to work our way back to windward, although we knew it would be practically labour in vain. The breeze increased to a gale, and instead of making any headway we had every prospect of drifting well to leeward; that was the usual result of trying to beat with the *Fram*. Rather annoyed though we were, we set to work to do what could be done, and with every square foot of canvas set the *Fram* pitched on her way close-hauled. To begin with, it looked as if we held our own more or less, but as the distance from land increased and the wind got more force, our bearings soon showed us that we were going the way the hen kicks. About midday we went about and stood in towards land again; immediately after came a violent squall which tore the outer jib to ribbons; with that we were also obliged to take in the mainsail, otherwise it would pretty soon have been caught aback, and there would have been further damage to the rigging. With the remaining sails any further attempt was useless; there was nothing left but to get as close under the lee of the land as we could and try with the help of the engine to hold our own till the weather moderated. How it blew that afternoon! One gust after another came dancing down the slopes of the hills, and tore at the rigging till the whole vessel shook. The feeling on board was, as might be expected, somewhat sultry, and found an outlet in various expressions the reverse

of gentle. Wind, weather, fate, and life in general
were inveighed against, but this availed little. The
peninsula that separated us from Storm Bay still lay
there firm and immovable, and the gale went on as if
it was in no hurry to let us get round. The whole day
went by, and the greater part of the night, without any
change taking place. Not till the morning of the 6th
did our prospects begin to improve. The wind became
lighter and went more to the south ; that was, of course,
the way we had to go, but by hugging the shore, where
we had perfectly smooth water, we succeeded in working
our way down to Tasman Island before darkness fell.
The night brought a calm, and that gave us our chance.
The engine worked furiously, and a slight favourable
current contributed to set us on our way. By dawn
on the 7th we were far up Storm Bay and could at last
consider ourselves masters of the situation.

It was a sunny day, and our faces shone in rivalry
with the sun ; all trace of the last two days' annoyances
had vanished. And soon the *Fram*, too, began to shine.
The white paint on deck had a thorough overhauling
with soap and water in strong solution. The Ripolin
was again as fresh as when new. When this had been
seen to, the outward appearance of the men also began
to undergo a striking change. The Iceland jackets and
" blanket costumes " from Horten gave way to " shore
clothes " of the most varied cut, hauled out after a two
years' rest ; razors and scissors had made a rich harvest,

and sailmaker Rönne's fashionable Burberry caps figured
on most heads. Even Lindström, who up to date had
held the position among the land party of being its
heaviest, fattest, and blackest member, showed unmistakable signs of having been in close contact with
water.

Meanwhile we were nearing a pilot station, and a
bustling little motor launch swung alongside. " Want
a pilot, captain ?" One positively started at the sound
of the first new human voice. Communication with the
outer world was again established. The pilot—a brisk,
good-humoured old man—looked about him in surprise
when he came up on to our deck. "I should never
have imagined things were so clean and bright on board
a Polar ship," he said; "nor should I have thought from
the look of you that you had come from Antarctica.
You look as if you had had nothing but a good time."
We could assure him of that, but as to the rest, it was
not our intention just yet to allow ourselves to be
pumped, and the old man could see that. He had no
objection to our pumping him, though he had no very
great store of news to give us. He had heard nothing
of the *Terra Nova;* on the other hand, he was able to
tell us that Dr. Mawson's ship, the *Aurora*, commanded
by Captain Davis, might be expected at Hobart any day.
They had been looking out for the *Fram* since the
beginning of February, and had given us up long ago.
That was a surprise, anyhow.

Our guest evidently had no desire to make the acquaintance of our cuisine; at any rate, he very energetically declined our invitation to breakfast. Presumably he was afraid of being treated to dog's flesh or similar original dishes. On the other hand, he showed great appreciation of our Norwegian tobacco. He had his handbag pretty nearly full when he left us.

Hobart Town lies on the bank of the Derwent River, which runs into Storm Bay. The surroundings are beautiful, and the soil evidently extremely fertile; but woods and fields were almost burnt up on our arrival; a prolonged drought had prevailed, and made an end of all green things. To our eyes it was, however, an unmixed delight to look upon meadows and woods, even if their colours were not absolutely fresh. We were not very difficult to please on that score.

The harbour of Hobart is an almost ideal one, large and remarkably well protected. As we approached the town, the usual procession of harbour-master, doctor, and Custom-house officers came aboard. The doctor soon saw that there was no work for his department, and the Custom-house officers were easily convinced that we had no contraband goods. The anchor was dropped, and we were free to land. I took my cablegrams, and accompanied the harbour-master ashore.

CHAPTER XV

THE EASTERN SLEDGE JOURNEY

By Lieutenant K. Prestrud

ON October 20, 1911, the southern party started on their long journey. The departure took place without much ceremony, and with the smallest possible expenditure of words. A hearty grasp of the hand serves the purpose quite as well on such occasions. I accompanied them to the place we called the starting-point, on the south side of the bay. After a final " Good luck " to our Chief and comrades—as sincere a wish as I have ever bestowed upon anyone—I cinematographed the caravan, and very soon after it was out of sight. Those fellows went southward at a great pace, Helmer Hanssen's quick-footed team leading as usual.

There I stood, utterly alone, and I cannot deny that I was a prey to somewhat mixed feelings. When should we see those five again, who had just disappeared from view on the boundless plain, and in what conditions ? What sort of a report would they bring of the result ? There was plenty of room for guesses here, and abundant

LIEUTENANT PRESTRUD.

opportunity for weighing every possibility, good and bad; but there was very little to be gained by indulging in speculations of that sort. The immediate facts first claimed attention. One fact, amongst others, was that Framheim was a good three miles away; another was that the cinematograph apparatus weighed a good many pounds; and a third that Lindström would be mightily put out if I arrived too late for dinner. Our *chef* insisted on a high standard of punctuality in the matter of meal-times. Homeward, then, at the best speed possible. The speed, however, was not particularly good, and I began to prepare for the consequences of a long delay. On the other side of the bay I could just make out a little black speck, that seemed to be in motion towards me. I thought at first it was a seal, but, fortunately, it turned out to be Jörgen Stubberud with six dogs and a sledge. This was quite encouraging: in the first place, I should get rid of my unmanageable burden, and in the second I might expect to get on faster. Stubberud's team consisted, however, of four intractable puppies, besides Puss and another courser of similar breed; the result was that our pace was a modest one and our course anything but straight, so that we arrived at Framheim two hours after the time appointed for dinner. Those who know anything of Master Lindström and his disposition will easily be able from this explanation to form an idea of his state of mind at the moment when we entered the door. Yes, he was undoubtedly angry, but we were at least equally hungry; and if anything can soften the heart of a Norwegian caterer, it is a ravenous appetite in those he has to feed, provided, of course, that he have enough to offer them, and Lindström's supplies were practically unlimited.

I remember that dinner well: at the same table where eight of us had sat for so many months, there were now only three left—Johansen, Stubberud, and I. We had more room, it is true, but that gain was a poor satisfaction. We missed those who had gone very badly, and our thoughts were always following them. The first thing we discussed on this occasion was how many miles they might be expected to do that day: nor was this the last dispute we had on the same theme. During the weeks and months that followed, it was constantly to the fore, and gave plenty of material for conversation when we had exhausted our own concerns. As regards these latter, my instructions were:

1. To go to King Edward VII. Land, and there carry out what exploration time and circumstances might permit.

2. To survey and map the Bay of Whales and its immediate surroundings.

3. As far as possible to keep the station at Framheim in order, in case we might have to spend another winter there.

As regards time, my orders were to be back at Framheim before we could reasonably expect the arrival of the *Fram*. This was, and would necessarily remain, somewhat uncertain. No doubt we all had a great idea of the *Fram's* capacity for keeping time, and Lieutenant Nilsen had announced his intention of being back by Christmas or the New Year; but nevertheless a year is a long time, and there are many miles in a trip round the world. If we assumed that no mishap had occurred to the *Fram*, and that she had left Buenos Aires at the time fixed in the plan—October 1, 1911—she would in all probability be able to arrive at the Bay of Whales about the middle of January, 1912. On the basis of this calculation we decided, if possible, to get the sledge journey to King Edward Land done before Christmas, while the surveying work around the bay would have to be postponed to the first half of January, 1912. I thought, however, seeing the advantages of working while the bay was still frozen over, that it would pay to devote a few days—immediately following the departure of the southern party—to the preparatory work of measuring. But this did not pay at all. We had reckoned without the weather, and in consequence were well taken in. When one thinks over it afterwards, it seems reasonable enough that the final victory of mild weather over the remains of the Antarctic winter cannot be accomplished without serious disturbances of the atmospheric conditions. The expulsion of one evil has to be effected by the help of another; and the weather was bad with a vengeance. During the two weeks that followed October 20 there were only three or four days that offered any chance of working with the theodolite and plane-table. We managed to get a base-line measured, 1,000 metres long, and to lay out the greater part of the east side of the bay, as well as the most prominent points round the camp; but one had positively to snatch one's opportunities by stealth, and every excursion ended regularly in bringing the instruments home well covered with snow.

If the bad weather thus put hindrances in the way of the work we were anxious to do, it made up for it by providing us with a lot of extra work which we could very well have done without. There was incessant shovelling of snow to keep any sort of passage open to the four dog-tents that were left standing, as well as to our own underground dwelling, over which the snow covering had been growing constantly higher. The fairly high wall that we had originally built on the east side of the entrance door was now entirely buried in the snow-drift. It had given us good protection; now the drift had unimpeded access, and the opening, like the descent into a cellar, that led down to the door, was filled up in the course of a few hours when the wind was in the right quarter. Lindström shook his head when we sometimes asked him how he would get on by himself if the weather continued in this way. "So long as there's nothing but snow in the way, I'll manage to get out," said he. One day he came and told us that he could no longer get at the coal, and on further investigation it looked rather difficult. The roof of the place where the coal was stored had yielded to the pressure of the mass of snow, and the whole edifice had collapsed. There was nothing to be done but to set to work at once, and after a great deal of hard labour we got the remainder of the precious fuel moved into the long snow tunnel that led from the house to the coal-store. With that our "black diamonds" were in safety for the time being. This job made us about as black as the "diamonds." When we came in the cook, as it happened, had just been doing a big wash on his own account—a comparatively rare event—and there was surprise on both sides. The cook was as much taken aback at seeing us so black as we were at seeing him so clean.

All the snow-shovelling that resulted from the continued bad weather, in conjunction with the necessary preparations for the sledge journey, gave us plenty of occupation, but I will venture to say that none of us would care to go through those days again. We were delayed in our real work. and delay, which is unpleasant enough in any circumstances, was all the more unwelcome down here, where time is so precious. As we only had two sledges on which to transport supplies for three men and sixteen dogs, besides all our outfit, and as on our trip we should have no depots to fall back on, the duration of the journey could not be extended much beyond six weeks. In order to be back again by Christmas, we had, therefore, to leave before the middle of November. It would do no harm, however, to be off before this, and as soon as November arrived we took the first opportunity of disappearing.

On account of getting on the right course, we preferred that the start should take place in clear weather. The fact was that we were obliged to go round by the depot in 80° S. As King Edward Land lies to the east, or rather north-east, of Framheim, this was a considerable detour; it had to be made, because in September we had left at this depot all the packed sledging provisions, a good deal of our personal equipment, and, finally, some of the necessary instruments.

On the way to the depot, about thirty geographical miles south of Framheim, we had the nasty crevassed surface that had been met with for the first time on the third depot journey in the autumn of 1911—in the month of April. At that time we came upon it altogether unawares, and it was somewhat remarkable that we escaped from it with the loss of two dogs. This broken surface lay in a depression about a mile to the west of the route originally marked out; but, however it may have been, it seems ever since that time to have exercised an irresistible attraction. On our first attempt to go south, in September, 1911, we came right into the middle of it, in spite of the fact that it was then perfectly clear. I afterwards heard that in spite of all their efforts, the southern party, on their last trip, landed in this dangerous region, and that one man had a very narrow escape of falling in with sledge and dogs. I had no wish to expose myself to the risk of such accidents — at any rate, while we were on familiar ground. That would have been a bad beginning to my first independent piece of work as a Polar explorer. A day or two of fine weather to begin with would enable us to follow the line originally marked out, and thus keep safe ground under our feet until the ugly place was passed.

In the opening days of November the weather conditions began to improve somewhat ; in any case, there was not the continual driving snow. Lindström asked us before we left to bring up a sufficient quantity of seals, to save him that work as long as possible. The supply we had had during the winter was almost exhausted ; there was only a certain amount of blubber left. We thought it only fair to accede to his wish, as it is an awkward business to transport those heavy beasts alone, especially when one has only a pack of unbroken puppies to drive. We afterwards heard that Lindström had some amusing experiences with them during the time he was left alone.

Leaving the transport out of the question, this seal-hunting is a very tame sport. An old Arctic hand or an Eskimo would certainly be astounded to see the placid calm with which the Antarctic seal allows itself to be shot and cut up. To them Antarctica would appear as a fairyland made real, a land flowing with milk and honey, where seals are to be found in quantities, and the difficulty of getting at them is reduced to *nil.* The fact is that these animals have once for all acquired the conviction that they are beyond the reach of any danger so long as they keep on land or on the ice. There they have never been attacked, and they are quite incapable of grasping the possibility of attack. Their natural enemies are in the water, and these enemies are not to be trifled with; that can clearly be seen from the gaping wounds that are often found on the seals' bodies. To avoid the attacks of these enemies the seals have only to get on to the ice, where for generations they have been accustomed to bask in the sun undisturbed, without other neighbours than the, to them, perfectly harmless penguins and skua gulls.

The sudden appearance of a man on the scene will therefore at first have very little effect on an Antarctic seal. One can go right up to it without its doing anything but staring with eyes that reflect a perfectly hopeless failure to comprehend the seriousness of the situation. It is only when one touches them with a ski-pole or something of the sort that they begin to fear danger. If the stirring-up is continued in a rather more pointed fashion, the seal soon shows the most manifest signs of terror. It groans, roars, and at the same time makes an attempt to get away from its unwelcome visitor;

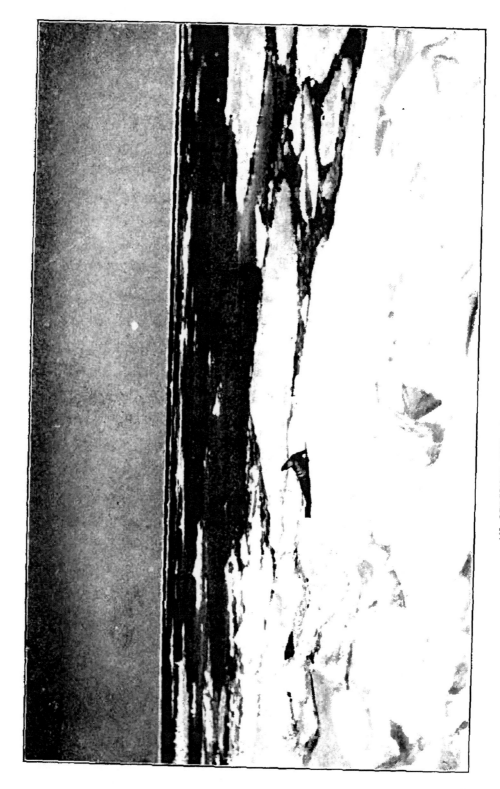

AN ORIGINAL INHABITANT OF THE ANTARCTIC.

but it seldom removes itself many yards at a time, for the motions of the seal are just as clumsy and slow on land as they are active and swift in the water. When it has crawled with great pains to a little distance, there is no sign that the interruption has made any lasting impression on it. It looks more as if it took it all as an unpleasant dream or nightmare, which it would be best to sleep off as soon as possible. If one shoots a single seal, this may happen without those lying round so much as raising their heads. Indeed, we could open and cut up a seal right before the noses of its companions without this making the slightest impression on them.

About the beginning of November the seals began to have their young. So far as we could make out, the females kept out of the water for several days without taking any food, until the young one was big enough to be able to go to sea; otherwise, it did not seem that the mothers cared very much for their little ones. Some, it is true, made a sort of attempt to protect their offspring if they were disturbed, but the majority simply left their young ones in the lurch.

As far as we were concerned, we left the females and their young as much as possible in peace. We killed two or three new-born seals to get the skins for our collection. It was another matter with the dogs. With them seal-hunting was far too favourite a sport for the opportunity to be neglected. Against a full-grown seal, however, they could do nothing; its body offered no particularly vulnerable spots, and the thick, tight-fitting skin was too much even for dogs' teeth. The utmost the rascals could accomplish was to annoy and torment the object of their attack. It was quite another matter when the young ones began to arrive. Among this small game the enterprising hunters could easily satisfy their inborn craving for murder, for the scoundrels only killed for the sake of killing; they were not at all hungry, as they had as much food as they liked. Of course, we did all we could to put a stop to this state of things, and so long as there were several of us at the hut, we saw that the whole pack was tied up; but when Lindström was left by himself, he could not manage to hold them fast. His tents were altogether snowed under in the weather that prevailed on the seaboard in December. There were not many dogs left in his charge, but I am afraid those few wrought great havoc among the young seals out on the ice of the bay. The poor mothers could hardly have done anything against a lot of dogs, even if they had been more courageous. Their enemies were too active. For them it was the work of a moment to snatch the young one from the side of its mother, and then they were able to take the poor thing's life undisturbed.

Unfortunately, there were no sea-leopards in the neighbourhood of Framheim. These, which are far quicker in their movements than the Weddell seal,

STUBBERUD REVIEWS THE SITUATION.

and are, moreover, furnished with a formidable set of teeth, would certainly have made the four-footed seal-hunters more careful in their behaviour.

After we had brought up to the house enough seals' carcasses to keep the ten or twelve dogs that would be left supplied for a good while, and had cut up a sufficient quantity for our own use on the way to 80° S., we took the first opportunity of getting away. Before I pass on to give an account of our trip, I wish to say a few words about my companions—Johansen and Stubberud. It goes without saying that it gave me, as a beginner, a great feeling of security to have with me such a man as Johansen, who possessed many years' experience of all that pertains to sledging expeditions; and as regards Stubberud, I could not have wished for a better travelling companion than him either—a first-rate fellow, steady and efficient in word and deed. As it turned out, we were not to encounter very many difficulties, but one never escapes scot-free on a sledge journey in these regions. I owe my comrades thanks for the way in which they both did their best to smooth our path.

Johansen and Stubberud drove their dog-teams; I myself acted as "forerunner." The drivers had seven dogs apiece. We took so many, because we were not quite sure of what the animals we had were fit for. As was right and proper, the southern party had picked out the best. Among those at our disposal there were several that had previously shown signs of being rather quickly tired. True, this happened under very severe conditions. As it turned out, our dogs exceeded all our expectations in the easier conditions of work that prevailed during the summer. On the first part of the way—as far as the depot in 80° S.—the loads were quite modest. Besides the tent, the sleeping-bags, our personal outfit, and instruments, we only had provisions for eight days—seals' flesh for the dogs, and tinned food for ourselves. Our real supplies were to be taken from the depot, where there was enough of everything.

On November 8 we left Framheim, where in future Lindström was to reside as monarch of all he surveyed. The weather was as fine as could be wished. I was out with the cinematograph apparatus, in order if possible to immortalize the start. To complete the series of pictures, Lindström was to take the forerunner, who was now, be it said, a good way behind those he was supposed to be leading. With all possible emphasis I enjoined Lindström only to give the crank five or six turns, and then started off to catch up the drivers. When I had nearly reached the provision store I pulled up, struck by a sudden apprehension. Yes, I was right: on looking back I discovered that incorrigible person still hard at work with the crank, as though he were going to be paid a pound for every yard of film showing the back view of the forerunner. By making threatening gestures with a ski-pole I stopped the too persistent cinematograph, and then went on to join Stubberud, who was only a few yards ahead. Johansen had disappeared like a meteor. The last I saw of him was the soles of his boots, as he quite unexpectedly made an elegant backward somersault off the sledge when it was passing over a little unevenness by the provision store. The dogs, of course, made off at full speed, and Johansen after them like the wind. We all met again safe and sound at the ascent to the Barrier. Here a proper order of march was formed, and we proceeded southward.

The Barrier greeted us with a fresh south wind, that now and then made an attempt to freeze the tip of one's nose; it did not succeed in this, but it delayed us a little. It does not take a great deal of wind on this level plain to diminish the rate of one's progress. But the sun shone too gaily that day to allow a trifle of wind to interfere very much with our enjoyment of life. The surface was so firm that there was hardly a sign of drift-snow. As it was perfectly clear, the mark-flags could be followed the whole time, thus assuring us that, at any rate, the first day's march would be accomplished without any deviation from the right track.

At five o'clock we camped, and when we had fed the dogs and come into the tent we could feel how much easier and pleasanter everything was at this season than on the former journeys in autumn and spring. We could move freely in a convenient costume; if we wished, there was nothing to prevent our performing all the work of the camp with bare hands and still preserving our finger-tips unharmed. As I had no dog-team to look after, I undertook the duty of attending to our own needs; that is to say, I acted as cook. This occupation also was considerably easier now than it had been when the temperature was below −60° F. At that time it took half an hour to turn the snow in the cooker into water; now it was done in ten minutes, and the cook ran no risk whatever of getting his fingers frozen in the process.

Ever since we landed on the Barrier in January, 1911, we had been expecting to hear a violent cannonade as the result of the movement of the mass of ice. We had now lived a whole winter at Framheim without having observed, as far as I know, the slightest sign of a sound. This was one of many indications that the ice round our winter-quarters was not in motion at all.

No one, I believe, had noticed anything of the expected noise on the sledge journeys either, but at the place where we camped on the night of November 8 we did hear it. There was a report about once in two minutes, not exactly loud, but still, there it was. It sounded just as if there was a whole battery of small guns in action down in the depths below us. A few hundred yards to the west of the camp there were a number of small hummocks, which might indicate the presence of crevasses, but otherwise the surface looked safe enough. The small guns kept up a lively crackle all through the night, and combined with a good deal of uproar among the dogs to shorten our sleep. But the first night of a sledge journey is almost always a bad one. Stubberud declared that he could not close his eyes on account of " that filthy row." He probably expected the ice to open and swallow him up every time he heard it. The surface, however, held securely, and we turned out to the finest day one could wish to see. It did not require any very great strength of mind to get out of one's sleeping-bag now. The stockings that had been hung up in the evening could be put on again as dry as a bone ; the sun had seen to that. Our ski boots were as soft as ever ; there was not a sign of frost on them. It is quite curious to see the behaviour of the dogs when the first head appears through the tent-door in the morning. They greet their lord and master with the most unmistakable signs of joy, although, of course, they must know that his arrival will be followed by many hours of toil, with, perhaps, a few doses of the whip thrown in ; but from the moment he begins to handle the sledge, the dogs look as if they had no desire in the world but to get into the harness as soon as possible and start away. On days like this their troubles would be few ; with the light load and good going we had no difficulty in covering nineteen geographical miles in eight hours. Johansen's team was on my heels the whole time, and Stubberud's animals followed faithfully behind.   From time to time we saw sledge-tracks quite plainly; we also kept the mark-flags in sight all day.   In the temperatures we now had to deal with our costume was comparatively light—certainly much lighter than most people imagine; for there is a kind of summer even in Antarctica, although the daily readings of the thermometer at this season would perhaps rather remind our friends at home of what they are accustomed to regard as winter.

In undertaking a sledge journey down there in autumn or spring, the most extraordinary precautions have to be taken to protect oneself against the cold. Skin clothing is then the only thing that is of any use; but at this time of year, when the sun is above the horizon for the whole twenty-four hours, one can go for a long time without being more heavily clad than a lumberman working in the woods.   During the march our clothing was usually the following: two sets of woollen underclothes, of which that nearest the skin was quite thin.   Outside the shirt we wore either an ordinary waistcoat or a comparatively light knitted woollen jersey.   Outside all came our excellent Burberry clothes—trousers and jacket.   When it was calm, with full sunshine, the Burberry jacket was too warm; we could then go all day in our shirt-sleeves.   To be provided for emergencies, we all had our thinnest reindeer - skin clothes with us; but, so far as I know, these were never used, except as pillows or mattresses.

The subject of sleeping-bags has no doubt been thoroughly threshed out on every Polar expedition. I do not know how many times we discussed this question, nor can I remember the number of more or less successful patents that were the fruit of these discussions. In any case, one thing is certain, that the adherents of one-man bags were in an overwhelming majority, and no doubt rightly. As regards two-man bags, it cannot be denied that they enable their occupants to keep warm longer; but it is always difficult to find room for two big men in one sack, and if the sack is to be used for sleeping in, and one of the big men takes to snoring into the other's ear, the situation may become quite unendurable. In the temperatures we had on the summer journeys there was no difficulty in keeping warm enough with the one-man bags, and they were used by all of us.

On the first southern journey, in September, Johansen and I used a double bag between us; in the intense cold that prevailed at that time we managed to get through the night without freezing; but if the weather is so cold that one cannot keep warmth in one's body in good, roomy one-man bags, then it is altogether unfit for sledging journeys.

November 10.—Immediately after the start this morning we tried how we could get on without a forerunner. As long as we were in the line of flags this answered very well; the dogs galloped from one flag to another, while I was able to adopt the easy method of hanging on to Stubberud's sledge. About midday we were abreast of the depression already mentioned, where, on the third depot journey last autumn, we ran into a regular net of crevasses. This time we were aware of the danger, and kept to the left; but at the last moment the leading team ran out to the wrong side, and we cut across the eastern part of the dangerous zone. Fortunately it was taken at full gallop. It is quite possible that I inwardly wished we were all a few pounds lighter, as our little caravan raced across those thin snow bridges, through which could be seen the blue colour of the ugly gulfs below. But after the lapse of a few long minutes we could congratulate ourselves on getting over with our full numbers.

Not for anything would I have gone that mile without ski on my feet; it would practically have meant falling in and going out. It is, perhaps, saying a good deal to claim that with ski on, one is absolutely secured against the danger these crevasses present; if misfortunes are abroad, anything may happen. But it would require a very considerable amount of bad luck for man and ski to fall through.

November 11.—In weather like this, going on the march is like going to a dance : tent, sleeping-bags, and clothes keep soft and dry as a bone. The thermometer

CAMP ON THE BARRIER : EASTERN EXPEDITION.

A BROKEN-OFF CAPE ON THE BARRIER.

is about − 4° F.   A fellow-man suddenly put down in
our midst from civilized surroundings would possibly
shake his head at so many degrees of frost, but it must
be remembered that we have long ago abandoned the
ordinary ideas of civilized people as to what is endurable
in the way of temperature.   We are enthusiastic about
the spring-like weather, especially when we remember
what it was like down here two months ago, when the
thermometer showed − 76° F., and the rime hung an inch
thick inside the tent, ready to drop on everything and
everybody at the slightest movement.   Now there is no
rime to be seen ; the sun clears it away.   For now there
is a sun ; not the feeble imitation of one that stuck its
red face above the northern horizon in August, but our
good old acquaintance of lower latitudes, with his wealth
of light and warmth.

After two hours' march we came in sight, at ten o'clock
in the morning, of the two snow-huts that were built
on the last trip.   We made straight for them, thinking
we might possibly find some trace of the southern party.
So we did, though in a very different way from what we
expected.   We were, perhaps, about a mile off when we
all three suddenly halted and stared at the huts.   " There
are men," said Stubberud.   At any rate there was something black that moved, and after confused thoughts of
Japanese, Englishmen, and the like had flashed through
our minds, we at last got out the glasses.   It was not
men, but a dog.   Well, the presence of a live dog here,

seventy-five miles up the Barrier, was in itself a remarkable thing. It must, of course, be one of the southern party's dogs, but how the runaway had kept himself alive all that time was for the present a mystery. On coming to closer quarters we soon found that it was one of Hassel's dogs, Peary by name. He was a little shy to begin with, but when he heard his name he quickly understood that we were friends come on a visit, and no longer hesitated to approach us. He was fat and round, and evidently pleased to see us again. The hermit had lived on the lamentable remains of poor Sara, whom we had been obliged to kill here in September. Sara's lean and frozen body did not seem particularly adapted for making anyone fat, and yet our newly-found friend Peary looked as if he had been feasting for weeks. Possibly he had begun by devouring Neptune, another of his companions, who had also given the southern party the slip on the way to the depot in 80° S. However this may be, Peary's rest cure came to an abrupt conclusion. Stubberud took him and put him in his team.

We had thought of reaching the depot before the close of the day, and this we could easily have done if the good going had continued ; but during the afternoon the surface became so loose that the dogs sank in up to their chests, and when—at about six in the evening—the sledge-meter showed twenty-one geographical miles, the animals were so done up that it was no use going on.

At eleven o'clock the next morning—Sunday, November 12—we reached the depot. Captain Amundsen had promised to leave a brief report when the southern party left here, and the first thing we did on arrival was, of course, to search for the document in the place agreed upon. There were not many words on the little slip of paper, but they gave us the welcome intelligence: " All well so far."

We had expected that the southern party's dogs would have finished the greater part, if not the whole, of the seal meat that was laid down here in April; but fortunately this was not the case. There was a great quantity left, so that we could give our own dogs a hearty feed with easy consciences. They had it, too, and it was no trifling amount that they got through. The four days' trot from Framheim had been enough to produce an unusual appetite. There was a puppy in Johansen's team that was exposed for the first time in his life to the fatigues of a sledge journey. This was a plucky little chap that went by the name of Lillegut. The sudden·change from short commons to abundance was too much for his small stomach, and the poor puppy lay shrieking in the snow most of the afternoon.

We also looked after ourselves that day, and had a good meal of fresh seal meat; after that we supplied ourselves from the large stores that lay here with the necessary provisions for a sledge journey of five weeks: three cases of dogs' pemmican, one case of men's pemmican, containing ninety rations, 20 pounds of dried milk, 55 pounds of oatmeal biscuits, and three tins of malted milk, besides instruments, Alpine rope, and clothing. The necessary quantity of chocolate had been brought with us from Framheim, as there was none of this to spare out in the field. Our stock of paraffin was $6\frac{1}{2}$ gallons, divided between two tanks, one on each sledge. Our cooking outfit was exactly the same as that used by the southern party.

The instruments we carried were a theodolite, a hypsometer, two aneroids, one of which was no larger than an ordinary watch, two thermometers, one chronometer watch, one ordinary watch, and one photographic camera (Kodak 3 x 3 inches), adapted for using either plates or films. We had three spools of film, and one dozen plates.

Our medical outfit was exceedingly simple. It consisted of nothing but a box of laxative pills, three small rolls of gauze bandage, and a small pair of scissors, which also did duty for beard-cutting. Both pills and gauze were untouched when we returned; it may therefore be safely said that our state of health during the journey was excellent.

While the drivers were packing and lashing their loads, which now weighed nearly 600 pounds, I wrote a report to the Chief, and took an azimuth observation to determine the direction of our course. According to our instructions we should really have taken a north-

OFF TO THE EAST.

easterly course from here ; but as our dogs seemed to be capable of more and better work than we had expected, and as there was believed to be a possibility that bare land was to be found due east of the spot where we were, it was decided to make an attempt in that direction.

Our old enemy the fog had made its appearance in the course of the night, and now hung, grey and disgusting, under the sky, when we broke camp at the depot on the morning of November 13. However, it was not so bad as to prevent our following the flags that marked the depot on the east.

My duty as forerunner was immediately found to be considerably lighter than before. With the greatly increased weight behind them the dogs had all they could do to follow, if I went at an ordinary walking pace. At 11 a.m. we passed the easternmost flag, at five geographical miles from the depot, and then we found ourselves on untrodden ground. A light southerly breeze appeared very opportunely and swept away the fog; the sun again shed its light over the Barrier, which lay before us, shining and level, as we had been accustomed to see it. There was, however, one difference : with every mile we covered there was the possibility of seeing something new. The going was excellent, although the surface was rather looser than one could have wished. The ski flew over it finely, of course, while dogs' feet and sledge-runners sank in. I hope I shall never have to go here without ski; that would be a terrible punishment; but with ski on one's feet and in such weather it was pure enjoyment.

Meanwhile the new sights we expected were slow in coming. We marched for four days due east without seeing a sign of change in the ground; there was the same undulating surface that we knew so well from previous expeditions. The readings of the hypsometer gave practically the same result day after day; the ascent we were looking for failed to appear.

Stubberud, who for the first day or two after leaving the depot had been constantly stretching himself on tiptoe and looking out for mountain-tops, finally gave it as his heartfelt conviction that this King Edward Land we were hunting for was only a confounded " Flyaway Land," which had nothing to do with reality. We others were not yet quite prepared to share this view; for my own part, in any case, I was loth to give up the theory that assumed a southward continuation of King Edward Land along the 158th meridian; this theory had acquired a certain force during the winter, and was mainly supported by the fact that on the second depot journey we had seen, between the 81st and 82nd parallels, some big pressure-ridges, which suggested the presence of bare land in a south-easterly direction.

On November 16 we found ourselves at the 158th meridian, but on every side the eye encountered the

level, uninterrupted snow surface and nothing else.
Should we go on? It was tempting enough, as the
probability was that sooner or later we should come
upon something; but there was a point in our instructions that had to be followed, and it said: Go to the
point where land is marked on the chart. This point
was now about 120 geographical miles to the north of
us. Therefore, instead of going on to the east in
uncertainty, we decided to turn to the left and go
north. The position of the spot where we altered our
course was determined, and it was marked by a snow
beacon 7 feet high, on the top of which was placed
a tin box containing a brief report.

On that part of the way which we now had before
us there was little prospect of meeting with surprises;
nor did any fall to our lot. In day's marches that
varied from seventeen to twenty geographical miles, we
went forward over practically level ground. The nature
of the surface was at first ideal; but as we came farther
north and thus nearer to the sea, our progress was
impeded by a great number of big snow-waves (*sastrugi*),
which had probably been formed during the long period
of bad weather that preceded our departure from Framheim. We did not escape damage on this bad surface.
Stubberud broke the forward part of the spare ski he
had lashed under his sledge, and Johansen's sledge also
suffered from the continual bumping against the hard
sastrugi. Luckily he had been foreseeing enough to

bring a little hickory bar, which came in very handy as a splint for the broken part.

As we were now following the direction of the meridian, or in other words, as our course was now true north, the daily observations of latitude gave a direct check on the readings of the sledge-meter. As a rule they agreed to the nearest minute. Whilst I was taking the noon altitude my companions had the choice of standing by the side of their sledges and eating their lunch, or setting the tent and taking shelter. They generally chose the latter alternative, making up for it by going an hour longer in the afternoon. Besides the astronomical observations, the barometric pressure, temperature, force and direction of the wind, and amount of cloud were noted three times daily; every evening a hypsometer reading was taken.

If I were to undertake the description of a long series of days like those that passed while we were travelling on the flat Barrier, I am afraid the narrative would be strikingly reminiscent of the celebrated song of a hundred and twenty verses, all with the same rhyme. One day was very much like another. One would think that this monotony would make the time long, but the direct opposite was the case. I have never known time fly so rapidly as on these sledge journeys, and seldom have I seen men more happy and contented with their existence than we three, when after a successful day's march we could set about taking our simple meal, with a pipe of cut plug to follow. The bill of fare was identically the same every day, perhaps a fault in the eyes of many; variety of diet is supposed to be the thing. Hang variety, say I; appetite is what matters. To a man who is really hungry it is a very subordinate matter *what* he shall eat; the main thing is to have *something* to satisfy his hunger.

After going north for seven days, we found that according to observations and sledge-meter we ought to be in the neighbourhood of the sea. This was correct. My diary for November 23 reads:

"To-day we were to see something besides sky and snow. An hour after breaking camp this morning two snowy petrels came sailing over us; a little while later a couple of skua gulls. We welcomed them as the first living creatures we had seen since leaving winter-quarters. The constantly increasing 'water-sky' to the north had long ago warned us that we were approaching the sea; the presence of the birds told us it was not far off. The skua gulls settled very near us, and the dogs, no doubt taking them for baby seals, were of course ready to break the line of march, and go off hunting, but their keenness soon passed when they discovered that the game had wings.

"The edge of the Barrier was difficult to see, and, profiting by previous experience of how easy it is to go down when the light is bad, we felt our way forward step by step. At four o'clock we thought we could see

the precipice.   A halt was made at a safe distance, and
I went in advance to look over.   To my surprise I found
that there was open water right in to the wall of ice.
We had expected the sea-ice to extend a good way out
still, seeing it was so early in summer; but there lay
the sea, almost free of ice as far as the horizon.   Black
and threatening it was to look at, but still a beneficent
contrast to the everlasting snow surface on which we
had now tramped for 300 geographical miles.

"The perpendicular drop of 100 feet that forms the
boundary between the dead Barrier and the sea, with
its varied swarm of life, is truly an abrupt and imposing transition.   The panorama from the top of the
ice-wall is always grand, and it can be beautiful as well.
On a sunny day, or still more on a moonlit night, it has
a fairylike beauty.   To-day a heavy, black sky hung
above a still blacker sea, and the ice-wall, which shines
in the light with a dazzling white purity, looked more
like an old white-washed wall than anything else.   There
was not a breath of wind; the sound of the surf at
the bottom of the precipice now and then reached my
ears—this was the only thing that broke the vast
silence.   One's own dear self becomes so miserably
small in these mighty surroundings; it was a sheer
relief to get back to the company of my comrades."

As things now were, with open water up to the
Barrier itself, our prospect of getting seals here at the
edge of the ice seemed a poor one.   Next morning,

however, we found, a few miles farther east, a bay about four miles long, and almost entirely enclosed. It was still frozen over, and seals were lying on the ice by the dozen. Here was food enough to give both ourselves and the dogs an extra feed and to replenish our supplies. We camped and went off to examine the ground more closely. There were plenty of crevasses, but a practicable descent was found, and in a very short time three full-grown seals and a fat young one were despatched. We hauled half a carcass up to the camp with the Alpine rope. As we were hard at work dragging our spoil up the steep slope, we heard Stubberud sing out, " Below, there !"—and away he went like a stone in a well. He had gone through the snow-bridge on which we were standing, but a lucky projection stopped our friend from going very far down, besides which he had taken a firm round turn with the rope round his wrist. It was, therefore, a comparatively easy matter to get him up on the surface again. This little intermezzo would probably have been avoided if we had not been without our ski, but the slope was so steep and smooth that we could not use them. After a few more hauls we had the seal up by the tent, where a large quantity of it disappeared in a surprisingly short time down the throats of fifteen hungry dogs.

The ice of the bay was furrowed by numerous leads, and while the hunters were busy cutting up the seals, I tried to get a sounding, but the thirty fathoms of

Alpine rope I had were not enough ; no bottom was reached. After having something to eat we went down again, in order if possible to find out the depth. This time we were better supplied with sounding tackle: two reels of thread, a marlinspike, and our geological hammer.

First the marlinspike was sent down with the thread as a line. An inquisitive lout of a seal did all it could to bite through the thread, but whether this was too strong or its teeth too poor, we managed after a lot of trouble to coax the marlinspike up again, and the interfering rascal, who had to come up to the surface now and then to take breath, got the spike of a ski-pole in his thick hide. This unexpected treatment was evidently not at all to his liking, and after acknowledging it by a roar of disgust, he vanished into the depths. Now we got on better. The marlinspike sank and sank until it had drawn with it 130 fathoms of thread. A very small piece of seaweed clung to the thread as we hauled it in again ; on the spike there was nothing to be seen. As its weight was rather light for so great a depth—a possible setting of current might have carried it a little to one side—we decided to try once more with the hammer, which was considerably heavier, in order to check the result. The hammer, on the other hand, was so heavy, that with the delicate thread as a line the probability of successfully carrying out the experiment seemed small, but we had to risk

IMPROVISED SOUNDING TACKLE.

it. The improvised sinker was well smeared with blubber, and this time it sank so rapidly to the bottom as to leave no doubt of the correctness of the sounding —130 fathoms again. By using extreme care we succeeded in getting the hammer up again in safety, but no specimen of the bottom was clinging to it.

On the way back to camp we dragged with us the carcass of the young seal. It was past three when we got into our sleeping-bags that night, and, in consequence, we slept a good deal later than usual the next morning. The forenoon was spent by Johansen and Stubberud in hauling up another seal from the bay and packing as much flesh on the sledges as possible. As fresh meat is a commodity that takes up a great deal of space in proportion to its weight, the quantity we were able to take with us was not large. The chief advantage we had gained was that a considerable supply could be stored on the spot, and it might be useful to fall back upon in case of delay or other mishaps.

I took the observation for longitude and latitude, found the height by hypsometer, and took some photographs. After laying down the depot and erecting beacons, we broke camp at 3 p.m. South of the head of the bay there were a number of elevations and pressure masses, exactly like the formations to be found about Framheim. To the east a prominent ridge appeared, and with the glass it could be seen to extend inland in a south-easterly direction. According to our observations this must be the same that Captain Scott has marked with land-shading on his chart.

We made a wide detour outside the worst pressure-ridges, and then set our course east-north-east towards the ridge just mentioned. It was a pretty steep rise, which was not at all a good thing for the dogs. They had overeaten themselves shockingly, and most of the seal's flesh came up again. So that their feast should not be altogether wasted, we stopped as soon as we had come far enough up the ridge to be able to regard the surface as comparatively safe; for in the depression round the bay it was somewhat doubtful.

On the following morning—Sunday, November 26—there was a gale from the north-east with sky and Barrier lost in driving snow. That put an end to our plans of a long Sunday march. In the midst of our disappointment I had a sudden bright idea. It was Queen Maud's birthday! If we could not go on, we could at least celebrate the day in a modest fashion. In one of the provision cases there was still a solitary Stavanger tin, containing salt beef and peas. It was opened at once, and its contents provided a banquet that tasted better to us than the most carefully chosen menu had ever done. In this connection I cannot help thinking of the joy it would bring to many a household in this world if its master were possessed of an appetite like ours. The wife would then have no need to dread the consequences, however serious the shortcomings of

the cuisine might be.   But to return to the feast.   Her
Majesty's health was drunk in a very small, but, at the
same time, very good tot of *aquavit*, served in enamelled
iron mugs.   Carrying alcohol was, of course, against
regulations, strictly speaking ; but, as everyone knows,
prohibition is not an easy thing to put into practice.
Even in Antarctica this proved to be the case.   Lindström
had a habit of sending a little surprise packet with each
sledging party that went out, and on our departure he
had handed us one of these, with the injunction that the
packet was only to be opened on some festive occasion ;
we chose as such Her Majesty's birthday.   On examination the packet was found to contain a little flask of
spirits, in which we at once agreed to drink the Queen's
health.

The 27th brought the same nasty weather, and the
28th was not much better, though not bad enough to
stop us.   After a deal of hard work in hauling our
buried belongings out of the snow, we got away and
continued our course to the north-eastward.   It was not
exactly an agreeable morning: a brisk wind with driving
snow right in one's face.   After trudging against this for
a couple of hours I heard Stubberud call "Halt!"—half
his team were hanging by the traces in a crevasse.   I
had gone across without noticing anything ; no doubt
owing to the snow in my face.   One would think the
dogs would be suspicious of a place like this ; but they
are not—they plunge on till the snow-bridge breaks

under them. Luckily the harness held, so that it was the affair of a moment to pull the poor beasts up again. Even a dog might well be expected to be a trifle shaken after hanging head downwards over such a fearful chasm; but apparently they took it very calmly, and were quite prepared to do the same thing over again.

For my own part I looked out more carefully after this, and although there were a good many ugly fissures on the remaining part of the ascent, we crossed them all without further incident.

Unpleasant as these crevasses are, they do not involve any direct danger, so long as the weather is clear and the light favourable. One can then judge by the appearance of the surface whether there is danger ahead; and if crevasses are seen in time, there is always a suitable crossing to be found. The case is somewhat different in fog, drift, or when the light is such that the small inequalities marking the course of the crevasse do not show up. This last is often the case in cloudy weather, when even a fairly prominent rise will not be noticed on the absolutely white surface until one falls over it. In such conditions it is safest to feel one's way forward with the ski-pole; though this mode of proceeding is more troublesome than effective.

In the course of the 28th the ascent came to an end, and with it the crevasses. The wind fell quite light, and the blinding drift was succeeded by clear sunshine. We had now come sufficiently high up to have a view of the sea far to the north-west. During the high wind a quantity of ice had been driven southward, so that for a great distance there was no open water to be seen, but a number of huge icebergs. From the distance of the sea horizon we guessed our height to be about 1,000 feet, and in the evening the hypsometer showed the guess to be very nearly right.

November 29.—Weather and going all that could be wished on breaking camp this morning; before us we had a level plateau, which appeared to be quite free from unpleasant obstructions. When we halted for the noon observation the sledge-meter showed ten geographical miles, and before evening we had brought the day's distance up to twenty. The latitude was then 77° 32′. The distance to the Barrier edge on the north was, at a guess, about twenty geographical miles. We were now a good way along the peninsula, the northern point of which Captain Scott named Cape Colbeck, and at the same time a good way to the east of the meridian in which he put land-shading on his chart. Our height above the sea, which was now about 1,000 feet, was evidence enough that we had firm land under us, but it was still sheathed in ice. In that respect the landscape offered no change from what we had learnt to know by the name of "Barrier." It cannot be denied that at this juncture I began to entertain a certain doubt of the existence of bare land in this quarter.

This doubt was not diminished when we had done

another good day's march to the eastward on November 30. According to our observations we were then just below the point where the Alexandra Mountains should begin, but there was no sign of mountain ranges; the surface was a little rougher, perhaps. However, it was still too soon to abandon the hope. It would be unreasonable to expect any great degree of accuracy of the chart we had to go by; its scale was far too large for that. It was, moreover, more than probable that our own determination of longitude was open to doubt.

Assuming the approximate accuracy of the chart, by holding on to the north-east we ought soon to come down to the seaboard, and with this object in view we continued our march. On December 1, in the middle of the day, we saw that everything agreed. From the top of an eminence the sea was visible due north, and on the east two domed summits were outlined, apparently high enough to be worthy of the name of mountains. They were covered with snow, but on the north side of them there was an abrupt precipice, in which many black patches showed up sharply against the white background. It was still too soon to form an idea as to whether they were bare rock or not; they might possibly be fissures in the mass of ice. The appearance of the summits agreed exactly with Captain Scott's description of what he saw from the deck of the *Discovery* in 1902. He assumed that the black patches were rocks emerging from the snow-slopes.

As will be seen later, our respected precursor was right.

In order to examine the nature of the seaboard, we began by steering down towards it; but in the meantime the weather underwent an unfavourable change. The sky clouded over and the light became as vile as it could be. The point we were anxious to clear up was whether there was any Barrier wall here, or whether the land and sea-ice gradually passed into each other in an easy slope. As the light was, there might well have been a drop of 100 feet without our seeing anything of it. Securely roped together we made our way down, until our progress was stopped by a huge pressure-ridge, which, as far as could be made out, formed the boundary between land and sea-ice. It was, however, impossible in the circumstances to get any clear view of the surroundings, and after trudging back to the sledges, which had been left up on the slope, we turned to the east to make a closer examination of the summits already mentioned. I went in front, as usual, in the cheerful belief that we had a fairly level stretch before us, but I was far out in my calculation. My ski began to slip along at a terrific speed, and it was advisable to put on the brake. This was easily done as far as I was concerned, but with the dogs it was a different matter. Nothing could stop them when they felt that the sledge was running by its own weight; they went in a wild gallop down the slope, the end of which could not at present be seen. I suppose it will sound like a tall story, but it is a fact, nevertheless, that to our eyes the surface appeared to be horizontal all the time. Snow, horizon and sky all ran together in a white chaos, in which all lines of demarcation were obliterated.

Fortunately nothing came of our expectation that the scamper would have a frightful ending in some insidious abyss. It was stopped quite naturally by an opposing slope, which appeared to be as steep as the one we had just slid down. If the pace had been rather too rapid before, there was now no ground of complaint on that score. Step by step we crawled up to the top of the ridge ; but the ground was carefully surveyed before we proceeded farther.

In the course of the afternoon we groped our way forward over a whole series of ridges and intervening depressions. Although nothing could be seen, it was obvious enough that our surroundings were now of an entirely different character from anything we had previously been accustomed to. The two mountain summits had disappeared in the fleecy mist, but the increasing unevenness of the ground showed that we were approaching them. Meanwhile I considered it inadvisable to come to close quarters with them so long as we were unable to use our eyes, and, remembering what happens when the blind leads the blind, we camped. For the first time during the trip I had a touch of snow-blindness that afternoon. This troublesome and rightly dreaded complaint was a thing that we had hitherto succeeded in keeping off by a judicious use of our excellent snow-goggles. Among my duties as forerunner was that of maintaining the direction, and this, at times, involved a very severe strain on the eyes. In thick weather it is only too easy to yield to the temptation of throwing off the protective goggles, with the idea that one can see better without them. Although I knew perfectly well what the consequence would be, I had that afternoon broken the commandment of prudence. The trifling smart I felt in my eyes was cured by keeping the goggles on for a couple of hours after we were in the tent. Like all other ills, snow-blindness may easily be dispelled by taking it in time.

Next morning the sun's disc could just be made out through a veil of thin stratus clouds, and then the light was more or less normal again. As soon as we could see what our surroundings were, it was clear enough that we had done right in stopping the game of blind man's buff we had been playing on the previous day. It might otherwise have had an unpleasant ending. Right across our line of route and about 500 yards from our camp the surface was so broken up that it was more like a sieve than anything else. In the background the masses of snow were piled in huge drifts down a steep slope on the north-west side of the two mountains. It was impossible to take the sledges any farther on the way we had hitherto been following, but in the course of the day we worked round by a long detour to the foot of the most westerly of the mountains. We were then about 1,000 feet above the sea; to the north of us we had the abrupt descent already mentioned, to the south it was quite flat. Our view to the east was shut in by the two mountains, and our first idea was to ascend to the tops of them, but the powers of the weather again opposed us with their full force. A stiff south-east wind set in and increased in the course of half an hour to a regular blizzard. Little as it suited our wishes, there was nothing to be done but to creep back into the tent. For a whole month now we had seen scarcely anything but fair weather, and the advance of summer had given us hopes that it would hold; but just when it suited us least of all came a dismal change.

The light Antarctic summer night ran its course, while the gusts of wind tugged and tore at the thin sides of our tent; no snowfall accompanied the south-easterly wind, but the loose snow of the surface was whirled up into a drift that stood like an impenetrable wall round the tent. After midnight it moderated a little, and by four o'clock there was comparatively fair weather. We were on our feet at once, put together camera, glasses, aneroids, axe, Alpine rope, with some lumps of pemmican to eat on the way, and then went off for a morning walk with the nearer of the two hills

as our goal. All three of us went, leaving the dogs
in charge of the camp. They were not so fresh now
that they would not gladly accept all the rest that
was offered them. We had no need to fear any
invasion of strangers; the land we had come to appeared to be absolutely devoid of living creatures of
any kind.

The hill was farther off and higher than it appeared
at first; the aneroid showed a rise of 700 feet when
we reached the top. As our camp lay at a height of
1,000 feet, this gave us 1,700 feet as the height of this
hill above the sea. The side we went up was covered
by *névé*, which, to judge from the depth of the
cracks, must have been immense. As we approached
the summit and our view over the surrounding ground
became wider, the belief that we should see so much as
a crag of this King Edward Land grew weaker and
weaker. There was nothing but white on every side,
not a single consolatory little black patch, however
carefully we looked. And to think that we had been
dreaming of great mountain masses in the style of
McMurdo Sound, with sunny slopes, penguins by the
thousand, seals and all the rest! All these visions were
slowly but surely sunk in an endless sea of snow, and
when at last we stood on the highest point, we certainly
thought there could be no chance of a revival of our
hopes.

But the unexpected happened after all. On the

precipitous northern side of the adjacent hill our eyes fell upon bare rock—the first glimpse we had had of positive land during the year we had been in Antarctica. Our next thought was of how to get to it and take specimens, and with this object we at once began to scale the neighbouring hill, which was a trifle higher than the one we had first ascended. The precipice was, however, perpendicular, with a huge snow cornice over-hanging it. Lowering a man on the rope would be rather too hazardous a proceeding; besides which, a length of thirty yards would not go very far. If we were to get at the rock, it would have to be from below. In the meantime we availed ourselves of the opportunity offered by the clear weather to make a closer examination of our surroundings. From the isolated summit, 1,700 feet high, on which we stood, the view was fairly extensive. Down to the sea on the north the distance was about five geographical miles. The surface descended in terraces towards the edge of the water, where there was quite a low Barrier wall. As might be expected, this stretch of the ice-field was broken by innumerable crevasses, rendering any passage across it impossible.

On the east extended a well-marked mountain-ridge, about twenty geographical miles in length, and some-what lower than the summit on which we stood. This was the Alexandra Mountains. It could not be called an imposing range, and it was snow-clad from one end to the other. Only on the most easterly spur was the rock just visible.

On the south and south-west nothing was to be seen but the usual undulating Barrier surface. Biscoe Bay, as Captain Scott has named it, was for the moment a gathering-place for numerous icebergs; one or two of these seemed to be aground. The inmost corner of the bay was covered with sea-ice. On its eastern side the Barrier edge could be seen to continue northward, as marked in Captain Scott's chart; but no indication of bare land was visible in that quarter.

Having built a snow beacon, 6 feet high, on the summit, we put on our ski again and went down the eastern slope of the hill at a whizzing pace. On this side there was an approach to the level on the north of the precipice, and we availed ourselves of it. Seen from below the mountain crest looked quite grand, with a perpendicular drop of about 1,000 feet. The cliff was covered with ice up to a height of about 100 feet, and this circumstance threatened to be a serious obstacle to our obtaining specimens of the rocks. But in one place a nunatak about 250 feet high stood out in front of the precipice, and the ascent of this offered no great difficulty.

A wall of rock of very ordinary appearance is not usually reckoned among things capable of attracting the attention of the human eye to any marked extent; nevertheless, we three stood and gazed at it, as though we had something of extraordinary beauty and interest before us. The explanation is very simple, if we remember the old saying about the charm of variety. A sailor, who for months has seen nothing but sea and sky, will lose himself in contemplation of a little islet, be it never so barren and desolate. To us, who for nearly a year had been staring our eyes out in a dazzling white infinity of snow and ice, it was indeed an experience to see once more a bit of the earth's crust. That this fragment was as poor and bare as it could be was not taken into consideration at the moment.

The mere sight of the naked rock was, however, only an anticipatory pleasure. A more substantial one was the feeling of again being able to move on ground that afforded a sure and trustworthy foothold. It is possible that we behaved rather like children on first reaching bare land. One of us, in any case, found immense enjoyment in rolling one big block after another down the steep slopes of the nunatak. At any rate, the sport had the interest of novelty.

This little peak was built up of very heterogenous materials. As the practical result of our visit, we brought away a fairly abundant collection of specimens of all the rocks to be found there. Not being a specialist, I cannot undertake any classification of the specimens. It will be the task of geologists to deal with them, and to obtain if possible some information as to the structure of the country. I will only mention

that some of the stones were so heavy that they must certainly have contained metallic ore of one kind or another. On returning to camp that evening, we tried them with the compass-needle, and it showed very marked attraction in the case of one or two of the specimens. These must, therefore, contain iron-ore.

This spur, which had been severely handled by ice-pressure and the ravages of time, offered a poor chance of finding what we coveted most—namely, fossils—and the most diligent search proved unsuccessful in this respect. From finds that have been made in other parts of Antarctica it is known that in former geological periods—the Jurassic epoch—even this desolate continent possessed a rich and luxurious vegetation. The leader of the Swedish expedition to Graham Land, Dr. Nordenskjöld, and his companion, Gunnar Andersson, were the first to make this exceedingly interesting and important discovery.

While it did not fall to our lot to furnish any proof of the existence of an earlier flora in King Edward Land, we found living plants of the most primitive form. Even on that tiny islet in the ocean of snow the rock was in many places covered with thick moss. How did that moss come there? Its occurrence might, perhaps, be quoted in support of the hypothesis of the genesis of organic life from dead matter. This disputed question must here be left open, but it may be mentioned in the same connection that we found the remains of birds' nests in many places among the rocks. Possibly the occupants of these nests may have been instrumental in the conveyance of the moss.

Otherwise, the signs of bird life were very few. One or two solitary snowy petrels circled round the summit while we were there; that was all.

It was highly important to obtain some successful photographs from this spot, and I was setting about the necessary preparations, when one of my companions made a remark about the changed appearance of the sky. Busy with other things, I had entirely neglected to keep an eye on the weather, an omission for which, as will be seen, we might have had to pay dearly. Fortunately, another had been more watchful than I, and the warning came in time. A glance was enough to convince me of the imminent approach of a snow-storm; the fiery red sky and the heavy ring round the sun spoke a language that was only too clear. We had a good hour's march to the tent, and the possibility of being surprised by the storm before we arrived was practically equivalent to never arriving at all.

We very soon put our things together, and came down the nunatak even more quickly. On the steep slopes leading up to the plateau on which the tent stood the pace was a good deal slower, though we made every possible effort to hurry. There was no need to trouble about the course; we had only to follow the

trail of our own ski—so long as it was visible. But the
drift was beginning to blot it out, and if it once did
that, any attempt at finding the tent would be hopeless.
For a long and anxious quarter of an hour it looked as
if we should be too late, until at last the tent came in
sight, and we were saved. We had escaped the blizzard
so far; a few minutes later it burst in all its fury, and
the whirling snow was so thick that it would have been
impossible to see the tent at a distance of ten paces, but
by then we were all safe and sound inside. Ravenously
hungry after the twelve hours that had passed since our
last proper meal, we cooked an extra large portion of
pemmican and the same of chocolate, and with this
sumptuous repast we celebrated the event of the day—
the discovery of land. From what we had seen in the
course of the day it might be regarded as certain that
we should be disappointed in our hopes of finding any
great and interesting field for our labours in this
quarter; King Edward Land was still far too well
hidden under eternal snow and ice to give us that. But
even the establishment of this, to us, somewhat unwelcome fact marked an increase of positive human
knowledge of the territory that bears the name of King
Edward VII.; and with the geological specimens that
we had collected, we were in possession of a tangible
proof of the actual existence of solid ground in a region
which otherwise bore the greatest resemblance to what
we called " Barrier " elsewhere, or in any case to the

Barrier as it appears in the neighbourhood of our winter-quarters at Framheim.

Monday, December 4.—The gale kept on at full force all night, and increased rather than moderated as the day advanced. As usual, the storm was accompanied by a very marked rise of temperature. At the noon observation to-day the reading was $+26 \cdot 6°$ F. This is the highest temperature we have had so far on this trip, and a good deal higher than we care about. When the mercury comes so near freezing-point as this, the floor of the tent is always damp.

To-day, for once in a way, we have falling snow, and enough of it. It is snowing incessantly—big, hard flakes, almost like hail. When the cooker was filled to provide water for dinner, the half-melted mass looked like sago. The heavy flakes of snow make a noise against the tent that reminds one of the safety-valve of a large boiler blowing off. Inside the tent it is difficult to hear oneself speak ; when we have anything to say to each other we have to shout.

These days of involuntary idleness on a sledge journey may safely be reckoned among the experiences it is difficult to go through without a good deal of mental suffering. I say nothing of the purely physical discomfort of having to pass the day in a sleeping-bag. That may be endured ; in any case, so long as the bag is fairly dry. It is a far worse matter to reconcile oneself to the loss of the many solid hours that might otherwise have been put to a useful purpose, and to the irritating consciousness that every bit of food that is consumed is so much wasted of the limited store. At this spot of all others we should have been so glad to spend the time in exploring round about, or still more in going farther. But if we are to go on, we must be certain of having a chance of getting seals at a reasonable distance from here. With our remaining supply of dogs' food we cannot go on for more than three days.

What we have left will be just enough for the return journey, even if we should not find the depot of seals' flesh left on the way. There remained the resource of killing dogs, if it was a question of getting as far to the east as possible, but for many reasons I shrank from availing myself of that expedient. We could form no idea of what would happen to the southern party's animals. The probability was that they would have none left on their return. Supposing their return were delayed so long as to involve spending another winter on the Barrier, the transport of supplies from the ship could hardly be carried out in the necessary time with the ten untrained puppies that were left with Lindström. We had picked out the useful ones, and I thought that, should the necessity arise, they could be used with greater advantage for this work than we should derive from slaughtering them here, and thereby somewhat prolonging the distance covered ; the more so as, to judge from all appearance, there was a poor prospect of our finding anything of interest within a reasonable time.

Tuesday, December 5.—It looks as if our patience is to be given a really hard trial this time. Outside the same state of things continues, and the barometer is going down. A mass of snow has fallen in the last twenty-four hours. The drift on the windward side of the tent is constantly growing ; if it keeps on a little longer it will be as high as the top of the tent. The sledges are completely snowed under, and so are the dogs ; we had to haul them out one by one in the middle of the day. Most of them are now loose, as there is nothing exposed to the attacks of their teeth. It is now blowing a regular gale ; the direction of the wind is about true east. Occasionally squalls of hurricane-like violence occur. Fortunately the big snow-drift keeps us comfortable, and we are under the lee of a hill, otherwise it would look badly for our tent. Hitherto it has held well, but it is beginning to be rather damp inside. The temperature remains very high ($+27 \cdot 2°$ F. at noon to-day), and the mass of snow pressing against the tent causes the formation of rime.

In order to while away the time to some extent under depressing circumstances like these, I put into my diary on leaving Framheim a few loose leaves of a Russian grammar ; Johansen solaced himself with a serial cut out of the *Aftenpost ;* as far as I remember, the title of it

FIRST IN KING EDWARD LAND.

IN KING EDWARD LAND : AFTER A THREE DAYS' STORM.

was "The Red Rose and the White." Unfortunately the story of the Two Roses was very soon finished ; but Johansen had a good remedy for that : he simply began it over again. My reading had the advantage of being incomparably stiffer. Russian verbs are uncommonly difficult of digestion, and not to be swallowed in a hurry. For lack of mental nutriment, Stubberud with great resignation consoled himself with a pipe, but his enjoyment must have been somewhat diminished by the thought that his stock of tobacco was shrinking at an alarming rate. Every time he filled his pipe, I could see him cast longing looks in the direction of my pouch, which was still comparatively full. I could not help promising a fraternal sharing in case he should run short ; and after that our friend puffed on with an easy mind.

Although I look at it at least every half-hour, the barometer will not go up. At 8 p.m. it was down to 27·30. If this means anything, it can only be that we shall have the pleasure of being imprisoned here another day. Some poor consolation is to be had in the thought of how lucky we were to reach the tent at the last moment the day before yesterday. A storm as lasting as this one would in all probability have been too much for us if we had not got in.

Wednesday, December 6.—The third day of idleness has at last crept away after its predecessors. We have done with it. It has not brought any marked variation. The weather has been just as violent, until now—8 p.m.—

the wind shows a slight tendency to moderate. It is, surely, time it did; three days and nights should be enough for it. The heavy snowfall continues. Big, wet flakes come dancing down through the opening in the drift in which the peak of the tent still manages to show itself. In the course of three days we have had more snowfall here than we had at Framheim in ten whole months. It will be interesting to compare our meteorological log with Lindström's; probably he has had his share of the storm, and in that case it will have given him some exercise in snow-shovelling.

The moisture is beginning to be rather troublesome now; most of our wardrobe is wet through, and the sleeping-bags will soon meet with the same fate. The snow-drift outside is now so high that it shuts out most of the daylight; we are in twilight. To-morrow we shall be obliged to dig out the tent, whatever the weather is like, otherwise we shall be buried entirely, and run the additional risk of having the tent split by the weight of snow. I am afraid it will be a day's work to dig out the tent and the two sledges; we have only one little shovel to do it with.

A slight rise of both barometer and thermometer tells us that at last we are on the eve of the change we have been longing for. Stubberud is certain of fair weather to-morrow, he says. I am by no means so sure, and offer to bet pretty heavily that there will be no change. Two inches of Norwegian plug tobacco is the stake, and with a heartfelt desire that Jörgen may win I await the morrow.

Thursday, December 7.—Early this morning I owned to having lost my bet, as the weather, so far as I could tell, was no longer of the same tempestuous character; but Stubberud thought the contrary. "It seems to me just as bad," said he. He was right enough, as a matter of fact, but this did not prevent my persuading him to accept payment. Meanwhile we were obliged to make an attempt to dig out the tent, regardless of the weather; the situation was no longer endurable. We waited all the forenoon in the hope of an improvement; but as none came, we set to work at twelve o'clock. Our implements showed some originality and diversity: a little spade, a biscuit-tin, and a cooker. The drift did its best to undo our work as fast as we dug, but we managed to hold our own against it. Digging out the tent-pegs gave most trouble. After six hours' hard work we got the tent set up a few yards to windward of its first position; the place where it had stood was now a well about seven feet deep. Unfortunately there was no chance of immortalizing this scene of excavation. It would have been amusing enough to have it on the plate; but drifting snow is a serious obstacle to an amateur photographer—besides which, my camera was on Stubberud's sledge, buried at least four feet down.

In the course of our digging we had had the misfortune to make two or three serious rents in the thin canvas of the tent, and the drift was not long in finding a way through these when the tent was up again. To conclude my day's work I had, therefore, a longish tailor's job, while the other two men were digging out a good feed for the dogs, who had been on half-rations for the last two days. That night we went rather short of sleep. Vulcan, the oldest dog in Johansen's team, was chiefly to blame for this. In his old age Vulcan was afflicted with a bad digestion, for even Eskimo dogs may be liable to this infirmity, hardy as they generally are. The protracted blizzard had given the old fellow a relapse, and he proclaimed this distressing fact by incessant howling. This kind of music was not calculated to lull us to sleep, and it was three or four in the morning before we could snatch a nap. During a pause I was just dropping off, when the sun showed faintly through the tent. This unwonted sight at once banished all further thoughts of sleep ; the Primus was lighted, a cup of chocolate swallowed, and out we went. Stubberud and Johansen set to work at the hard task of digging out the sledges ; they had to go down four feet to get hold of them. I dragged our wet clothes, sleeping-bags, and so forth out of the tent, and hung them all up to dry. In the course of the morning observations were taken for determining the geographical longitude and latitude, as well as a few photographs, which will give some idea of what our camp looked like after the blizzard.

Having made good the damage and put everything

ON SCOTT'S NUNATAK.

To face page 238, Vol. II.

SCOTT'S NUNATAK.

fairly in order, we hurried away to our peaks, to secure
some photographs while the light was favourable. This
time we were able to achieve our object. "Scott's
Nunataks," as they were afterwards named—after Captain
Scott, who first saw them—were now for the first time
recorded by the camera. Before we left the summit the
Norwegian flag was planted there, a snow beacon erected,
and a report of our visit deposited in it. The weather
would not keep clear; before we were back at the camp
there was a thick fog, and once more we had to thank
the tracks of our ski for showing us the way. During
the time we had been involuntarily detained at this
spot, our store of provisions had decreased alarmingly;
there was only a bare week's supply left, and in less than
a week we should hardly be able to make home;
probably it would take more than a week, but in that
case we had the depot at our Bay of Seals to fall back
upon. In the immediate neighbourhood of our present
position we could not reckon on being able to replenish
our supply in the continued unfavourable state of the
weather. We therefore made up our minds on the
morning of December 9 to break off the journey and
turn our faces homeward. For three days more we had
to struggle with high wind and thick snow, but as things
now were, we had no choice but to keep going, and by
the evening of the 11th we had dragged ourselves fifty
geographical miles to the west. The weather cleared
during the night, and at last, on December 12, we had

a day of real sunshine. All our discomforts were forgotten; everything went easily again. In the course of nine hours we covered twenty-six geographical miles that day, without any great strain on either dogs or men.

At our midday rest we found ourselves abreast of the bay, where, on the outward journey, we had laid down our depot of seals' flesh. I had intended to turn aside to the depot and replenish our supply of meat as a precaution, but Johansen suggested leaving out this detour and going straight on. We might thereby run the risk of having to go on short rations; but Johansen thought it a greater risk to cross the treacherous ground about the bay, and, after some deliberation, I saw he was right. It was better to go on while we were about it.

From this time on we met with no difficulty, and rapidly drew near to our destination in regular daily marches of twenty geographical miles. After men and dogs had received their daily ration on the evening of the 15th, our sledge cases were practically empty; but, according to our last position, we should not have more than twenty geographical miles more to Framheim.

Saturday, December 16.—We broke camp at the usual time, in overcast but perfectly clear weather, and began what was to be our last day's march on this trip. A dark water-sky hung over the Barrier on the west and north-west, showing that there was open sea off the mouth of the Bay of Whales. We went on till 10.30, our course being true west, when we made out far to the north-west an ice-cape that was taken to be the extreme point on the western side of the bay. Immediately after we were on the edge of the Barrier, the direction of which was here south-west and north-east. We altered our course and followed the edge at a proper distance until we saw a familiar iceberg that had broken off to the north of Framheim, but had been stopped by the sea-ice from drifting out. With this excellent mark in view the rest of the way was plain sailing. The sledge-meter showed 19·5 geographical miles, when in the afternoon we came in sight of our winter home. Quiet and peaceful it lay there, if possible more deeply covered in snow than when we had left it. At first we could see no sign of life, but soon the glasses discovered a lonely wanderer on his way from the house to the "meteorological institute." So Lindström was still alive and performing his duties.

When we left, our friend had expressed his satisfaction at "getting us out of the way"; but I have a suspicion that he was quite as pleased to see us back again. I am not quite certain, though, that he did see us for the moment, as he was about as snow-blind as a man can be. Lindström was the last person we should have suspected of that malady. On our asking him how it came about, he seemed at first unwilling to give any explanation; but by degrees it came out that the misfortune had happened a couple of days before, when

he had gone out after seals. His team, composed of
nothing but puppies, had run away and pulled up at
a big hummock out by the western cape, ten miles from
the station. But Lindström, who is a determined man,
would not give up before he had caught the runaways;
and this was too much for his eyes, as he had no goggles
with him. "When I got home 1 couldn't see what the
time was," he said; "but it must have been somewhere
about six in the morning." When we had made him
put on plenty of red eye-ointment and supplied him
with a proper pair of goggles, he was soon cured.

Framheim had had the same protracted storms with
heavy snowfall. On several mornings the master of the
house had had to dig his way out through the snow-
wall outside the door; but during the last three fine
days he had managed to clear a passage, not only to
the door, but to the window as well. Daylight came
down into the room through a well nine feet deep. This
had been a tremendous piece of work; but, as already
hinted, nothing can stop Lindström when he makes
up his mind. His stock of seals' flesh was down to
a minimum; the little there was vanished on the appearance of our ravenous dogs. We ourselves were in
no such straits; sweets were the only things in special
demand.

We stayed at home one day. After bringing up two
loads of seals' flesh, filling our empty provision cases,
carrying out a number of small repairs, and checking

our watches, we were again on the road on Monday the 18th. We were not very loth to leave the house; indoor existence had become rather uncomfortable on account of constant dripping from the ceiling. In the course of the winter a quantity of ice had formed in the loft. As the kitchen fire was always going after our return, the temperature became high enough to melt the ice, and the water streamed down. Lindström was annoyed and undertook to put a stop to it. He disappeared into the loft, and sent down a hail of ice, bottle-straw, broken cases, and other treasures through the trap-door. We fled before the storm and drove away. This time we had to carry out our instructions as to the exploration of the long eastern arm of the Bay of Whales. During the autumn several Sunday excursions had been made along this remarkable formation; but although some of these ski-runs had extended as far as twelve miles in one direction, there was no sign of the hummocks coming to an end. These great disturbances of the ice-mass must have a cause, and the only conceivable one was that the subjacent land had brought about this disruption of the surface. For immediately to the south there was undoubtedly land, as there the surface rose somewhat rapidly to a height of 1,000 feet; but it was covered with snow. There was a possibility that the rock might project among the evidences of heavy pressure at the foot of this slope; and with this possibility in view we made a five days' trip, following the great fissure, or "bay," as we generally called it, right up to its head, twenty-three geographical miles to the east of our winter-quarters.

Although we came across no bare rock, and in that respect the journey was a disappointment, it was nevertheless very interesting to observe the effects of the mighty forces that had here been at work, the disruption of the solid ice-sheath by the still more solid rock.

The day before Christmas Eve we were back at Framheim. Lindström had made good use of his time in our absence. The ice had disappeared from the loft, and therewith the rain from the ceiling. New linoleum had been laid down over half the floor, and marks of the paint-brush were visible on the ceiling. These efforts had possibly been made with an eye to the approaching festival, but in other respects we abstained from any attempt at keeping Christmas. It did not agree with the time of year ; constant blazing sunshine all through the twenty-four hours could not be reconciled with a northerner's idea of Christmas. And for that reason we had kept the festival six months before. Christmas Eve fell on a Sunday, and it passed just like any ordinary Sunday. Perhaps the only difference was that we used a razor that day instead of the usual beard-clipper. On Christmas Day we took a holiday, and Lindström prepared a banquet of skua gulls. Despise this dish as one may, it tasted undeniably of—bird.

The numerous snow-houses were now in a sad way.

Under the weight of the constantly increasing mass, the
roofs of most of the rooms were pressed so far in that
there was just enough space to crawl on hands and
knees. In the Crystal Palace and the Clothing Store
we kept all our skin clothing, besides a good deal of
outfit, which it was intended to take on board the *Fram*
when she and the southern party arrived. If the sinking
continued, it would be a long business digging these
things out again, and in order to have everything ready
we made up our minds to devote a few days to this
work at once. We hauled the snow up from these two
rooms through a well twelve feet deep by means of
tackles. It was a long job, but when we had finished
this part of the labyrinth was as good as ever. We had
no time to deal with the vapour-bath or the carpenter's
shop just then. There still remained the survey of the
south-western corner of the Bay of Whales and its
surroundings. On an eight days' sledge journey, starting at the New Year, we ranged about this district,
where we were surprised to find the solid Barrier divided
into small islands, separated by comparatively broad
sounds. These isolated masses of ice could not possibly
be afloat, although the depth in one or two places, where
we had a chance of making soundings, proved to be as
much as 200 fathoms. The only rational explanation
we could think of was that there must be a group of
low-lying islands here, or in any case shoals. These
" ice islands," if one may call them so, had a height of

90 feet and sloped evenly down to the water on the greater part of their circumference.   One of the sounds, that penetrated into the Barrier a short distance inside the western cape of the bay, continued southward and gradually narrowed to a mere fissure.   We followed this until it lost itself, thirty geographical miles within the Barrier.

The last day of this trip—Thursday, January 11—will always be fixed in our memory; it was destined to bring us experiences of the kind that are never forgotten.   Our start in the morning was made at exactly the same time and in exactly the same way as so many times before.   We felt pretty certain of reaching Framheim in the course of the day, but that prospect was for the moment of minor importance.   In the existing state of the weather our tent offered us as comfortable quarters as our snowed-up winter home.   What made us look forward to our return with some excitement was the possibility of seeing the *Fram* again, and this thought was no doubt in the minds of all of us that January morning, though we did not say much about it.

After two hours' march we caught sight of West Cape, at the entrance to the bay, in our line of route, and a little later we saw a black strip of sea far out on the horizon.   As usual, a number of bergs of all sizes were floating on this strip, in every variety of shade from white to dark grey, as the light fell on them.   One particular lump appeared to us so dark that it could hardly be made of ice ; but we had been taken in too many times to make any remark about it.

As the dogs now had a mark to go by, Johansen was driving in front without my help ; I went by the side of Stubberud's sledge. The man at my side kept staring out to sea, without uttering a word. On my asking him what in the world he was looking at, he replied : "I could almost swear it was a ship, but of course it's only a wretched iceberg." We were just agreed upon this, when suddenly Johansen stopped short and began a hurried search for his long glass. " Are you going to look at the *Fram*?" I asked ironically. " Yes, I am," he said ; and while he turned the telescope upon the doubtful object far out in Ross Sea, we two stood waiting for a few endless seconds. " It's the *Fram* sure enough, as large as life !" was the welcome announcement that broke our suspense. I glanced at Stubberud and saw his face expanding into its most amiable smile. Though I had not much doubt of the correctness of Johansen's statement, I borrowed his glass, and a fraction of a second was enough to convince me. That ship was easily recognized ; she was our own old *Fram* safely back again.

We had still fourteen long miles to Framheim and an obstinate wind right in our faces, but that part of the way was covered in a remarkably short time. On arriving at home at two in the afternoon we had some expectation of finding a crowd of people in front of the

house; but there was not a living soul to be seen.
Even Lindström remained concealed, though as a rule
he was always about when anyone arrived. Thinking
that perhaps our friend had had a relapse of snow-
blindness, I went in to announce our return. Lindström
was standing before his range in the best of health
when I entered the kitchen. "The *Fram's* come!" he
shouted, before I had shut the door. "Tell me something I don't know," said I, "and be so kind as to give
me a cup of water with a little syrup in it if you can."
I thought somehow that the cook had a sly grin on his
face when he brought what I asked for, but with the
thirst I had after the stiff march, I gave a great part of
my attention to the drink. I had consumed the best
part of a quart, when Lindström went off to his bunk
and asked if I could guess what he had hidden there.
There was no time to guess anything before the blankets
were thrown on to the floor, and after them bounded a
bearded ruffian clad in a jersey and a pair of overalls of
indeterminable age and colour. "Hullo!" said the
ruffian, and the voice was that of Lieutenant Gjertsen.
Lindström was shaking with laughter while I stood
open-mouthed before this apparition; I had been given
a good surprise. We agreed to treat Johansen and
Stubberud in the same way, and as soon as they were
heard outside, Gjertsen hid himself again among the
blankets. But Stubberud had smelt a rat in some way
or other. "There are more than two in this room," he

THE " FRAM " AT THE ICE EDGE, JANUARY, 1912.

said, as soon as he came in. It was no surprise to him to find a man from the *Fram* in Lindström's bunk.

When we heard that the visitor had been under our roof for a whole day, we assumed that in the course of that time he had heard all about our own concerns from Lindström. We were therefore not inclined to talk about ourselves; we wanted news from without, and Gjertsen was more than ready to give us them. The *Fram* had arrived two days before, all well. After lying at the ice edge for a day and a night, keeping a constant lookout for the "natives," Gjertsen had grown so curious to know how things were at Framheim that he had asked Captain Nilsen for "shore leave." The careful skipper had hesitated a while before giving permission; it was a long way up to the house, and the sea-ice was scored with lanes, some of them fairly wide. Finally Gjertsen had his way, and he left the ship, taking a signal flag with him. He found it rather difficult to recognize his surroundings, to begin with; one ice cape was very like another, and ugly ideas of calvings suggested themselves, until at last he caught sight of Cape Man's Head, and then he knew that the foundations of Framheim had not given way. Cheered by this knowledge, he made his way towards Mount Nelson, but on arriving at the top of this ridge, from which there was a view over Framheim, the eager explorer felt his heart sink. Where our new house had made such a brave show a year before on the surface of the Barrier, there was now no

house at all to be seen. All that met the eyes of the
visitor was a sombre pile of ruins. But his anxiety
quickly vanished when a man emerged from the confusion. The man was Lindström, and the supposed ruin
was the most ingenious of all winter-quarters. Lindström
was ignorant of the *Fram's* arrival, and the face he
showed on seeing Gjertsen must have been worth some
money to look at.

When our first curiosity was satisfied, our thoughts
turned to our comrades on board the *Fram.* We
snatched some food, and then went down to the sea-ice,
making our way across the little bay due north of the
house. Our well-trained team were not long in getting
there, but we had some trouble with them in crossing
the cracks in the ice, as some of the dogs, especially the
puppies, had a terror of water.

The *Fram* was cruising some way out, but when we
came near enough for them to see us, they made all
haste to come in to the ice-foot. Yes, there lay our
good little ship, as trim as when we had last seen her;
the long voyage round the world had left no mark
on her strong hull. Along the bulwarks appeared a row
of smiling faces, which we were able to recognize in spite
of the big beards that half concealed many of them.
While clean-shaven chins had been the fashion at
Framheim, almost every man on board appeared with
a flowing beard. As we came over the gangway
questions began to hail upon us. I had to ask for a

moment's grace to give the captain and crew a hearty shake of the hand, and then I collected them all about me and gave a short account of the most important events of the past year. When this was done, Captain Nilsen pulled me into the chart-house, where we had a talk that lasted till about four the next morning—to both of us certainly one of the most interesting we have ever had. On Nilsen's asking about the prospects of the southern party, I ventured to assure him that in all probability we should have our Chief and his companions back in a few days with the Pole in their pockets.

Our letters from home brought nothing but good news. What interested us most in the newspapers was, of course, the account of how the expedition's change of route had been received.

At 8 a.m. we left the *Fram* and returned home. For the next few days we were occupied with the work of surveying and charting, which went comparatively quickly in the favourable weather. When we returned after our day's work on the afternoon of the 17th, we found Lieutenant Gjertsen back at the hut. He asked us if we could guess the news, and as we had no answer ready, he told us that the ship of the Japanese expedition had arrived. We hurriedly got out the cinematograph apparatus and the camera, and went off as fast as the dogs could go, since Gjertsen thought this visit would not be of long duration.

When we caught sight of the *Fram* she had her flag

up, and just beyond the nearest cape lay the *Kainan Maru*, with the ensign of the Rising Sun at the peak. *Banzai!* We had come in time. Although it was rather late in the evening, Nilsen and I decided to pay her a visit, and if possible to see the leader of the expedition. We were received at the gangway by a young, smiling fellow, who beamed still more when I produced the only Japanese word I knew: *Oheio*—Good-day. There the conversation came to a full stop, but soon a number of the inquisitive sons of Nippon came up, and some of them understood a little English. We did not get very far, however. We found out that the *Kainan Maru* had been on a cruise in the direction of King Edward VII. Land; but we could not ascertain whether any landing had been attempted or not.

As the leader of the expedition and the captain of the ship had turned in, we did not want to disturb them by prolonging our visit; but we did not escape before the genial first officer had offered us a glass of wine and a cigar in the chart-house. With an invitation to come again next day, and permission to take some photographs, we returned to the *Fram*; but nothing came of the projected second visit to our Japanese friends. Both ships put out to sea in a gale that sprang up during the night, and before we had another opportunity of going on board the *Kainan Maru* the southern party had returned.

The days immediately preceding the departure of the expedition for the north fell about the middle of the

THE "KAINAN MARU."

short Antarctic summer, just at the time when the comparatively rich animal life of the Bay of Whales shows itself at its best.

The name of the Bay of Whales is due to Shackleton, and is appropriate enough; for from the time of the break-up of the sea-ice this huge inlet in the Barrier forms a favourite playground for whales, of which we often saw schools of as many as fifty disporting themselves for hours together. We had no means of disturbing their peaceful sport, although the sight of all these monsters, each worth a small fortune, was well calculated to make our fingers itch. It was the whaling demon that possessed us.

For one who has no special knowledge of the industry it is difficult to form an adequate opinion as to whether this part of Antarctica is capable of ever becoming a field for whaling enterprise. In any case, it will probably be a long time before such a thing happens. In the first place, the distance to the nearest inhabited country is very great—over 2,000 geographical miles— and in the second, there is a serious obstruction on this route in the shape of the belt of pack-ice, which, narrow and loose as it may be at times, will always necessitate the employment of timber-built vessels for the work of transport.

The conditions prevailing in the Bay of Whales must presumably offer a decisive obstacle to the establishment of a permanent station. Our winter house was snowed under in the course of two months, and to us this was only a source of satisfaction, as our quarters became all the warmer on this account; but whether a whaling station would find a similar fate equally convenient is rather doubtful.

Lastly, it must be said that, although in the bay itself huge schools of whales were of frequent occurrence, we did not receive the impression that there was any very great number of them out in Ross Sea. The species most commonly seen was the Finner; after that the Blue Whale.

As regards seals, they appeared in great quantities along the edge of the Barrier so long as the sea-ice still lay there; after the break-up of the ice the Bay of Whales was a favourite resort of theirs all through the summer. This was due to its offering them an easy access to the dry surface, where they could abandon themselves to their favourite occupation of basking in the sunshine.

During our whole stay we must have killed some two hundred and fifty of them, by far the greater number of which were shot in the autumn immediately after our arrival. This little inroad had no appreciable effect. The numerous survivors, who had been eye-witnesses of their companions' sudden death, did not seem to have the slightest idea that the Bay of Whales had become for the time being a somewhat unsafe place of residence.

As early as September, while the ice still stretched

SEALS ON SEA-ICE NEAR THE BARRIER.

SEALS : MOTHER AND CALF.

To face page 274, Vol. II.

for miles out into Ross Sea, the first seal found occasion to come up into daylight through one of the numerous pressure cracks in the bay. To us this was the first sure sign of spring; for the seal it was a leap into eternity.

Of the three different species we met with—the Weddell, the sea-leopard, and the crab-eater—the first-named was by far the most numerous. The Weddell seal is an extremely awkward and clumsy animal, that fully understands the art of not hurrying; this, of course, applies only to its movements out of the water. A full-grown bull is almost as large as a walrus, and must certainly weigh something like 8 hundredweight. A ridiculously small head is set upon its heavy body, and its mouth is provided with teeth about as innocuous as those of the domestic cow. The skins vary from light grey to brownish black.

The sea-leopard was far more rare in these parts. In the bay itself it was not found; the few specimens we saw were met with in the pack-ice. As far as I know, we only secured a couple of them. The sea-leopard is a far more dangerous fellow than his cousin the Weddell seal. He is almost as big, but his body is very much more lithe and agile; he has a mouth full of long, sharp teeth, and is always ready to use this weapon. He is not to be approached without a certain caution, and in the water he must be an extremely unpleasant opponent.

The name crab-eater may possibly evoke ideas of some ferocious creature ; in that case it is misleading. The animal that bears it is, without question, the most amicable of the three species. It is of about the same size as our native seal, brisk and active in its movements, and is constantly exercising itself in high jumps from the water on to the ice-foot. Even on the ice it can work its way along so fast that it is all a man can do to keep up. Its skin is extraordinarily beautiful—grey, with a sheen of silver and small dark spots.

One is often asked whether seal's flesh does not taste of train oil. It seems to be a common assumption that it does so. This, however, is a mistake ; the oil and the taste of it are only present in the layer of blubber, an inch thick, which covers the seal's body like a protective armour. The flesh itself contains no fat ; on the other hand, it is extremely rich in blood and its taste in consequence reminds one of black-puddings. The flesh of the Weddell seal is very dark in colour ; in the frying-pan it turns quite black. The flesh of the crab-eater is of about the same colour as beef, and to us, at any rate, its taste was equally good. We therefore always tried to get crab-eater when providing food for ourselves.

We found the penguins as amusing as the seals were useful. So much has been written recently about these remarkable creatures, and they have been photographed and cinematographed so many times, that everyone is acquainted with them. Nevertheless, anyone who sees a living penguin for the first time will always be attracted and interested, both by the dignified Emperor penguin, with his three feet of stature, and by the bustling little Adélie.

Not only in their upright walk, but also in their manners and antics, these birds remind one strikingly of human beings. It has been remarked that an Emperor is the very image of "an old gentleman in evening dress," and the resemblance is indeed very noticeable. It becomes still more so when the Emperor—as is always his habit—approaches the stranger with a series of ceremonious bows; such is their good breeding!

When this ceremony is over, the penguin will usually come quite close; he is entirely unsuspecting and is not frightened even if one goes slowly towards him. On the other hand, if one approaches rapidly or touches him, he is afraid and immediately takes to flight. It sometimes happens, though, that he shows fight, and then it is wiser to keep out of range of his flippers; for in these he has a very powerful weapon, which might easily break a man's arm. If you wish to attack him, it is better to do so from behind; both flippers must be seized firmly at the same time and bent backwards along his back; then the fight is over.

The little Adélie is always comic. On meeting a flock of these little busybodies the most ill-humoured observer is forced to burst into laughter. During the first weeks of our stay in the Bay of Whales, while we were still unloading stores, it was always a welcome distraction to see a flock of Adélie penguins, to the number of a dozen or so, suddenly jump out of the water, as though at a word of command, and then sit still for some moments, stiff with astonishment at the extraordinary things they saw. When they had recovered from the first surprise, they generally dived into the sea again, but their intense curiosity soon drove them back to look at us more closely.

In contradistinction to their calm and self-controlled relative, the Emperor penguin, these active little creatures have an extremely fiery temperament, which makes them fly into a passion at the slightest interference with their affairs; and this, of course, only makes them still more amusing.

The penguins are birds of passage; they spend the winter on the various small groups of islands that are scattered about the southern ocean. On the arrival of spring they betake themselves to Antarctica, where they have their regular rookeries in places where there is bare ground. They have a pronounced taste for roaming, and as soon as the chicks are grown they set out, young and old together, on their travels. It was only as tourists that the penguins visited Framheim and its environs; for there was, of course, no bare land in our neighbourhood that might offer them a place of

A GROUP OF ADÉLIE PENGUINS.

A QUIET PIPE.

To face page 278, *Vol. II.*

residence.   For this reason we really saw comparatively little of them ; an Emperor was a very rare visitor ; but the few occasions on which we met these peculiar "bird people" of Antarctica will remain among the most delightful memories of our stay in the Bay of Whales.

CHAPTER XVI

THE VOYAGE OF THE "FRAM"

By First-Lieutenant Thorvald Nilsen

I.

FROM NORWAY TO THE BARRIER.

AFTER the *Fram* had undergone extensive repairs in Horten Dockyard, and had loaded provisions and equipment in Christiania, we left the latter port on June 7, 1910. According to the plan we were first to make an oceanographical cruise of about two months in the North Atlantic, and then to return to Norway, where the *Fram* was to be docked and the remaining outfit and dogs taken on board.

This oceanographical cruise was in many respects successful. In the first place, we gained familiarity with the vessel, and got everything shipshape for the long voyage to come; but the best of all was, that we acquired valuable experience of our auxiliary engine. This is a 180 h.p. Diesel motor, constructed for solar oil, of which we were taking about 90,000 litres (about 19,800 gallons). In this connection it may be mentioned that

FIRST-LIEUTENANT THORVALD NILSEN, NORWEGIAN NAVY.

To face page 280, *Vol. II.*

we consumed about 500 litres (about 110 gallons) a day, and that the *Fram's* radius of action was thus about six months. For the first day or two the engine went well enough, but after that it went slower and slower, and finally stopped of its own accord. After this it was known as the " Whooping Cough." This happened several times in the course of the trip ; the piston-rods had constantly to be taken out and cleared of a thick black deposit. As possibly our whole South Polar Expedition would depend on the motor doing its work properly, the result of this was that the projected cruise was cut short, and after a lapse of three weeks our course was set for Bergen, where we changed the oil for refined paraffin, and at the same time had the motor thoroughly overhauled.

Since then there has never been anything wrong with the engine.

From Bergen we went to Christiansand, where the *Fram* was docked, and, as already mentioned, the remaining outfit, with the dogs and dog-food, was taken on board.

The number of living creatures on board when we left Norway was nineteen men, ninety-seven dogs, four pigs, six carrier pigeons, and one canary.

At last we were ready to leave Christiansand on Thursday, August 9, 1910, and at nine o'clock that evening the anchor was got up and the motor started. After the busy time we had had, no doubt we were all glad to get off. As our departure had not been made public, only the pilot and a few acquaintances accompanied us a little way out. It was glorious weather, and everyone stayed on deck till far into the light night, watching the land slowly disappear. All the ninety-seven dogs were chained round the deck, on which we also had coal, oil, timber and other things, so that there was not much room to move about.

The rest of the vessel was absolutely full. To take an example, in the fore-saloon we had placed forty-three sledging cases, which were filled with books, Christmas presents, underclothing, and the like. In addition to these, one hundred complete sets of dog-harness, all our ski, ski-poles, snow-shoes, etc. Smaller articles were stowed in the cabins, and every man had something. When I complained, as happened pretty often, that I could not imagine where this or that was to be put, the Chief of the expedition used generally to say: " Oh, that's all right; you can just put it in your cabin!" Thus it was with every imaginable thing—from barrels of paraffin and new-born pups to writing materials and charts.

As the story of this voyage has already been told, it may be rapidly passed over here. After much delay through headwinds in the Channel, we picked up the north-east trade in about the latitude of Gibraltar, and arrived at Madeira on September 6.

At 9 p.m. on September 9 we weighed anchor for the

last time, and left Madeira. As soon as we were clear of the land we got the north-east trade again, and it held more or less fresh till about lat. 11° N.

After our departure from Madeira I took over the morning watch, from 4 to 8 a.m.; Prestrud and Gjertsen divided the remainder of the twenty-four hours.

In order if possible to get a little more way on the ship, a studding-sail and a skysail were rigged up with two awnings; it did not increase our speed very much, but no doubt it helped a little.

The highest temperature we observed was 84° F. In the trade winds we constantly saw flying-fish, but as far as I know not one was ever found on deck; those that came on board were of course instantly snapped up by the dogs.

In about lat. 11° N. we lost the north-east trade, and thus came into the "belt of calms," a belt that extends on each side of the Equator, between the north-east and south-east trades. Here, as a rule, one encounters violent rain-squalls; to sailing ships in general and ourselves in particular this heavy rain is welcome, as water-tanks can be filled up. Only on one day were we lucky enough to have rain, but as it was accompanied by a strong squall of wind, we did not catch all the water we wanted. All hands were on deck carrying water, some in oilskins, some in Adam's costume; the Chief in a white tropical suit, and, as far as I remember, clogs. As the latter were rather slippery, and the *Fram* suddenly gave an unexpected lurch, he was carried off his legs, and left sitting on the deck, while his bucket of water poured all over him. But "it was all in his country's cause," so he did not mind. We caught about 3 tons of water, and then had our tanks full, or about 30 tons, when the shower passed off; later in the voyage we filled a bucket now and again, but it never amounted to much, and if we had not been as careful as we were, our water-supply would hardly have lasted out.

On October 4 we crossed the Equator. The southeast trade was not so fresh as we had expected, and the engine had to be kept going the whole time.

At the beginning of November we came down into the west wind belt, or the "Roaring Forties," as they are called, and from that time we ran down our easting at a great rate. We were very lucky there, and had strong fair winds for nearly seven weeks at a stretch. In the heavy sea we found out what it was to sail in the *Fram;* she rolls incessantly, and there is never a moment's rest. The dogs were thrown backwards and forwards over the deck, and when one of them rolled into another, it was taken as a personal insult, and a fight followed at once. But for all that the *Fram* is a first-rate sea boat, and hardly ever ships any water. If this had been otherwise, the dogs would have been far worse off than they were.

THE SECOND IN COMMAND TAKES A NAP.

THE "FRAM" SIGHTED

The weather in the " Foggy Fifties " varied between gales, calms, fogs, snowstorms, and other delights. As a rule, the engine was now kept constantly ready, in case of our being so unlucky as to come too near an iceberg. Fortunately, however, we did not meet any of these until early on the morning of January 1, 1911, when we saw some typical Antarctic bergs ; that is to say, entirely tabular. Our latitude was then a little over 60° S., and we were not far off the pack. On the 1st and 2nd we sailed southward without seeing anything but scattered bergs and a constantly increasing number of lumps of ice, which showed us we were getting near. By 10 p.m. on the 2nd we came into slack drift-ice ; the weather was foggy, and we therefore kept going as near as might be on the course to the Bay of Whales, which was destined to be our base.

A good many seals were lying on the ice-floes, and as we went forward we shot some. As soon as the first seal was brought on board, all our dogs had their first meat meal since Madeira ; they were given as much as they wanted, and ate as much as they could. We, too, had our share of the seal, and from this time forward we had fresh seal-steak for breakfast at least every day ; it tasted excellent to us, who for nearly half a year had been living on nothing but tinned meat. With the steak whortleberries were always served, which of course helped to make it appreciated. The biggest seal we got in the pack-ice was about 12 feet long, and

weighed nearly half a ton.   A few penguins were also
shot, mostly Adélie penguins ; these are extraordinarily
amusing, and as inquisitive as an animal can be.   When
any of them saw us, they at once came nearer to get
a better view of the unbidden guests.   If they became
too impertinent, we did not hesitate to take them, for
their flesh, especially the liver, was excellent.   The
albatrosses, which had followed us through the whole
of the west wind belt, had now departed, and in their
place came the beautiful snowy petrels and Antarctic
petrels.

We had more or less fog all through the pack-ice.
Only on the night of the 5th did we have sun and fine
weather, when we saw the midnight sun for the first
time.   A more beautiful morning it would be difficult
to imagine : radiantly clear, with thick ice everywhere,
as far as the eye could see ; the lanes of water between
the floes gleamed in the sun, and the ice-crystals glittered like thousands of diamonds.   It was a pure delight to go on deck and drink in the fresh air ; one felt
altogether a new man.   I believe everyone on board
found this passage through the pack the most interesting
part of the whole voyage, and, of course, it all had the
charm of novelty.   Those who had not been in the ice
before, myself among them, and who were hunting for
the first time, ran about after seals and penguins, and
amused themselves like children.

At 10 p.m. on the 6th we were already out of the

ice after a passage of exactly four days; we had been extremely lucky, and the *Fram* went very easily through the ice.

After coming out of the pack, our course was continued through the open Ross Sea to the Bay of Whales, which from the previous description was to be found in about long. 164° W. On the afternoon of the 11th we had strong ice-blink ahead, by which is meant the luminous stripe that is seen above a considerable accumulation of ice; the nearest thing one can compare it to is the glare that is always seen over a great city on approaching it at night. We knew at once that this was the glare of the mighty Ross Barrier, named after Sir James Clark Ross, who first saw it in 1841. The Barrier is a wall of ice, several hundred miles long, and about 100 feet high, which forms the southern boundary of Ross Sea. We were, of course, very intent upon seeing what it looked like, but to me it did not appear so imposing as I had imagined it. Possibly this was because I had become familiar with it, in a way, from the many descriptions of it. From these descriptions we had expected to find a comparatively narrow opening into Balloon Bight, as shown in the photographs we had before us; but as we went along the Barrier, on the 12th, we could find no opening. In long. 164° W., on the other hand, there was a great break in the wall, forming a cape (West Cape); from here to the other side of the Barrier was about eight geographical miles, and southward, as far as we could see, lay loose bay ice.   We held on to the east outside this drift-ice and along the eastern Barrier till past midnight, but as Balloon Bight was not to be found, we returned to the above-mentioned break or cape, where we lay during the whole forenoon of the 13th, as the ice was too thick to allow us to make any progress.   After midday, however, the ice loosened, and began to drift out ; at the same time we went in, and having gone as far as possible, the *Fram* was moored to the fast ice-foot on the western side of the great bay we had entered.   It proved that Balloon Bight and another bight had merged to form a great bay, exactly as described by Sir Ernest Shackleton, and named by him the Bay of Whales.

After mooring here, the Chief and one or two others went on a reconnoitring tour; but it began to snow pretty thickly, and, as far as I am aware, nothing was accomplished beyond seeing that the Barrier at the southernmost end of the bay sloped evenly down to the sea-ice; but between the latter and the slope there was open water, so that they could not go any farther. We lay all night drifting in the ice, which was constantly breaking up, and during this time several seals and penguins were shot.   Towards morning on the 14th it became quite clear, and we had a splendid view of the surroundings.   Right over on the eastern side of the bay it looked as if there was more open water; we therefore went along the fast ice-foot and moored off the eastern Barrier at about three in the afternoon. The cape in the Barrier, under which we lay, was given the name of " Man's Head," on account of its resemblance to a human profile. All the time we were going along the ice we were shooting seals, so that on arrival at our final moorings we already had a good supply of meat.

For my part I was rather unlucky on one of these hunts. Four seals were lying on the ice-foot, and I jumped down with rifle and five cartridges; to take any cartridges in reserve did not occur to me, as, of course, I regarded myself as a mighty hunter, and thought that one shot per seal was quite enough. The three first died without a groan; but the fourth took the alarm, and made off as fast as it could. I fired my fourth cartridge, but it did not hit as it ought to have done, and the seal was in full flight, leaving a streak of blood behind it. I was not anxious to let a wounded seal go, and as I had only one cartridge left, and the seal had its tail turned towards me, I wanted to come to close quarters to make sure of it. I therefore ran as hard as I could, but the seal was quicker, and it determined the range. After running half-way to the South Pole, I summoned my remaining strength and fired the last shot. Whether the bullet went above or below, I have no idea. All I know is, that on arriving on board I was met by scornful smiles and had to stand a good deal of chaff.

As already mentioned, we left Norway on August 9, 1910, and arrived at our final moorings on January 14, 1911, in the course of which time we had only called at Madeira. The Barrier is 16,000 geographical miles from Norway, a distance which we took five months to cover. From Madeira we had had 127 days in open sea, and therewith the first part of the voyage was brought to an end.

II.

OFF THE BARRIER.

As soon as we had moored, the Chief, Prestrud, Johansen and I went up on to the Barrier on a tour of reconnaissance. The ascent from the sea-ice to the Barrier was fine, a perfectly even slope. When no more than a mile from the ship, we found a good site for the first dog-camp, and another mile to the south it was decided that the house was to stand, on the slope of a hill, where it would be least exposed to the strong south-easterly gales which might be expected from previous descriptions. Up on the Barrier all was absolutely still, and there was not a sign of life; indeed, what should anything live on ? This delightful ski-run was extended a little farther to the south, and after a couple of hours we returned on board. Here in the meantime the slaughtering of seals had been going on, and there were plenty to be had, as several hundreds of them lay about on the ice.

After the rather long sea voyage, and the cramped quarters on board, I must say it was a pleasure to have firm ground under one's feet and to be able to move about a little. The dogs evidently thought the same; when they came down on to the ice, they rolled in the snow and ran about, wild with delight. During our whole stay a great part of the time was spent in ski-runs and seal-hunts, and an agreeable change it was.

Sunday the 15th was spent in setting up tents at the first dog-camp and at Framheim, as the winter station was named. A team of dogs was used, and, as they were unused to being driven, it is not surprising that some lay down, others fought, a few wanted to go on board, but hardly any of them appreciated the serious-ness of the situation or understood that their good time had come to an end. On Monday all the dogs were landed, and on the following day the supplies began to be put ashore.

The landing of the cases was done in this way: the sea-party brought up on deck as many cases as the drivers could take in one journey; as the sledges came down to the vessel, the cases were sent down on to the ice on skids, so that it all went very rapidly. We would not put the cases out on the ice before the sledges came back, as, in case the ice should break up, we should be obliged to heave them all on board again, or we might even lose them. At night no one was ever allowed to stay on the ice.

Before we reached the ice, we had counted on having 50 per cent. of idle days—that is, from previous descriptions we had reckoned on having such bad weather half the time that the *Fram* would be obliged to leave her moorings. In this respect we were far luckier than we expected, and only had to put out twice. The first time was on the night of January 25, when we had a stiff breeze from the north with some sea, so that the vessel was bumping rather hard against the ice. Drifting floes came down upon us, and so as not to be caught by any iceberg that might suddenly come sailing in from the point of the Barrier we called Man's Head, we took our moorings on board and went. When the shore party next morning came down as usual at a swinging pace, they saw to their astonishment that the *Fram* was gone. In the course of the day the weather became fine, and we tried to go back about noon; but the bay was so full of drift-ice that we could not come in to the fast ice-foot. About nine in the evening we saw from the crow's nest that the ice was loosening; we made the attempt, and by midnight we were again moored.

But the day was not wasted by the shore party, for on the day before Kristensen, L. Hansen and I had been out on ski and had shot forty seals, which were taken up to the station while we were away.

ON THE ICE EDGE, JANUARY, 1911.

To face page 292, *Vol. II.*

Only once or twice more did we have to leave our berth, until on February 7, when almost all the ice had left the bay, we were able to moor alongside the low, fast Barrier, where we lay in peace until we went for good.

There was a great deal of animal life about us. A number of whales came close in to the vessel, where they stayed still to look at the uninvited guests. On the ice seals came right up to the ship, as did large and small flocks of penguins, to have a look at us. These latter were altogether extraordinarily inquisitive creatures. Two Emperor penguins often came to our last moorings to watch us laying out an ice-anchor or hauling on a hawser, while they put their heads on one side and jabbered, and they were given the names of "the Harbour-master and his Missis."

A great number of birds, skua gulls, snowy petrels and Antarctic petrels, flew round the ship and gave us many a good "roast ptarmigan."

On the morning of February 4, about 1 a.m., the watchman, Beck, came and called me with the news that a vessel was coming in. I guessed at once, of course, that it was the *Terra Nova*; but I must confess that I did not feel inclined to turn out and look at her. We hoisted the colours, however.

As soon as she was moored, Beck told me, some of her party went ashore, presumably to look for the house. They did not find it, though, and at 3 a.m. Beck came below again, and said that now they were coming on board. So then I turned out and received them. They were Lieutenant Campbell, the leader of Captain Scott's second shore party, and Lieutenant Pennell, the commander of the *Terra Nova*. They naturally asked a number of questions, and evidently had some difficulty in believing that it was actually the *Fram* that was lying here. We had at first been taken for a whaler. They offered to take our mail to New Zealand; but we had no mail ready, and had to decline the offer with thanks. Later in the day a number of the *Terra Nova's* officers went to breakfast at Framheim, and the Chief, Prestrud and I lunched with them. At about two in the afternoon the *Terra Nova* sailed again.

On Friday, February 16, a number of the shore party started on the first trip to lay down depots. We cleared up, filled our water-tanks with snow, and made the ship ready for sea. We had finished this by the evening of the 14th.

III.

From the Bay of Whales to Buenos Aires.

The sea party consisted of the following ten men: Thorvald Nilsen, L. Hansen, H. Kristensen and J. Nödtvedt; H. F. Gjertsen, A. Beck, M. Rönne,

OUR LAST MOORINGS ON THE ICE-FOOT.

A HUNTING EXPEDITION AT THE FOOT OF THE BARRIER.

A. Kutschin and O. K. Sundbeck. The first four formed one watch, from eight to two, and the last five the other, from two to eight. Last, but not least, comes K. Olsen, cook.

Having made ready for sea, we let go our moorings on the Ice Barrier at 9 a.m. on February 15, 1911. Hassel, Wisting, Bjaaland, and Stubberud came down to see us off. As in the course of the last few days the ice had broken up right to the end of the bay, we went as far south as possible to take a sounding; the shallowest we got was $155\frac{3}{4}$ fathoms (285 metres). The bay ended in a ridge of ice on the east, which was continued in a northerly direction, so that at the spot where we were stopped by the Barrier, we reached the most southerly point that a vessel can attain, so long as the Barrier remains as it is now. Highest latitude 78° 41′ S. When the *Terra Nova* was here, her latitude and ours was 78° 38′ S.

The last two days before our departure had been calm, and a thick, dense sludge lay over the whole bay; so dense was it that the *Fram* lost her way altogether, and we had to keep going ahead and astern until we came out into a channel. Seals by the hundred were lying on the floes, but as we had a quantity of seal's flesh, we left them in peace for a change.

Before the Chief began the laying out of depots, I received from him the following orders:

"To First-Lieutenant Thorvald Nilsen.

"With the departure of the *Fram* from the Ice Barrier, you will take over the command on board. In accordance with the plan we have mutually agreed upon:

"1. You will sail direct to Buenos Aires, where the necessary repairs will be executed, provisions taken on board, and the crew completed. When this has been done,

"2. You will sail from Buenos Aires to carry out oceanographical observations in the South Atlantic Ocean. It would be desirable if you could investigate the conditions between South America and Africa in two sections. These investigations must, however, be dependent on the prevailing conditions, and on the time at your disposal. When the time arrives you will return to Buenos Aires, where the final preparations will be made for

"3. Your departure for the Ice Barrier to take off the shore party. The sooner you can make your way in to the Barrier in 1912, the better. I mention no time, as everything depends on circumstances, and I leave it to you to act according to your judgment.

"In all else that concerns the interests of the Expedition, I leave you entire freedom of action.

"If on your return to the Barrier you should find that I am prevented by illness or death from taking over the leadership of the Expedition, I place this in your hands, and beg you most earnestly to endeavour to carry out the original plan of the Expedition—the exploration of the North Polar basin.

" With thanks for the time we have spent together, and in the hope that when we meet again we shall have reached our respective goals,

" I am,

" Yours sincerely,

" ROALD AMUNDSEN."

When Sir James Ross was in these waters for the first time, in 1842, he marked " Appearance of land " in long. 160° W., and lat. about 78° S. Afterwards, in 1902, Captain Scott named this land " King Edward VII. Land." One of the *Terra Nova's* objects was to explore this land; but when we met the ship on February 4, they told us on board that on account of the ice conditions they had not been able to land. As no one had ever been ashore there, I thought it might be interesting to go and see what it looked like. Consequently our course was laid north-eastward along the Barrier. During the night a thick sea-fog came on, and it was only now and then that we could see the Barrier over our heads. All of a sudden we were close upon a lofty iceberg, so that we had to put the helm hard over to go clear. The *Fram* steers splendidly, however, when she is in proper trim, and turns as if on a pivot; besides which, it was calm.

As the day advanced, the weather cleared more and more, and by noon it was perfectly clear. The sight that then met us was the lofty Barrier to starboard, and elsewhere all round about some fifty icebergs, great and small. The Barrier rose from about 100 feet at its edge to something like 1,200 feet.

We followed the Barrier for some distance, but in the neighbourhood of Cape Colbeck we met the drift-ice, and as I had no wish to come between this and the Barrier, we stood out in a north-westerly direction. There is, besides, the disadvantage about a propeller like ours, that it is apt to wear out the brasses, so that these have to be renewed from time to time. It was imperative that this should be done before we came into the pack-ice, and the sooner the better. When, therefore, we had gone along the Barrier for about a day and a half without seeing any bare land, we set our course north-west in open water, and after we had come some way out we got a slant of easterly wind, so that the sails could be set. We saw the snow-covered land and the glare above it all night.

The date had not yet been changed, but as this had to be done, it was changed on February 15.*

---

* A vessel sailing continuously to the eastward puts the clock on every day, one hour for every fifteen degrees of longitude; one sailing westward puts it back in the same way. In long. 180° one of them has gone twelve hours forward, the other twelve hours back; the differ-

At noon on the 16th the propeller was lifted, and by the evening of the 17th the job was done—a record in spite of the temperature. Capital fellows to work, our engineers.

On the night of the 15th we saw the midnight sun unfortunately for the last time. The same night something dark was sighted on the port bow ; in that light it looked very like an islet. The sounding apparatus was got ready, and we who were on watch of course saw ourselves in our minds as great discoverers. I was already wondering what would be the most appropriate name to give it, but, alas ! the "discovery" became clearer and the name—well, it was a rather prosaic one : "Dead Whale Islet" ; for it turned out to be a huge inflated whale, that was drifting, covered with birds.

We went rather slowly north-westward under sail alone. On the morning of the 17th we saw ice-blink on the starboard bow, and about noon we were close to the pack itself ; it was here quite thick, and raised by pressure, so that an attempt to get through it was out of the question. We were, therefore, obliged to follow the ice to the west. Due aft we saw in the sky the same glare as above the great Ice Barrier, which may possibly show that the Barrier turns towards the north

---

ence is thus twenty-four hours. In changing the longitude, therefore, one has to change the date, so that, in passing from east to west longitude, one will have the same day twice over, and in passing from west to east longitude a day must be missed.

and north-west; besides which, the masses of pressure-ice that collect here must go to show that it encounters an obstruction, probably the Barrier. When we went out in 1912 the ice lay in exactly the same place and in the same way.

Our course was still to the west along the pack-ice, and it was not till the 20th that we could turn her nose northward again. For a change we now had a stiff breeze from the south-east, with thick snow, so we got on very well. On the whole, the *Fram* goes much more easily through the water now than on the way south. Her bottom has probably been cleaned by the cold water and all the scraping against the ice; besides which, we have no more than a third of the load with which we left Norway.

On the night of the 20th we had to light the binnacle-lamps again, and now the days grew rapidly shorter. It may possibly be a good thing to have dark nights on land, but at sea it ought always to be light, especially in these waters, which are more or less unknown, and full of drifting icebergs.

At 4 p.m. on the 22nd we entered the drift-ice in lat. 70·5° S., long. 177·5° E. The ice was much higher and uglier than when we were going south, but as there was nothing but ice as far as we could see both east and west, and it was fairly loose, we had to make the attempt where there seemed to be the best chance of getting through.

The seals, which to the south of the ice had been following us in decreasing numbers, had now disappeared almost entirely, and curiously enough we saw very few seals in the pack. Luckily, however, Lieutenant Gjertsen's watch got three seals, and for a week we were able to enjoy seal-beef, popularly known as "crocodile beef," three times a day. Seal-beef and fresh whortleberries—*delicioso!*

We went comparatively well through the ice, though at night—from eleven to one—we had to slacken speed, as it was impossible to steer clear on account of the darkness, and towards morning we had a heavy fall of snow, so that nothing could be seen, and the engine had to be stopped. When it cleared, at about 9 a.m., we had come into a dam, out of which we luckily managed to turn fairly easily, coming out into a bay. This was formed by over a hundred icebergs, many of which lay in contact with each other and had packed the ice close together. On the west was the outlet, which we steered for, and by 10 p.m. on February 23 we were already out of the ice and in open water. Our latitude was then 69° S., longitude 175·5° E.

It is very curious to find such calm weather in Ross Sea; in the two months we have been here we have hardly had a strong breeze. Thus, when I was relieved at 2 a.m. on the 25th, I wrote in my diary: '. . . It is calm, not a ripple on the water. The three men forming the watch walk up and down the deck. Now and then one hears the penguins' cry, *kva, kva,* but except these there is no other sound than the *tuff, tuff* of the motor, 220 times a minute. Ah, that motor! it goes unweariedly. It has now gone for 1,000 hours without being cleaned, while on our Atlantic cruise last year it stopped dead after going for eighty hours. . . . Right over us we have the Southern Cross, all round glow the splendid southern lights, and in the darkness can be seen the gleaming outline of an iceberg. . . ."

On the 26th we crossed the Antarctic Circle, and the same day the temperature both of air and water rose above 32° F.

It was with sorrow in our hearts that we ate our last piece of "crocodile beef," but I hoped we should get a good many albatrosses, which we saw as soon as we came out of the ice. They were mostly the sooty albatross, that tireless bird that generally circles alone about the ship and is so difficult to catch, as he seldom tries to bite at the pork that is used as bait. When I saw these birds for the first time, as a deck boy, I was told they were called parsons, because they were the souls of ungodly clergymen, who had to wait down here till doomsday without rest.

More or less in our course to Cape Horn there are supposed to be two groups of islands, the Nimrod group in about long. 158° W., and Dougherty Island in about long. 120° W. They are both marked "D" (Doubtful) on the English charts.   Lieutenant Shackleton's vessel, the *Nimrod*, Captain Davis, searched for both, but found neither; Dougherty Island, however, is said to have been twice sighted.   The *Fram's* course was therefore laid for the Nimrod group.   For a time things went very well, but then we had a week of northerly winds—that is, head winds—and when at last we had a fair wind again, we were so far to the south-east of them that there was no sense in sailing back to the north-west to look for doubtful islands; it would certainly have taken us weeks.   Consequently, our course was laid for Dougherty Island.   We had westerly winds for about two weeks, and were only two or three days' sail from the island in question, when suddenly we had a gale from the north-east, which lasted for three days, and ended in a hurricane from the same quarter.   When this was over, we had come according to dead reckoning about eighty nautical miles to the south-east of the island; the heavy swell, which lasted for days, made it out of the question to attempt to go against it with the motor.   We hardly had a glimpse of sun or stars, and weeks passed without our being able to get an observation, so that for that matter we might easily be a degree or two out in our reckoning.   For the present, therefore, we must continue to regard these islands as doubtful.

Moral: Don't go on voyages of discovery, my friend; you're no good at it!

As soon as we were out of Ross Sea and had entered the South Pacific Ocean, the old circus started again—in other words, the *Fram* began her everlasting rolling from one side to the other. When this was at its worst, and cups and plates were dancing the fandango in the galley, its occupant's only wish was, "Oh, to be in Buenos Aires!" For that matter, it is not a very easy job to be cook in such circumstances, but ours was always in a good humour, singing and whistling all day long. How well the *Fram* understands the art of rolling is shown by the following little episode.

One afternoon a couple of us were sitting drinking coffee on a tool-box that stood outside the galley. As ill-luck would have it, during one of the lurches the lashing came loose, and the box shot along the deck. Suddenly it was checked by an obstacle, and one of those who were sitting on it flew into the air, through the galley door, and dashed past the cook with a splendid tiger's leap, until he landed face downwards at the other end of the galley, still clinging like grim death to his cup, as though he wanted something to hold on to. The face he presented after this successful feat of aviation was extremely comical, and those who saw it had a hearty fit of laughter.

As has already been said, we went very well for a time after reaching the Pacific, a fair wind for fourteen days together, and I began to hope that we were once more in what are called the "westerlies." However,

BECK STEERS THE "FRAM" THROUGH UNKNOWN WATERS.

OUR COOK, CHEERFUL AND CONTENTED AS USUAL.

nothing is perfect in this world, and we found that out here, as we had icebergs every day, and were constantly bothered by snow-squalls or fog; the former were, of course, to be preferred, as it was at any rate clear between the squalls; but fog is the worst thing of all. It sometimes happened that all hands were on deck the whole night to work the ship at a moment's notice, and there were never less than two men on the lookout forward. The engine, too, was always ready to be started instantly. A little example will show how ready the crew were at any time.

One Sunday afternoon, when Hansen, Kristensen and I were on watch, the wind began to draw ahead, so that we had to beat. It was blowing quite freshly, but I did not want to call the watch below, as they might need all the sleep they could get, and Hansen and I were to put the ship about. Kristensen was steering, but gave us a hand when he could leave the wheel. As the ship luffed up into the wind and the sails began to flap pretty violently, the whole of the watch below suddenly came rushing on deck in nothing but their unmentionables and started to haul. Chance willed it that at the same moment an iceberg came out of the fog, right in front of our bows. It was not many minutes, either, before we were on the other tack, and the watch below did not linger long on deck. With so few clothes on it was no pleasure to be out in that cold, foggy air. They slept so lightly, then, that it took no more noise than that to wake them.   When I afterwards asked one of them—I think it was Beck—what made them think of coming up, he replied that they thought we were going to run into an iceberg and were trying to get out of the way.

It has happened at night that I have seen the ice-blink as far off as eight miles, and then there is nothing to fear ; but sometimes in the middle of the day we have sailed close to icebergs that have only been seen a few minutes before we were right on them.   As the voyage was long, we sailed as fast as we could, as a rule ; but on two or three nights we had to reduce our way to a minimum, as we could not see much farther than the end of the bowsprit.

After two or three weeks' sailing the icebergs began gradually to decrease, and I hoped we should soon come to the end of them ; but on Sunday, March 5, when it was fairly clear, we saw about midday a whole lot of big bergs ahead.   One of the watch below, who had just come on deck, exclaimed : " What the devil is this beastly mess you fellows have got into ?"   He might well ask, for in the course of that afternoon we passed no less than about a hundred bergs.   They were big tabular bergs, all of the same height, about 100 feet, or about as high as the crow's-nest of the *Fram*.   The bergs were not the least worn, but looked as if they had calved quite recently.   As I said, it was clear enough, we even got an observation that day (lat. 61° S., long. 150° W.), and as we had a west wind, we twisted quite elegantly past one iceberg after another. The sea, which during the morning had been high enough for the spray to dash over the tops of the bergs, gradually went down, and in the evening, when we were well to leeward of them all, it was as smooth as if we had been in harbour. In the course of the night we passed a good many more bergs, and the next day we only saw about twenty.

In the various descriptions of voyages in these waters, opinions are divided as to the temperature of the water falling in the neighbourhood of icebergs. That it falls steadily as one approaches the pack-ice is certain enough, but whether it falls for one or a few scattered icebergs, no doubt depends on circumstances.

One night at 12 o'clock we had a temperature in the water of 34·1° F., at 4 a.m. 33·8° F., and at 8 a.m. 33·6° F.; at 6 a.m. we passed an iceberg. At 12 noon the temperature had risen to 33·9° F. In this case one might say that the temperature gave warning, but, as a rule, in high latitudes it has been constant both before and after passing an iceberg.

On Christmas Eve, 1911, when on our second trip southward we saw the first real iceberg, the temperature of the water fell in four hours from 35·6° F. to 32·7° F., which was the temperature when the bergs were passed, after which it rose rather rapidly to 35° F.

In the west wind belt I believe one can tell with some degree of certainty when one is approaching ice. In the middle of November, 1911, between Prince

Edward Island and the Crozet Islands (about lat. 47° S.) the temperature fell. Towards morning I remarked to someone : " The temperature of the water is falling as if we were getting near the ice." On the forenoon of the same day we sailed past a very small berg ; the temperature again rose to the normal, and we met no more ice until Christmas Eve.

On Saturday, March 4, the day before we met that large collection of bergs, the temperature fell pretty rapidly from 33·9° F. to 32·5° F. We had not then seen ice for nearly twenty-four hours. At the same time the colour of the water became unusually green, and it is possible that we had come into a cold current. The temperature remained as low as this till Sunday morning, when at 8 a.m. it rose to 32·7° F. ; at 12 noon, close to a berg, to 32·9° F., and a mile to lee of it, to 33° F. It continued to rise, and at 4 p.m., when the bergs were thickest, it was 33·4° F. ; at 8 p.m. 33·6° F., and at midnight 33·8° F. If there had been a fog, we should certainly have thought we were leaving the ice instead of approaching it ; it is very curious, too, that the temperature of the water should not be more constant in the presence of such a great quantity of ice ; but, as I have said, it may have been a current.

In the course of the week following March 5 the bergs became rarer, but the same kind of weather prevailed. Our speed was irreproachable, and in one day's work (from noon to noon) we covered a distance of

200 nautical miles, or an average of about 8½ knots an hour, which was the best day's work the *Fram* had done up to that time. The wind, which had been westerly and north-westerly, went by degrees to the north, and ended in a hurricane from the north-east on Sunday, March 12. I shall quote here what I wrote about this in my diary on the 13th:

" Well, now we have experienced the first hurricane on the *Fram*. On Saturday afternoon, the 11th, the wind went to the north-east, as an ordinary breeze with rain. The barometer had been steady between 29·29 inches (744 millimetres) and 29·33 inches (745 millimetres). During the afternoon it began to fall, and at 8 p.m. it was 29·25 inches (743 millimetres) without the wind having freshened at all. The outer jib was taken in, however. By midnight the barometer had fallen to 29·0 inches (737 millimetres), while the wind had increased to a stiff breeze. We took in the foresail, mainsail, and inner jib, and had now only the top-sail and a storm-trysail left. The wind gradually increased to a gale. At 4 a.m. on Sunday the barometer had fallen again to 28·66 inches (728 millimetres), and at 6 a.m. the topsail was made fast.*

* For the benefit of those who know what a buntline on a sail is, I may remark that besides the usual topsail buntlines we had six extra buntlines round the whole sail, so that when it was clewed up it was, so to speak, made fast. We got the sail clewed up without its going to pieces, but it took us over an hour. We had to take this precaution, of having so many buntlines, as we were short-handed.

"The wind increased and the seas ran higher, but we did not ship much water.   At 8 a.m. the barometer was 28·30 inches (719 millimetres), and at 9 a.m. 28·26 inches (718 millimetres), when at last it stopped going down and remained steady till about noon, during which time a furious hurricane was blowing.   The clouds were brown, the colour of chocolate; I cannot remember ever having seen such an ugly sky.   Little by little the wind went to the north, and we sailed large under two storm-trysails.   Finally, we had the seas on our beam, and now the *Fram* showed herself in all her glory as the best sea-boat in the world.   It was extraordinary to watch how she behaved.   Enormous seas came surging high to windward, and we, who were standing on the bridge, turned our backs to receive them, with some such remark as : ' Ugh, that's a nasty one coming.'   But the sea never came.   A few yards from the ship it looked over the bulwarks and got ready to hurl itself upon her.   But at the last moment the *Fram* gave a wriggle of her body and was instantly at the top of the wave, which slipped under the vessel.   Can anyone be surprised if one gets fond of such a ship ?   Then she went down with the speed of lightning from the top of the wave into the trough, a fall of fourteen or fifteen yards.   When we sank like this, it gave one the same feeling as dropping from the twelfth to the ground-floor in an American express elevator, ' as if everything inside you was coming up.'   It was so quick that we seemed

to be lifted off the deck.   We went up and down like
this all the afternoon and evening, till during the night
the wind gradually dropped and it became calm.   That
the storm would not be of long duration might almost
be assumed from its suddenness, and the English rule—

> " ' Long foretold, long last ;
> Short notice, soon past '—

may thus be said to have held good.

"When there is a strong wind on her beam, the
Fram does not roll so much as usual, except for an
occasional leeward lurch ; nor was any excessive quantity
of water shipped in this boisterous sea.   The watch went
below as usual when they were relieved, and, as somebody very truly remarked, all hands might quite well
have turned in, if we had not had to keep a lookout for
ice.   And fortune willed it that the day of the hurricane
was the first since we had left the Barrier that we did
not see ice—whether this was because the spray was so
high that it hid our view, or because there really was
none.   Be that as it may, the main thing was that we
saw no ice. · During the night we had a glimpse of the
full moon, which gave the man at the wheel occasion to
call out ' Hurrah !'—and with good reason, as we had
been waiting a long time for the moon to help us in
looking out for ice.

" In weather like this one notices nothing out of the
ordinary below deck.   Here hardly anything is heard of
the wind, and in the after-saloon, which is below the

water-line, it is perfectly comfortable.   The cook, who
resides below, therefore reckons 'ugly weather' according to the motion of the vessel, and not according to
storms, fog, or rain.   On deck we do not mind much
how it blows, so long as it is only clear, and the wind is
not against us.   How little one hears below deck may
be understood from the fact that yesterday morning,
while it was blowing a hurricane, the cook went about
as usual, whistling his two verses of 'The Whistling
Bowery Boy.'   While he was in the middle of the first,
I came by and told him that it was blowing a hurricane
if he cared to see what it looked like.   'Oh, yes,' he
said, 'I could guess it was blowing, for the galley fire
has never drawn so well ; the bits of coal are flying up
the chimney'; and then he whistled through the second
verse.   All the same, he could not resist going up to
see.   It was not long before he came down again, with
a 'My word, it *is* blowing, and waves up to the sky !'
No ; it was warmer and more cosy below among his
pots and pans.

   " For dinner, which was eaten as usual amid cheerful
conversation, we had green-pea soup, roast sirloin, with
a glass of aquavit, and caramel pudding ; so it may be
seen that the cook was not behindhand in opening tins,
even in a hurricane.   After dinner we enjoyed our usual
Sunday cigar, while the canary, which has become Kristensen's pet, and hangs in his cabin, sang at the top of
its voice."

On March 14 we saw the last iceberg; during the whole trip we had seen and passed between 500 and 600 bergs.

The wind held steady from the north-east for a week and a half, and I was beginning to think we should be stuck down here to play the Flying Dutchman. There was every possible sign of a west wind, but it did not come. On the night of the 17th it cleared; light cirrus clouds covered the sky, and there was a ring about the moon. This, together with the heavy swell and the pronounced fall of the barometer, showed that something might be expected. And, sure enough, on Sunday, March 19, we were in a cyclone. By manœuvring according to the rules for avoiding a cyclone in the southern hemisphere, we at any rate went well clear of one semicircle. About 4 p.m. on Sunday afternoon the barometer was down to 27·56 inches (700 millimetres), the lowest barometer reading I have ever heard of. From noon to 4 p.m. there was a calm, with heavy sea. Immediately after a gale sprang up from the north-west, and in the course of a couple of days it slowly moderated to a breeze from the same quarter.

Sunday, March 5, a hundred icebergs; Sunday March 12, a hurricane; and Sunday, March 19, a cyclone: truly three pleasant " days of rest."

The curves given on the next page, which show the course of barometric pressure for a week, from Monday to Monday, are interesting.

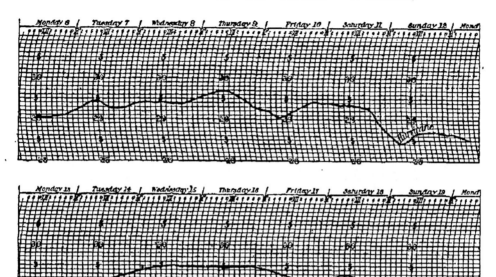

By way of comparison a third curve is given from the north-east trade, where there is an almost constant breeze and fine weather.

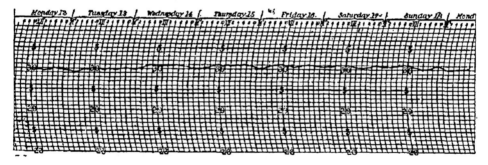

On this trip the fore-saloon was converted into a sail-loft, where Rönne and Hansen carried on their work, each in his watch. The after-saloon was used as a common mess-room, as it is warmer, and the motion is far less felt than forward.

From the middle of March it looked as if the equi-
noctial gales were over, for we had quite fine weather
all the way to Buenos Aires. Cape Horn was passed
on March 31 in the most delightful weather—a light
westerly breeze, not a cloud in the sky, and only a very
slight swell from the west. Who would have guessed
that such splendid weather was to be found in these
parts ?—and that in March, the most stormy month of
the year.

Lieutenant Gjertsen and Kutschin collected plankton
all the time ; the latter smiled all over his face whenever
he chanced to get one or two " tadpoles " in his tow-net.

From the Falkland Islands onward the *Fram* was
washed and painted, so that we might not present too
" Polar " an appearance on arrival at Buenos Aires.

It may be mentioned as a curious fact that the snow
with which we filled our water-tanks on the Barrier did
not melt till we were in the River La Plata, which
shows what an even temperature is maintained in the
Fram's hold.

About midday on Easter Sunday we were at the mouth
of the River La Plata, without seeing land, however.
During the night the weather became perfect, a breeze
from the south, moonlight and starry, and we went up
the river by soundings and observations of the stars
until at 1 a.m. on Monday, when we had the Recalada
light-ship right ahead. We had not seen any light
since we left Madeira on September 9. At 2.30 the

same morning we got a pilot aboard, and at seven in the evening we anchored in the roads of Buenos Aires.

We had then been nearly once round the world, and for over seven months the anchor had not been out.

We had reckoned on a two months' voyage from the ice, and it had taken us sixty-two days.

IV.

THE OCEANOGRAPHICAL CRUISE.

According to the programme, the *Fram* was to go on an oceanographical cruise in the South Atlantic, and my orders were that this was to be arranged to suit the existing circumstances. I had reckoned on a cruise of about three months. We should have to leave Buenos Aires at the beginning of October to be down in the ice at the right time (about the New Year).

As we were too short-handed to work the ship, take soundings, etc., the following four seamen were engaged: H. Halvorsen, A. Olsen, F. Steller, and J. Andersen.

At last we were more or less ready, and the *Fram* sailed from Buenos Aires on June 8, 1911, the anniversary of our leaving Horten on our first hydrographic cruise in the North Atlantic. I suppose there was no one on board on June 8, 1910, who dreamed that a year later we should go on a similar cruise in the South.

We had a pilot on board as far as Montevideo, where we arrived on the afternoon of the 9th; but on account of an increasing wind (pampero) we had to lie at anchor here for a day and a half, as the pilot could not be taken off. On Saturday afternoon, the 10th, he was fetched off by a big tug-boat, on board of which was the Secretary of the Norwegian Consulate. This gentleman asked us if we could not come into the harbour, as " people would like to see the ship." I promised to come in on the way back, " if we had time."

On Sunday morning, the 11th, we weighed anchor, and went out in the most lovely weather that can be imagined. Gradually the land disappeared, and in the course of the evening we lost the lights; we were once more out in the Atlantic, and immediately everything resumed its old course.

In order to save our supply of preserved provisions as much as possible, we took with us a quantity of live poultry, and no fewer than twenty live sheep, which were quartered in the " farmyard " on the port side of the vessel's fore-deck. Sheep and hens were all together, and there was always a most beautiful scent of hay, so that we had not only sea air, but " country air." In spite of all this delightful air, three or four of the crew were down with influenza, and had to keep their berths for some days.

I reckoned on being back at Buenos Aires by the beginning of September, and on getting, if possible, one station a day. The distance, according to a rough calculation, was about 8,000 nautical miles, and I laid down the following plan : To go about east by north with the prevailing northerly and north-westerly winds to the coast of Africa, and there get hold of the south-east trade. If we could not reach Africa before that date, then to turn on July 22 and lay our course with the south-east trade for St. Helena, which we could reach before August 1 ; from there again with the same wind to South Trinidad (August 11 or 12) ; on again with easterly and north-easterly winds on a south-westerly course until about August 22, when the observations were to be concluded, and we should try to make Buenos Aires in the shortest time.

That was the plan that we attempted. On account of the fresh water from the River La Plata, we did not begin at once to take samples of water, and with a head-wind, north-east, we lay close-hauled for some days. We also had a pretty stiff breeze, which was another reason for delaying the soundings until the 17th.

For taking samples of water a winch is used, with a sounding-line of, let us say, 5,000 metres (2,734 fathoms), on which are hung one or more tubes for catching water ; we used three at once to save time. Now, supposing water and temperatures are to be taken at depths of 300, 400, and 500 metres (164, 218, and 273 fathoms), Apparatus III. (see diagram) is first hung on, about 20 metres (10 fathoms) from the end of the line, where a small weight (*a*) hangs ; then it is lowered until the indicator-wheel, over which the line passes, shows 100 metres (54 fathoms); Apparatus II. is then put on, and it is lowered again for another 100 metres, when Apparatus I. is put on and the line paid out for 300 metres (164 fathoms)—that is, until the indicator-wheel shows 500 metres (273 fathoms). The upper Apparatus (I.) is then at 300 metres (164 fathoms), No. II. at 400 metres (218 fathoms), and No. III. at 500 metres (273 fathoms). Under Apparatus I. and II. is hung a slipping sinker (about 8 centimetres, or 3¼ inches, long, and 3 centimetres, or 1¼ inches, in diameter). To the water-samplers are attached thermometers (*b*) in tubes arranged for the purpose.

The water-samplers themselves consist of a brass cylinder (*c*), about 38 centimetres (15 inches) long and 4 centimetres (1½ inches) in diameter (about half a litre of water), set in a frame (*d*). At about the middle of the cylinder are pivots, which rest in bearings on the frame, so that the cylinder can be swung 180 degrees (straight up and down).

The cylinder, while being lowered in an inverted position, is open at both ends, so that the water can pass through. But at its upper and lower ends are valves, working on hinges and provided with packing. When the apparatus is released, the cylinder swings round, and these valves then automatically close the ends of the cylinder. The water that is thus caught in the cylinder at the required depth remains in it while it is being heaved up, and is collected in bottles.   When the apparatus is released, the column of mercury in the thermometer is broken, and the temperature of the water is read at the same depth as the water is taken from.

The release takes place in the following manner: when all the cylinders have been lowered to the required depths, they are left hanging for a few minutes, so that the thermometers may be set at the right temperature before the column of mercury is broken.   Then a slipping sinker is sent down the line.   When this sinker strikes the first apparatus, a spring is pressed, a hook (e) which has held the cylinder slips loose, and the cylinder turns completely over (Apparatus I.).   As it does this, the valves, as already mentioned, close the ends of the cylinder, which is fixed in its new position by a hook in the bottom of the frame.   At the same instant the slipping sinker that hangs under Apparatus I. is released, and continues the journey to Apparatus II., where the same thing happens.   It is then repeated with Apparatus III.   When they are all ready, they are heaved in.

By holding one's finger on the line one can feel, at all events in fairly calm weather, when the sinkers strike against the cylinders; but I used to look at my watch, as it takes about half a minute for the sinker to go down 100 metres.

The necessary data are entered in a book.

On the morning of the 17th, then, the sails were clewed up, and the *Fram* began to roll even worse than with the sails set. We first tried taking soundings with a sinker of 66 pounds, and a tube for taking specimens of the sea-bed. At 2,000 metres (1,093 fathoms) or more the line (piano wire) broke, so that sinker, tube, and over 2,000 metres of line continued their way unhindered to the bottom. I had thought of taking samples of water at 4,000, 3,000, and 2,000 metres (2,187, 1,639, 1,093 fathoms), and so on, and water-cylinders were put on from 0 to 2,000 metres. This, however, took six hours. Next day, on account of the heavy sea, only a few samples from 0 to 100 metres (54 fathoms) were taken. On the third day we made another attempt to get the bottom. This time we got specimens of the sea-bed from about 4,500 metres (about 2,500 fathoms); but the heaving in and taking of water samples and temperatures occupied eight hours, from 7 a.m. till 3 p.m., or a third part of the twenty-four hours. In this way we should want at least nine months on the route that had been laid down; but as, unfortunately, this time was not at our disposal, we at once gave up taking specimens of the bottom and samples of water at greater depths than 1,000 metres (546 fathoms). For the remainder of the trip we took temperatures and samples of water at the following depths: 0, 5, 10, 25, 50, 75, 100, 150, 200, 250, 300, 400, 500, 750, and 1,000 metres (0, $2\frac{3}{4}$, $5\frac{1}{2}$, $13\frac{1}{2}$, 27, 41, 54, 81, 108, 135, 164, 218, 273,

410, and 546 fathoms), in all, fifteen samples from each station, and from this time forward we went on regularly with one station every day. Finally, we managed to heave up two water-cylinders on the same line by hand without great difficulty. At first this was done with the motor and sounding-machine, but this took too long, and we afterwards used nothing but a light hand-winch. Before very long we were so practised that the whole business only took two hours.

These two hours were those we liked best of the twenty-four. All kinds of funny stories were told, especially about experiences in Buenos Aires, and every day there was something new. Here is a little yarn:

One of the members of the expedition had been knocked down by a motor-car in one of the busiest streets; the car stopped and of course a crowd collected at once. Our friend lay there, wondering whether he ought not to be dead, or at least to have broken a leg, so as to get compensation. While he lay thus, being prodded and examined by the public, he suddenly remembered that he had half a dollar in his pocket. With all that money it didn't matter so much about the compensation; up jumped our friend like an india-rubber ball, and in a second he had vanished in the crowd, who stood open-mouthed, gazing after the "dead" man.

Our speed on this cruise was regulated as nearly as possible so that there might be about 100 nautical miles

between each station, and I must say we were uncommonly lucky in the weather. We made two
fairly parallel sections with comparatively regular
intervals between the stations; as regular, in any
case, as one can hope to get with a vessel like the
Fram, which really has too little both of sail area and
engine power. The number of stations was 60 in all
and 891 samples of water were taken. Of plankton
specimens 190 were sent home. The further examination of these specimens in Norway will show whether
the material collected is of any value, and whether the
cruise has yielded satisfactory results.

As regards the weather on the trip, it was uniformly
good the whole time; we had a good deal of wind now
and then, with seas and rolling, but for the most part
there was a fresh breeze. In the south-east trade we
sailed for four weeks at a stretch without using the
engine, which then had a thorough overhauling. At
the same time we had a good opportunity of smartening
up the ship, which she needed badly. All the iron was
freed from rust, and the whole vessel painted both
below and above deck. The decks themselves were
smeared with a mixture of oil, tar and turpentine, after
being scoured. All the rigging was examined. At the
anchorage at Buenos Aires nearly the whole ship was
painted again, masts and yards, the outside of the vessel
and everything inboard, both deck-houses, the boats and
the various winches, pumps, etc. In the engine-room

everything was either shining bright or freshly painted, everything hung in its place and such order and cleanliness reigned that it was a pleasure to go down there. The result of all this renovating and smartening up was that, when we fetched up by the quay at Buenos Aires, the *Fram* looked brighter than I suppose she has ever done since she was new.

During the trip the holds were also cleaned up, and all the provisions re-stowed and an inventory made of them.

A whole suit of sails was completely worn out on this voyage ; but what can one expect when the ship is being worked every single day, with clewing up, making fast and setting of sails both in calms and winds? This work every day reminded me of the corvette *Ellida*, when the order was " all hands aloft." As a rule, though, it was only clewing up the sails that had to be done, as we always had to take soundings on the weather side, so that the sounding-line should not foul the bottom of the vessel and smash the apparatus. And we did not lose more than one thermometer in about nine hundred soundings.

On account of all this wear and tear of sails Rönne was occupied the whole time, both at sea and in Buenos Aires, in making and patching sails, as there was not much more than the leeches left of those that had been used, and on the approaching trip (to the Ice Barrier) we should have to have absolutely first-class things in the " Roaring Forties."

June 30, 1911, is a red-letter day in the *Fram's* history, as on that day we intersected our course from Norway to the Barrier, and the *Fram* thus completed her first circumnavigation of the globe. Bravo, *Fram!* It was well done, especially after the bad character you have been given as a sailer and a sea-boat. In honour of the occasion we had a better dinner than usual, and the *Fram* was congratulated by all present on having done her work well.

On the evening of July 29 St. Helena was passed. It was the first time I had seen this historic island. It was very strange to think that "the greatest spirit of a hundred centuries," as some author has called Napoleon, should have ending his restless life on this lonely island of the South Atlantic.

On August 12, when daylight came, we sighted the little Martin Vaz Islands ahead, and a little later South Trinidad (in 1910 this island was passed on October 16). We checked our chronometers, which, however, proved to be correct. From noon till 2 p.m., while we were lying still and taking our daily hydrographic observations, a sailing ship appeared to the north of us, lying close-hauled to the south. She bore down on us and ran up her flag, and we exchanged the usual greetings; she was a Norwegian barque bound for Australia. Otherwise we did not see more than four or five ships on the whole voyage, and those were pretty far off.

Never since leaving Madeira (September, 1910) had

we been troubled with animals or insects of any kind whatever; but when we were in Buenos Aires for the first time, at least half a million flies came aboard to look at the vessel. I hoped they would go ashore when the *Fram* sailed; but no, they followed us, until by degrees they passed peacefully away on fly-paper.

Well, flies are one thing, but we had something else that was worse—namely, rats—our horror and dread, and for the future our deadly enemies. The first signs of them I found in my bunk and on the table in the fore-saloon; they were certainly not particular. What I said on that occasion had better not be printed, though no expression could be strong enough to give vent to one's annoyance at such a discovery. We set traps, but what was the use of that, when the cargo consisted exclusively of provisions?

One morning, as Rönne was sitting at work making sails, he observed a " shadow " flying past his feet, and, according to his account, into the fore-saloon. The cook came roaring: " There's a rat in the fore-saloon !" Then there was a lively scene; the door was shut, and all hands started hunting. All the cabins were emptied and rummaged, the piano, too; everything was turned upside down, but the rat had vanished into thin air.

About a fortnight later I noticed a corpse-like smell in Hassel's cabin, which was empty. On closer sniffing and examination it turned out to be the dead rat, a big black one, unfortunately a male rat. The poor brute, that had starved to death, had tried to keep itself alive by devouring a couple of novels that lay in a locked drawer. How the rat got into that drawer beats me.

On cleaning out the provision hold nests were found with several rats in them : six were killed, but at least as many escaped, so now no doubt we have a whole colony. A reward was promised of ten cigars for each rat; traps were tried again, but all this did very little good. When we were in Buenos Aires for the second time we got a cat on board; it certainly kept the rats down, but it was shot on the Barrier. At Hobart we provided a few traps, which caught a good many; but we shall hardly get rid of them altogether until we have landed most of the provisions, and smoked them out.

We have also had a lot of moth; at present they have done nothing beyond eating a couple of holes in my best trousers.

During the whole of this cruise we had a fishing-line hanging out, but it hung for a whole month without there being a sign of a fish, in spite of the most delicate little white. rag that was attached to the hook. One morning the keenest of our fishermen came up as usual and felt the line. Yes, by Jove! at last there was one, and a big one, too, as he could hardly haul in the line by himself. There was a shout for assistance. " Hi, you beggar! come and lend a hand ; there's a big fish !" Help came in a second, and they both hauled for all they were worth. "Ah! he's a fine, glistening fish; it'll be grand to get fresh fish for dinner!" At last the fish appeared over the rail; but, alas! it was seen to have no head. It was an ordinary stockfish, about three-quarters of a yard long, that some joker had hung on the line during the night. That we all had a hearty laugh goes without saying, the fishermen included, as they took it all in good part.

As a fishing-boat the *Fram* is on the whole not very successful. The only fish we caught, besides the above-mentioned stockfish, was a real live fish; but, unfortunately, it fell off the hook as it was being hauled in. According to the account of eye-witnesses, this fish was . . . six feet long and one broad.

Now we don't fish any more.

On August 19 the hydrographic observations were brought to an end, and a course was laid for Buenos Aires, where we anchored in the roads at midnight on September 1.

V.

AT BUENOS AIRES.

To arrive at Buenos Aires in the early part of 1911 was not an unmixed pleasure, especially when one had no money. The *Fram* Expedition was apparently not very popular at that time, and our cash balance amounted to about forty pesos (about £3 10s.), but that would not go very far; our supply of provisions had shrunk to almost nothing, and we had not enough to be able to leave the port. I had been told that a sum had been placed to the credit of the *Fram* for our stay in Buenos Aires, but I neither saw nor heard anything of it while we were there, and it was no doubt somewhat imaginary.

If we were to be at all able to go down and take off the shore party money must be found. We had come to the end of sail-cloth and ropes, we had too little food and a minimum of oil; all this would have to be provided. At the worst the oceanographical cruise could be cut out, and we could lie still at Buenos Aires; then, as our comrades could not very well be left to perish on the ice, enough would have to be sent us from Norway to enable us to go down there; but that would finish the whole expedition, as in such a case the *Fram* had orders to go back to Norway.

As usual, however, the *Fram's* luck helped her again. A few days before we left Norway our distinguished compatriot in Buenos Aires, Don Pedro Christophersen, had cabled that he would supply us with what provisions we might require, if, after leaving Madeira, we would call at Buenos Aires. Of course, he did not know at that time that the voyage would be extended to include the South Pole, and that the *Fram* on arrival at Buenos Aires would be almost empty instead of having a full cargo, but that did not prevent his helping us. I immediately called on him and his brother, the

Norwegian Minister; fortunately, they were both very enthusiastic about our Chief's change of plan.

When, on a subsequent occasion, I expressed my astonishment at not hearing from home, I was told that the funds of the Expedition were exhausted, and Mr. Christophersen promised me, on hearing what straits we were in, to pay all our expenses in Buenos Aires, and to supply us with provisions and fuel. That brought us out of our difficulties at a bound, and we had no more need to take thought for the morrow.

Everyone on board received a sum of money for his personal expenses from the Norwegian colony of the River Plate, and we were invited to their dinner on Independence Day, May 17.

Our second stay at Buenos Aires was very pleasant; everyone was amiability itself, and festivities were even got up for us. We took on board provisions that had been sent out from Norway by Mr. Christophersen's orders, about 50,000 litres (11,000 gallons) of petroleum, ship's stores, and so on; enough for a year. But this was not all. Just before we sailed Mr. Christophersen said he would send a relief expedition, if the *Fram* did not return to Australia by a certain date; but, as everyone knows, this was happily unnecessary.

During the three weeks we were lying at the quay in Buenos Aires we were occupied in getting everything on board, and making the vessel ready for sea. We had finished this by the afternoon of Wednesday,

October 4, and next morning the *Fram* was ready to continue her second circumnavigation of the globe.

In Buenos Aires we lay at the same quay as the *Deutschland*, the German Antarctic Expedition's ship.

A. Kutschin and the second engineer, J. Nödtvedt, went home, and seaman J. Andersen was discharged.

VI.

FROM BUENOS AIRES TO THE ROSS BARRIER.

On the trip from Buenos Aires to the Barrier the watches were divided as follows: From eight to two: T. Nilsen, L. Hansen, H. Halvorsen, and A. Olsen. From two to eight: H. Gjertsen, A. Beck, M. Rönne, and F. Steller. In the engine-room: K. Sundbeck and H. Kristensen. Lastly, K. Olsen, cook. In all eleven men.

It is said that "well begun is half done," and it almost seems as if a bad beginning were likely to have a similar continuation. When we left the northern basin on the morning of October 5, there was a head wind, and it was not till twenty-four hours later that we could drop the pilot at the Recalada lightship. After a time it fell calm, and we made small progress down the River La Plata, until, on the night of the 6th, we were clear of the land, and the lights disappeared on the horizon.

Properly speaking, we ought to have been in the west wind belt as soon as we came out, and the drift of the clouds and movement of the barograph were examined at least twenty-four times a day, but it still remained calm.   At last, after the lapse of several days, we had a little fresh south-westerly wind with hail showers, and then, of course, I thought we had made a beginning; but unfortunately it only lasted a night, so that our joy was short-lived.

We took with us from Buenos Aires fifteen live sheep and fifteen live little pigs, for which two houses were built on the after-deck; as, however, one of the pigs was found dead on the morning after the south-westerly breeze just mentioned, I assumed that this was on account of the cold, and another house was at once built for them between decks (in the work-room), where it was very warm.   They were down here the whole time; but as their house was cleaned out twice a day and dry straw put on the floor, they did not cause us much inconvenience;   besides which, their house was raised more than half a foot above the deck itself, so that the space below could always be kept clean.   The pigs thrived so well down here that we could almost see them growing;   on arrival at the Barrier we had no fewer than nine alive.

The sheep had a weather-tight house with a tarpaulin over the roof, and they grew fatter and fatter; we had every opportunity of noticing this, as we killed one of them regularly every Saturday until we came into the pack-ice and got seal-meat. We had four sheep left on reaching the Barrier.

We did wretchedly in October—calms and east winds, nothing but east winds; as regards distance it was the worst month we had had since leaving Norway, notwithstanding that the *Fram* had been in dry dock, had a clean bottom and a light cargo. When close-hauled with any head sea, we scarcely move; a stiff fair wind is what is wanted if we are to get on. Somebody said we got on so badly because we had thirteen pigs on board; another said it was because we caught so many birds, and I had caught no less than fourteen albatrosses and four Cape pigeons. Altogether there is quite enough of what I will call superstition at sea. One particular bird brings fine weather, another storms; it is very important to notice which way the whale swims or the dolphin leaps; the success of seal-hunting depends on whether the first seal is seen ahead or astern, and so on. Enough of that.

October went out and November came in with a fresh breeze from the south-south-west, so that we did nine and a half knots. This promised well for November, but the promise was scarcely fulfilled. We had northerly wind or southerly wind continually, generally a little to the east of north or south, and I believe I am not saying too much when I state that in the " west wind belt " with an *easterly* course we lay close-hauled on one tack or the other for about two-thirds of the way. For only three days out of three months did we have a real west wind, a wind which, with south-westerly and north-westerly winds, I had reckoned on having for 75 per cent. of the trip from Buenos Aires to about the longitude of Tasmania.

In my enthusiasm over the west wind in question, I went so far as to write in my diary at 2 a.m. on November 11 : "'There is a gale from the west, and we are making nine knots with foresail and topsail. The sea is pretty high and breaking on both sides of the vessel, so that everything about us is a mass of spray. In spite of this, not a drop of water comes on deck, and it is so dry that the watch are going about in clogs. For my part I am wearing felt slippers, which will not stand wet. Sea-boots and oilskins hang ready in the chart-house, in case it should rain. On a watch like to-night, when the moon is kind enough to shine, everyone on deck is in the best of humours, whistling, chattering, and singing. Somebody comes up with the remark that ' She took that sea finely,' or ' Now she's flying properly.' 'Fine' is almost too feeble an expression ; one ought to say 'lightly and elegantly' when speaking of the *Fram*. . . . What more can one wish ?" etc.

But whatever time Adam may have spent in Paradise, we were not there more than three days, and then the same wretched state of things began again. What I wrote when there was a head wind or calm, I should be

Woe to him who then came and said it was fine weather.

It was lucky for us that the *Fram* sails so much more easily now than in 1910, otherwise we should have taken six months to reach the Barrier.   When we had wind, we used it to the utmost; but we did not do this without the loss of one or two things; the new jib-sheet broke a couple of times, and one night we carried away the outer bobstay of the jib-boom.   The foresail and topsail were neither made fast nor reefed during the whole trip.

The last time the jib-sheet broke there was a strong breeze from the south-west with a heavy sea; all sail was set with the exception of the spanker, as the ship would not steer with that.   There was an extra preventer on the double jib-sheet, but in spite of that the sheets broke and the jib was split with a fearful crack. Within a minute the mainsail and gaff-topsail were hauled down, so that the ship might fall off, and the jib hauled down.   This was instantly unbent and a new one bent. · The man at the helm, of course, got the blame for this, and the first thing he said to me was: "I couldn't help it, she was twisting on the top of a wave."   We were then making ten knots, and more than that we shall not do.

The *Fram* rolled well that day.   A little earlier in the afternoon, at two o'clock, when the watch had gone below to dinner and were just eating the sweet, which

on that occasion consisted of preserved pears, we felt
that there was an unusually big lurch coming. Although,
of course, we had fiddles on the table, the plates, with
meat, potatoes, etc., jumped over the fiddles, which they
didn't care a button for, into Beck's cabin. I caught
one of the pears in its flight, but the plate with the rest
of them went on its way. Of course there was a great
shout of laughter, which stopped dead as we heard a
violent noise on deck, over our heads; I guessed at once
it was an empty water-tank that had broken loose, and
with my mouth full of pear I yelled " Tank !" and flew
on deck with the whole watch below at my heels. A sea
had come in over the after-deck, and had lifted the tank
up from its lashings. All hands threw themselves upon
the tank, and held on to it till the water had poured off
the deck, when it was again fixed in its place. When
this was done, my watch went below again and lit their
pipes as if nothing had happened.

On November 13 we passed the northernmost of the
Prince Edward Islands, and on the 18th close to Penguin
Island, the most south-westerly of the Crozets. In the
neighbourhood of the latter we saw a great quantity of
birds, a number of seals and penguins, and even a little
iceberg. I went close to the land to check the
chronometers, which an observation and bearings of the
islands showed to be correct.

Our course was then laid for Kerguelen Island, but
we went too far north to see it, as for two weeks the

wind was south-easterly and southerly, and the leeway we made when sailing close-hauled took us every day a little to the north of east. When we were in the same waters in 1910, there was gale after gale; then we did not put in at Kerguelen on account of the *force* of the wind; this time we could not approach the island because of the wind's *direction*. In no respect can the second trip be compared with the first; I should never have dreamed that there could be so much difference in the " Roaring Forties " in two different years at the same season. In the " Foggy Fifties " the weather was calm and fine, and we had no fog until lat. 58° S.

As regards the distance sailed, November, 1911, is the best month the *Fram* has had.

In December, which began with a speed of one and a half knots, calm, swell against us, and the engine at full speed, we had a fair wind for three days, all the rest calms and head winds; the first part of the month from the north-east and east, so that we came much too far south; even in long. 150 E. we were in lat. 60° S. In Christmas week we had calms and light winds from the south-east, so that we managed to steal eastward to long. 170° E. and lat. 65° S., where, on the edge of the pack-ice, we had a stiff breeze from the north-north-east, that is, straight on to the ice.

Between Buenos Aires and the pack-ice we caught, as I have said, a good many birds, mostly albatrosses, and about thirty skins were prepared by L. Hansen. The

largest albatross we got measured twelve feet between the
tips of its wings, and the smallest bird was of a land
species, not much bigger than a humming-bird.

Talking of albatrosses, it is both amusing and interesting to watch their elegant flight in a high wind. Without a movement of the wings they sail, now with, now
against, the wind ; at one instant they touch the surface
of the water with the points of their wings, at the next
they go straight into the air like an arrow. An
interesting and instructive study for an aviator.

In a wind, when there is generally a number of them
hovering about the vessel, they will dash down after
anything that is thrown overboard ; but of course it is
useless to try to catch them when the ship has so much
way. This must be done the next day, when the wind
is lighter.

The birds are caught with an iron triangle, which
ought to be enclosed in wood, so that it will float on the
water. At the apex, which is very acute, the iron is
filed as sharp as a knife, and pork is hung on each of the
sides. When this is thrown in the wake of the ship,
the bird settles on the water to feed. The upper part of
its beak is hooked like that of a bird of prey, and as the
albatross opens its beak and bites at the pork, you give
a jerk, so that the triangle catches the upper part of the
beak by two small notches, and the bird is left hanging.
If the line should break, the whole thing simply falls off
and the bird is unharmed. In hauling in, therefore, you

have to be very careful to hold the line quite tight, even if the bird flies towards you, otherwise it will easily fall off. A bird may be pulled half-way in several times, and will immediately take the bait again.

On the night of December 11 an unusually beautiful aurora was seen; it lasted over an hour, and moved in a direction from west to east.

On the 14th all the white paint was washed; the temperature was 43° F., and we were in shirt-sleeves.

For a whole week before Christmas the cook was busy baking Christmas cakes. I am bound to say he is industrious; and the day before Christmas Eve one of the *little* pigs, named Tulla, was killed. The swineherd, A. Olsen, whose special favourite this pig was, had to keep away during the operation, that we might not witness his emotion.

Early on the morning of Christmas Eve we saw the three first icebergs; there was an absolute calm all day, with misty air.

To keep Christmas the engine was stopped at 5 p.m., and then all hands came to dinner. Unfortunately we had no gramophone to sing to us, as in 1910; as a substitute the " orchestra " played " Glade Jul, hellige Jul," when all were seated. The orchestra was composed of Beck on the violin, Sundbeck on the mandolin, and the undersigned on the flute. I puffed out my cheeks as much as I could, and that is not saying a little, so that the others might see how proficient I was.

I hardly think it was much of a musical treat; but the public was neither critical nor ceremonious, and the prevalent costume was jerseys. The dinner consisted of soup, roast pork, with fresh potatoes and whortleberries, ten-years-old aquavit and Norwegian bock beer, followed by wine-jelly and "kransekake," with—champagne. The toasts of their Majesties the King and Queen, Don Pedro Christophersen, Captain Amundsen, and the *Fram* were drunk.

I had decorated the saloon in a small way with artificial flowers, embroideries, and flags, to give a little colour. Dinner was followed by cigars and the distribution of Christmas presents. L. Hansen played the accordion, and Lieutenant Gjertsen and Rönne danced "folk dances"; the latter was, as usual, so amusing that he kept us in fits of laughter.

At ten o'clock it was all over, the engine was started again, one watch went to bed and the other on deck; Olsen cleaned out the pigsty, as usual at this time of night. That finished Christmas for this year.

As has been said before, Sir James Ross was down here in the 1840's. Two years in succession he sailed from the Pacific into Ross Sea with two ships that had no auxiliary steam-power. I assumed, therefore, that if he could get through so easily, there must be some place between South Victoria Land and the Barrier (or land) on the other side, where there was little or no ice. Following this assumption, I intended to go down to the western pack-ice (that lying off South Victoria Land) and steer along it till we were in Ross Sea, or, at all events, until we found a place where we could easily get through. It is quite possible that Ross was very lucky in the time at which he encountered the ice, and that he only sailed in clear weather. We had no time to spare, however, but had to make use of whatever wind there was, even if we could not see very far.

As early as December 28, at 5 p.m., in lat. 65° S. and long. 171·5° E., it was reported that we were off the pack. I was a good deal surprised, as recent expeditions had not met the pack until 66·5° S., or about one hundred nautical miles farther south, nor had there been any sign of our being so near the ice. The wind for the last few days had been south-easterly, but for the moment it was calm; we therefore held on to the east along the edge of the pack, with the ice to starboard. About midnight the wind freshened from the north, and we lay close-hauled along the edge of the ice till midday on the 29th, when the direction of the ice became more southerly. The northerly wind, which gradually increased to a stiff breeze, was good enough for getting us on, but it must inevitably bring fog and snow in its train. These came, sure enough, as thick as a wall, and for a couple of days we sailed perfectly blindly.

Outside the pack-ice proper lie long streams of floes and loose scattered lumps, which become more frequent

as one nears the pack.   For two days we sailed simply
by the lumps of ice; the more of them we saw, the
more easterly was our course, until they began to
decrease, when we steered more to the south.   In
this way we went in forty-eight hours from lat. 65° S.
and long. 174° E. to lat. 69° S. and long. 178° E.,
a distance of about two hundred and fifty nautical
miles, without entering the pack.   Once we very
nearly went into the trap, but fortunately got out
again.   The wind was so fresh that we did as much as
eight and a half knots; when sailing at such a rate
through a loose stream of ice, we sometimes ran upon a
floe, which went under the ship's bottom, and came up
alongside the other way up.

During the afternoon of the 31st the streams of ice
became closer and closer, and then I made the mistake
of continuing to sail to the eastward; instead of this,
I ought to have stood off, and steered due south or
to the west of south, with this ice on our *port* side.
The farther we advanced, the more certain I was that
we had come into the eastern pack-ice.   It must be
remembered, however, that owing to fog and thick
snow we had seen nothing for over two days.   Observations there were none, of course; our speed had varied
between two and eight and a half knots, and we had
steered all manner of courses.   That our dead reckoning
was not very correct in such circumstances goes without saying, and an observation on January 2 showed

us that we were somewhat farther to the east than we
had reckoned. On the evening of December 31 the fog
lifted for a while, and we saw nothing but ice all round.
Our course was then set due south. We had come
right down in lat. 69·5° S., and I hoped soon to be
clear altogether; in 1910 we got out of the ice in 70° S.,
and were then in the same longitude as now.

Now, indeed, our progress began to be slow, and the
old year went out in a far from pleasant fashion. The
fog was so thick that I may safely say we did not see
more than fifty yards from the ship, whereas we ought
to have had the midnight sun; ice and snow-sludge were
so thick that at times we lay still. The wind had,
unfortunately, fallen off, but we still had a little
breeze from the north, so that both sails and engine
could be used. We went simply at haphazard; now
and then we were lucky enough to come into great
open channels and even lakes, but then the ice closed
again absolutely tight. It could hardly be called real ice,
however, but was rather a snow-sludge, about two feet
thick, and as tough as dough; it looked as if it had all
just been broken off a single thick mass. The floes lay
close together, and we could see how one floe fitted
into the other. The ice remained more or less close
until we were right down in lat. 73° S. and long. 179°
W.; the last part of it was old drift-ice.

From here to the Bay of Whales we saw a few
scattered streams of floes and some icebergs.

A few seals were shot in the ice, so that we had fresh meat enough, and could save the sheep and pigs until the shore party came on board. I was sure they would appreciate fresh roast pork.

The chart of Ross Sea has been drawn chiefly as a guide to future expeditions. It may be taken as certain that the best place to go through the ice is between long. 176° E. and 180°, and that the best time is about the beginning of February.

Take, for instance, our southward route in 1911-1912: as has been said, the ice was met with as early as in 65° S., and we were not clear of it till about 73° S.; between 68° S. and 69° S. the line is interrupted, and it was there that I ought to have steered to the south.

Now follow the course from the Bay of Whales in 1912. Only in about 75° S. was ice seen (almost as in 1911), and we followed it. After that time we saw absolutely no more ice, as the chart shows; therefore in the course of about a month and a half all the ice that we met when going south had drifted out.

The stippled line shows how I *assume* the ice to have lain; the heavy broken line shows what our course ought to have been.

The midnight sun was not seen till the night of January 7, 1912, to the south of lat. 77° S.; it was already 9·5° above the horizon.

On the night of January 8 we arrived off the Barrier in extremely bitter weather. South-westerly

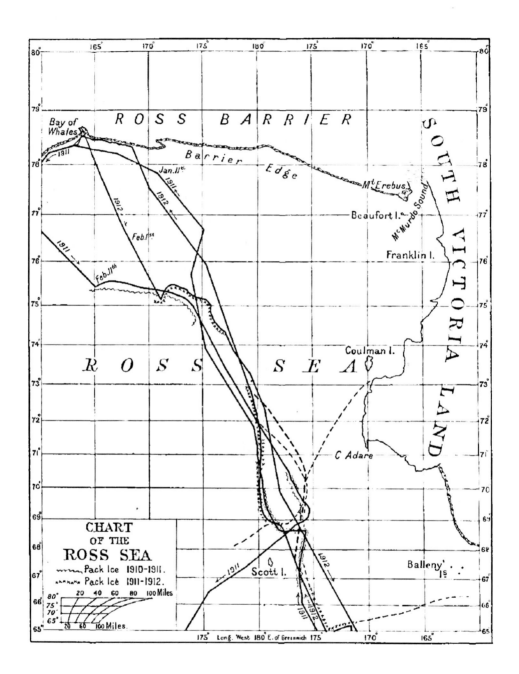

CHART
OF THE
ROSS SEA

Pack Ice 1910-1911.
Pack Ice 1911-1912.

and southerly winds had held for a few days, with fair weather; but that night there was thick snow, and the wind gradually fell calm, after which a fresh breeze sprang up from the south-east, with biting snow, and at the same time a lot of drift-ice. The engine went very slowly, and the ship kept head to wind. About midnight the weather cleared a little, and a dark line, which proved to be the Barrier, came in sight. The engine went ahead at full speed, and the sails were set, so that we might get under the lee of the perpendicular wall. By degrees the ice-blink above the Barrier became lighter and lighter, and before very long we were so close under it that we only just had room to go about. The Barrier here runs east and west, and with a south-easterly wind we went along it to the east. The watch that had gone below at eight o'clock, when we were still in open sea, came up again at two to find us close to the long-desired wall of ice.

Some hours passed in the same way, but then, of course, the wind became easterly—dead ahead—so that we had tack after tack till 6 p.m. the same day, when we were at the western point of the Bay of Whales.

The ice lay right out to West Cape, and we sailed across the mouth of the bay and up under the lee of the eastern Barrier, in order, if possible, to find slack ice or open water; but no, the fast ice came just as far on that side. It turned out that we could not get farther south than 78° 30'—that is, eleven nautical miles farther north than the previous year, and no less than fifteen nautical miles from Framheim, taking into consideration the turn in the bay.

We were thus back at the same place we had left on February 14, 1911, and had since been round the world. The distance covered on this voyage of circumnavigation was 25,000 nautical miles, of which 8,000 belong to the oceanographical cruise in the South Atlantic.

We did not lie under the lee of the eastern Barrier for more than four hours; the wind, which had so often been against us, was true to its principles to the last. Of course it went to the north and blew right up the bay; the drift-ice from Ross Sea came in, and at midnight (January 9-10) we stood out again.

I had thought of sending a man up to Framheim to report that we had arrived, but the state of the weather did not allow it. Besides, I had only one pair of private ski on board and should therefore only have been able to send one man. It would have been better if several had gone together.

During the forenoon of the 10th it gradually cleared, the wind fell light and we stood inshore again. As at the same time the barometer was rising steadily, Lieutenant Gjertsen went ashore on ski about one o'clock.

Later in the afternoon a dog came running out across the sea-ice, and I thought it had come down on Lieutenant Gjertsen's track; but I was afterwards told

it was one of the half-wild dogs that ran about on the
ice and did not show themselves up at the hut.

Meanwhile the wind freshened again ; we had to put
out for another twenty-four hours and lay first one way
and then the other with shortened sail ; then there was
fine weather again and we came in.   At 4 p.m. on the
11th Lieutenant Gjertsen returned with Lieutenant
Prestrud, Johansen and Stubberud.   Of course we were
very glad to see one another again and all sorts of
questions were asked on both sides.   The Chief and the
southern party were not yet back.   They stayed on
board till the 12th, got their letters and a big pile of
newspapers and went ashore again ; we followed them
with the glasses as far as possible, so as to take them on
board again if they could not get across the cracks in
the ice.

During the days that followed we lay moored to the
ice or went out, according to the weather.

At 7 p.m. on the 16th we were somewhat surprised
to see a vessel bearing down.   For my part, I guessed
her to be the *Aurora*, Dr. Mawson's ship.   She came
very slowly, but at last what should we see but the
Japanese flag !   I had no idea that expedition was out
again.   The ship came right in, went past us twice and
moored alongside the loose ice.   Immediately afterwards ten men armed with picks and shovels went up
the Barrier, while the rest rushed wildly about after
penguins, and their shots were heard all night.   Next

morning the commander of the *Kainan Maru*, whose name was Homura, came on board. The same day a tent was set up on the edge of the Barrier, and cases, sledges, and so on, were put out on the ice. *Kainan Maru* means, I have been told, "the ship that opens the South."

Prestrud and I went on board her later in the day, to see what she was like, but we met neither the leader of the expedition nor the captain of the ship. Prestrud had the cinematograph apparatus with him, and a lot of photographs were also taken.

The leader of the Japanese expedition has written somewhere or other that the reason of Shackleton's losing all his ponies was that the ponies were not kept in tents at night, but had to lie outside. He thought the ponies ought to be in the tents and the men outside. From this one would think they were great lovers of animals, but I must confess that was not the impression I received. They had put penguins into little boxes to take them alive to Japan! Round about the deck lay dead and half-dead skua gulls in heaps. On the ice close to the vessel was a seal ripped open, with part of its entrails on the ice; but the seal was still alive. Neither Prestrud nor I had any sort of weapon that we could kill the seal with, so we asked the Japanese to do it, but they only grinned and laughed. A little way off two of them were coming across the ice with a seal in front of them; they drove it on with two long poles, with which they pricked it when it would not go.   If it fell into a crack, they dug it up again as you would see men quarrying stone at home ; it had not enough life in it to be able to escape its tormentors.   All this was accompanied by laughter and jokes.   On arrival at the ship the animal was nearly dead, and it was left there till it expired.

On the 19th we had a fresh south-westerly wind and a lot of ice went out.   The Japanese were occupied most of the night in going round among the floes and picking up men, dogs, cases, and so on, as they had put a good deal on to the ice in the course of the day.   As the ice came out, so the *Fram* went in, right up to lat. 78° 35′ S., while the *Kainan Maru* drifted farther and farther out, till at last she disappeared.   Nor did we see the vessel again, but a couple of men with a tent stayed on the Barrier as long as we were in the bay.

On the night of the 24th there was a stiff breeze from the west, and we drifted so far out in the thick snow that it was only on the afternoon of the 27th that we could make our way in again through a mass of ice.   In the course of these two days so much ice had broken up that we came right in to lat. 78° 39′ S., or almost to Framheim, and that was very lucky.   As we stood in over the Bay of Whales, we caught sight of a big Norwegian naval ensign flying on the Barrier at Cape Man's Head, and I then knew that the southern party had arrived.   We went therefore as far south as possible and blew our powerful siren; nor was it very long before eight men came tearing down. There was great enthusiasm. The first man on board was the Chief; I was so certain he had reached the goal that I never asked him. Not till an hour later, when we had discussed all kinds of other things, did I enquire: " Well, of course you have been at the South Pole ?"

We lay there for a couple of days; on account of the short distance from Framheim, provisions, outfit, etc., were brought on board. If such great masses of ice had not drifted out in the last few days, it would probably have taken us a week or two to get the same quantity on board.

At 9.30 p.m. on January 30, 1912, in a thick fog, we took our moorings on board and waved a last farewell to the mighty Barrier.

VII.

From the Barrier to Buenos Aires, via Hobart.

THE first day after our departure from the Barrier everything we had taken on board was stowed away, so that one would not have thought our numbers were doubled, or that we had taken several hundred cases and a lot of outfit on board. The change was only noticed on deck, where thirty-nine powerful dogs made an uproar all day long, and in the fore-saloon, which

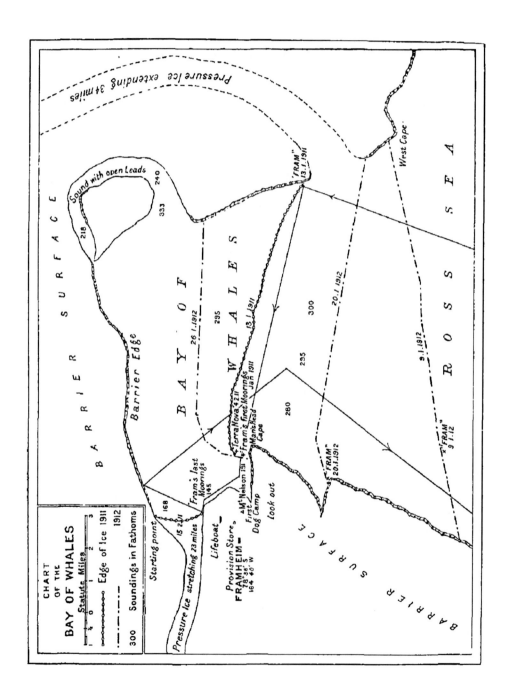

CHART
OF THE
BAY OF WHALES

Statute Miles

Edge of Ice 1911
1912
300   Soundings in Fathoms

BARRIER SURFACE

Pressure Ice extending 34 miles

Sound with open Leads
218   333   240

BAY   OF   WHALES

Barrier Edge

BARRIER

26.1.1912
295

"FRAM"
13.1.1911

Starting point
15 2 11
168

Fram's last
Moorings
145

Lifeboat

Provision Store
FRAMHEIM
78°38′S
164 40 W

Pressure Ice stretching 23 miles

△Mⁿ Nelson 151
Fram's First Moorings
Jan 1911
TerraNova 42 II

First
Dog Camp

Manhead
Cape

Look out

300
20.1.1912

"FRAM"
20.1.1912

295

280

"FRAM"
9.1.12

9.1.1912

West Cape

ROSS   SEA

BARRIER SURFACE

was entirely changed. This saloon, after being deserted for a year, was now full of men, and it was a pleasure to be there; especially as everyone had something to tell—the Chief of his trip, Prestrud of his, and Gjertsen and I of the *Fram's*.

However, there was not very much time for yarning. The Chief at once began writing cablegrams and lectures, which Prestrud and I translated into English, and the Chief then copied again on a typewriter. In addition to this I was occupied the whole time in drawing charts, so that on arrival at Hobart everything was ready; the time passed quickly, though the voyage was fearfully long.

As regards the pack-ice we were extremely lucky. It lay in exactly the same spot where we had met with it in 1911—that is, in about lat. 75° S. We went along the edge of it for a very short time, and then it was done with. To the north of 75° we saw nothing but a few small icebergs.

We made terribly slow progress to the northward, how slow may perhaps be understood if I quote my diary for February 27:

"This trip is slower than anything we have had before; now and then we manage an average rate of two knots an hour in a day's run. In the last four days we have covered a distance that before would have been too little for a single day. We have been at it now for nearly a month, and are still only between lat. 52° and 53° S. Gales from the north are almost the order of the day," etc. However, it is an ill wind that blows nobody any good, and the time was well employed with all we had to do.

After a five weeks' struggle we at last reached Hobart and anchored in the splendid harbour on March 7.

Our fresh provisions from Buenos Aires just lasted out ; the last of the fresh potatoes were finished a couple of days before our arrival, and the last pig was killed when we had been at Hobart two days.

The *Fram* remained here for thirteen days, which were chiefly spent in repairing the propeller and cleaning the engine ; in addition to this the topsail-yard, which was nearly broken in the middle, was spliced, as we had no opportunity of getting a new one.

The first week was quiet on board, as, owing to the circumstances, there was no communication with the shore ; but after that the ship was full of visitors, so that we were not very sorry to get away again.

Twenty-one of our dogs were presented to Dr. Mawson, the leader of the Australian expedition, and only those dogs that had been to the South Pole and a few puppies, eighteen in all, were left on board.

While we lay in Hobart, Dr. Mawson's ship, the *Aurora*, came in. I went aboard her one day, and have thus been on board the vessels of all the present Antarctic expeditions. On the *Terra Nova*, the British, on February 4, 1911, in the Bay of Whales ; on the

Deutschland, the German, in September and October, 1911, in Buenos Aires; on the *Kainan Maru*, the Japanese, on January 17, 1912, in the Bay of Whales; and finally on the *Aurora* in Hobart. Not forgetting the *Fram*, which, of course, I think best of all.

On March 20 the *Fram* weighed anchor and left Tasmania.

We made very poor progress to begin with, as we had calms for nearly three weeks, in spite of its being the month of March in the west wind belt of the South Pacific. On the morning of Easter Sunday, April 7, the wind first freshened from the north-west and blew day after day, a stiff breeze and a gale alternately, so that we went splendidly all the way to the Falkland Islands, in spite of the fact that the topsail was reefed for nearly five weeks on account of the fragile state of the yard. I believe most of us wanted to get on fast; the trip was now over for the present, and those who had families at home naturally wanted to be with them as soon as they could; perhaps that was why we went so well.

On April 1 Mrs. Snuppesen gave birth to eight pups; four of these were killed, while the rest, two of each sex, were allowed to live.

On Maundy Thursday, April 4, we were in long. 180° and changed the date, so that we had two Maundy Thursdays in one week; this gave us a good many holidays running, and I cannot say the effect is altogether cheerful; it was a good thing when Easter Tuesday came round as an ordinary week-day.

On May 6 we passed Cape Horn in very fair weather; it is true we had a snow-squall of hurricane violence, but it did not last much more than half an hour. For a few days the temperature was a little below freezing-point, but it rose rapidly as soon as we were out in the Atlantic.

From Hobart to Cape Horn we saw no ice.

After passing the Falkland Islands we had a head wind, so that the last part of the trip was nothing to boast of.

On the night of May 21 we passed Montevideo, where the Chief had arrived a few hours before. From here up the River La Plata we went so slowly on account of head wind that we did not anchor in the roads of Buenos Aires till the afternoon of the 23rd, almost exactly at the same time as the Chief landed at Buenos Aires. When I went ashore next morning and met Mr. P. Christophersen, he was in great good-humour. "This is just like a fairy tale," he said; and it could not be denied that it was an amusing coincidence. The Chief, of course, was equally pleased.

On the 25th, the Argentine National Fête, the *Fram* was moored at the same quay that we had left on October 5, 1911. At our departure there were exactly seven people on board to say good-bye, but, as far as I could see, there were more than this when we arrived;

and I was able to make out, from newspapers and other sources, that in the course of a couple of months the third *Fram* Expedition had grown considerably in popularity.

In conclusion I will give one or two data. Since the *Fram* left Christiania on June 7, 1910, we have been two and a half times round the globe; the distance covered is about 54,400 nautical miles; the lowest reading of the barometer during this time was 27·56 inches (700 millimetres) in March, 1911, in the South Pacific, and the highest 30·82 inches (783 millimetres) in October, 1911, in the South Atlantic.

On June 7, 1912, the second anniversary of our leaving Christiania, all the members of the Expedition, except the Chief and myself, left for Norway, and the first half of the Expedition was thus brought to a fortunate conclusion.

APPENDIX I

THE "FRAM"

By Commodore Christian Blom

Colin Archer says in his description of the *Fram*, in Fridtjof Nansen's account of the Norwegian Arctic Expedition, 1893-1896, that the successful result of an expedition such as that planned and carried out by Dr. Nansen in the years 1893-1896 must depend on the care with which all possible contingencies are foreseen, and precautions taken to meet them, and the choice of every detail of the equipment with special regard to the use to which it will be put. To no part of the equipment, he says, could this apply with greater force than to the ship which was to carry Dr. Nansen and his companions on their adventurous voyage.

Colin Archer then built the ship—*Fram* was her name—and she showed—first on Fridtjof Nansen's famous voyage, and afterwards on Sverdrup's long wintering expedition in Ellesmere Land, that she answered her purpose completely, nay, she greatly exceeded the boldest expectations.

Then Roald Amundsen decided to set out on a voyage not less adventurous than the two former, and he looked about for a suitable ship. It was natural that he should think of the *Fram*, but she was old—about sixteen years—and had been exposed to many a hard buffet; it was said that she was a good deal damaged by decay.

Roald Amundsen, however, did not allow himself to be discouraged by these misgivings, but wished to see for himself what

356

kind of a craft the *Fram* was after her two commissions. He therefore came down to Horten with Colin Archer on June 1, 1908, and made a thorough examination of the vessel. He then, in the spring of 1909, requested the Naval Dockyard at Horten to repair the ship and carry out the alterations he considered necessary for his enterprise.

Before giving an account of the repairs and alterations to the vessel in 1909-1910, we shall briefly recapitulate, with the author's permission, a part of the description of the *Fram* in Fridtjof Nansen's work, especially as regards the constructive peculiarities of the vessel.

The problem which it was sought to solve in the construction of the *Fram* was that of providing a ship which could survive the crushing embrace of the Arctic drift-ice. To fit her for this was the object before which all other considerations had to give way.

But apart from the question of mere strength of construction, there were problems of design and model which, it was thought, would play an important part in the attainment of the chief object. It is sometimes prudent in an encounter to avoid the full force of a blow instead of resisting it, even if it could be met without damage ; and there was reason to think that by a judicious choice of model something might be done to break the force of the ice-pressure, and thus lessen its danger. Examples of this had been seen in small Norwegian vessels that had been caught in the ice near Spitzbergen and Novaya Zemlya. It often happens that they are lifted right out of the water by the pressure of the ice without sustaining serious damage ; and these vessels are not particularly strong, but have, like most small sailing-ships, a considerable dead rising and sloping sides. The ice encounters these sloping sides and presses in under the bilge on both sides, until the ice-edges meet under the keel, and the ship is raised up into the bed that is formed by the ice itself.

In order to turn this principle to account, it was decided to depart entirely from the usual flat-bottomed frame-section, and to adopt a form that would offer no vulnerable point on the ship's side, but would cause the increasing horizontal pressure of the ice to effect a raising of the ship, as described above. In the construction of the *Fram* it was sought to solve this problem by avoiding plane or concave surfaces, thus giving the vessel as far as possible round and full lines. Besides increasing the power of resistance to external pressure, this form has the advantage of making it easy for the ice to glide along the bottom in any direction.

The *Fram* was a three-masted fore-and-aft schooner with an auxiliary engine of 200 indicated horse-power, which was calculated to give her a speed of 6 knots, when moderately loaded, with a coal consumption of 2·8 tons a day.

The vessel was designed to be only large enough to carry the necessary coal-supply, provisions, and other equipment for a period of five years, and to give room for the crew.

Her principal dimensions are:

Length of keel	103·3 English feet.
Length of waterline	119 ,,
Length over all	128 ,,
Beam on waterline	34 ,,
Greatest beam	36 ,,
Depth	17·2 ,,

Her displacement, with a draught of 15·6 feet, is 800 tons. The measurements are taken to the outside of the planks, but do not include the ice-skin. By Custom-house measurement she was found to be 402 gross tons register, and 307 tons net.

The ship, with engines and boilers, was calculated to weigh about 420 tons. With the draught above mentioned, which gives a freeboard of 3 feet, there would thus be 380 tons available for cargo. This weight was actually exceeded by 100 tons, which left a freeboard of only 20 inches when the ship sailed on her first voyage. This additional immersion could only have awkward effects when the ship came into the ice, as its effect would then be to retard the lifting by the ice, on which the safety of the ship was believed to depend in a great measure. Not only was there a greater weight to lift, but there was a considerably greater danger of the walls of ice, that would pile themselves against the ship's sides, falling over the bulwarks and covering the deck before the ice began to raise her. The load would, however, be lightened by the time the ship was frozen fast. Events showed that she was readily lifted when the ice-pressure set in, and that the danger of injury from falling blocks of ice was less than had been expected. The *Fram's* keel is of American elm in two lengths, 14 inches square; the room and space is 2 feet. The frame-timbers are almost all of oak obtained from the Naval Dockyard at Horten, where they had lain for many years, thus being perfectly seasoned. The timbers were all grown to shape. The frames consist of two tiers of timbers everywhere, each timber measuring 10 to 11 inches fore and aft; the two tiers of timbers are fitted together and bolted, so that they form a solid and compact whole. The joints of the frame-timbers are covered with iron plates. The lining consists of pitch-pine in good lengths and of varying thickness from 4 to 6 inches. The keelson is also of pitch-pine, in two layers, one above the other; each layer 15 inches square from the stem to the engine-room. Under the boiler and engine there was only room for one keelson. There are two decks. The beams of the main-deck are of American or German oak, those of the lower deck and half-deck of pitch-pine and Norwegian fir. All the deck planks are of Norwegian fir, 4 inches in the main-deck and 3 inches elsewhere. The beams are fastened to the ship's sides by knees of Norwegian spruce, of which about 450 were used. Wooden knees were, as a rule, preferred to iron ones, as they are more elastic. A good many iron knees were used, however, where wood was less suitable. In the boiler and engine room the beams of the lower deck had to be raised about 3 feet to give sufficient height for the engines. The upper deck was similarly raised from the stern-post to the mainmast, forming a half-deck, under which the cabins were placed. On this half-deck, immediately forward of the funnel, a deck-house was placed, arranged as a chart-house, from which two companions (one on each side) led down to the cabins. Besides the ice-skin, there is a double layer of outside planking of oak. The two first strakes (garboard strakes), however, are single, 7 inches thick, and are bolted both to the keel and to the frame-timbers. The first (inner) layer of planks is 3 inches thick, and is only fastened with nails; outside this comes a layer of 4-inch planks, fastened with oak trenails and through bolts, as usual. The two top strakes are single again, and 6 inches thick. The ice-skin is of greenheart, and covers the whole ship's side from the keel to 18 inches from the sheer strake. It is only fastened with nails and jagged bolts. Each layer of planks was caulked and pitched before the next one was laid. Thus only about 3 or 4 inches of the keel projects below the planking, and this part of the keel is rounded off so as not to hinder the ice from passing under the ship's bottom. The intervals between the timbers were filled with a mixture of coal-tar, pitch, and sawdust, heated together and put in warm. The ship's side thus forms a compact mass varying in thickness from 28 to 32 inches. As a consequence of all the intervals between the timbers being filled up, there is no room for bilge-water under the lining. A loose bottom was therefore laid a few inches above the lining on each side of the keelson. In order to strengthen the ship's sides still more, and especially to prevent stretching, iron braces were placed on the lining, running from the clamps of the top deck down to well past the floor-timbers.

The stem consists of three massive oak beams, one inside the other, forming together 4 feet of solid oak fore and aft, with a breadth of 15 inches. The three external plankings as well as the lining are all rabbeted into the stem. The propeller-post is in two thicknesses, placed side by side, and measures 26 inches athwart-ship and 14 inches fore and aft. It will be seen from the plan that the overhang aft runs out into a point, and that there is thus no transom. To each side of the stern-post is fitted a stout stern-timber parallel to the longitudinal midship section, forming, so to speak, a double stern-post, and the space between them forms a well, which goes right up through the top deck. The rudder-post is placed in the middle of this well, and divides it into two parts, one for the propeller and one for the rudder. In this way it is possible to lift both the rudder and the screw out of the water. The rudder is so hung that the rudder-stock, which is cylindrical, turns on its own axis, to prevent the rudder being jammed if the well should be filled with ice. Aft of the rudder-well the space between the stern-timbers is filled with solid wood, and the whole is securely bolted together with bolts running athwart-ship. The frame-timbers join the stern-timbers in this part, and are fastened to them by means of knees. The stem and stern-post are connected to the keelson and to the keel by stout knees of timber, and both the ship's sides are bound together with solid breasthooks and crutches of wood or iron.

Although the *Fram* was not specially built for ramming, it was probable that now and then she would be obliged to force her way through the ice. Her bow and stern were therefore shod in the usual way. On the forward side of the stem a segment-shaped iron was bolted from the bobstay-bolt to some way under the keel. Outside this iron plates (3 × ¾ inches) were fastened over the stem, and for 6 feet on each side of it. These iron plates were placed close together, and thus formed a continuous armour-plating to a couple of feet from the keel. The sharp edge of the stern was protected in the same way, and the lower sides of the well were lined with thick iron plates. The rudder-post, which owing to its exposed position may be said to form the Achilles' heel of the ship, was strengthened with three heavy pieces of iron, one in the opening for the screw and one on each side of the two posts and the keel, and bolted together with bolts running athwart-ship.

Extraordinary precautions were taken for strengthening the ship's sides, which were particularly exposed to destruction by ice-pressure, and which, on account of their form, compose the weakest part of the hull. These precautions will best be seen in the sections (Figs. 3 and 4). Under each beam in both decks were placed diagonal stays of fir (6 × 10 inches), almost at right angles to the ship's sides, and securely fastened to the sides and to the beams by wooden knees. There are 68 of these stays distributed over the ship. In addition, there are under the beams three rows of vertical stanchions between decks, and one row in the lower hold from the keelson. These are connected to the keelson, to the beams, and to each other by iron bands. The whole of the ship's interior is thus filled with a network of braces and stays, arranged in such a way as to transfer and distribute the pressure from without, and give rigidity to the whole construction. In the engine and boiler room it was necessary to modify the arrangement of stays, so as to give room for the engines and boiler. All the iron, with the exception of the heaviest forgings, is galvanized.

When Otto Sverdrup was to use the *Fram* for his Polar expedition, he had a number of alterations carried out. The most important of these consisted in laying a new deck in the fore part of the ship, from the bulkhead forward of the engine-room to the stem, at a height of 7 feet 4 inches (to the upper side of the planks) above the old fore-deck. The space below the new deck was fitted as a fore-cabin, with a number of state-rooms leading out of it, a large workroom, etc. The old chart-house immediately forward of the funnel was removed, and in its place a large water-tank was fitted. The foremast was raised and stepped in the lower deck. A false keel, 10 inches deep and 12 inches broad, was placed below the keel. A number of minor alterations were also carried out.

After the *Fram* returned in 1902 from her second expedition under Captain Sverdrup, she was sent down to Horten to be laid up in the Naval Dockyard.

Not long after the vessel had arrived at the dockyard, Captain Sverdrup proposed various repairs and alterations. The repairs were carried out in part, but the alterations were postponed pending a decision as to the future employment of the vessel.

The *Fram* then lay idle in the naval harbour until 1905, when she was used by the marine artillery as a floating magazine. In the same year a good deal of the vessel's outfit (amongst other things all her sails and most of her rigging) was lost in a fire in one of the naval storehouses, where these things were stored.

In 1903 the ship's keel and stem (which are of elm and oak) were sheathed with zinc, while the outer sheathing (ice-skin), which is of greenheart, was kept coated with coal-tar and copper composition. In 1907 the whole outer sheathing below the water-line was covered with zinc; this was removed in 1910 when the ship was prepared for her third commission under Roald Amundsen.

In 1907 a thorough examination of the vessel was made, as it was suspected that the timber inside the thick cork insulation that surrounded the cabins had begun to decay.

On previous expeditions the cabins, provision hold aft, and workrooms forward of the fore-cabin, had been insulated with several thicknesses of wooden panelling. The interstices were filled with finely-divided cork, alternately with reindeer hair and thick felt and linoleum. In the course of years damp had penetrated into the non-conducting material, with the result that fungus and decay had spread in the surrounding woodwork. Thus it was seen during the examination in 1907 that the panelling and ceiling of the cabins in question were to a great extent rotten or attacked by fungus. In the same way the under side of the upper deck over these cabins was partly attacked by fungus, as were its beams, knees, and carlings. The lower deck, on the other hand, was better preserved. The filling-in timbers of spruce or fir between the frame-timbers in the cabins were damaged by fungus, while the frame-timbers themselves, which were of oak, were good. The outer lining outside the insulated parts was also somewhat damaged by fungus.

In the coal-bunkers over the main-deck the spruce knees were partly rotten, as were some of the beams, while the lining was here fairly good.

The masts and main-topmast were somewhat attacked by decay, while the rest of the spars were good.

During and after the examination all the panelling and insulation was removed, the parts attacked by fungus or decay were also removed, and the woodwork coated with carbolineum or tar. The masts and various stores and fittings were taken ashore at the same time.

It was found that the rest of the vessel—that is, the whole of the lower part of the hull right up to the cabin deck—was perfectly sound, and as good as new. Nor was there any sign of strain anywhere. It is difficult to imagine any better proof of the excellence of the vessel's construction; after two protracted expeditions to the most northern regions to which any ship has ever penetrated, where the vessel was often exposed to the severest ice-pressure, and in spite of her being (in 1907) fifteen years old, the examination showed that her actual hull, the part of the ship that has to resist the heavy strain of water and ice, was in just as good condition as when she was new.

The vessel was then left in this state until, as already mentioned, Roald Amundsen and her builder, Colin Archer, came down to the dockyard on June 1, 1908, and with the necessary assistance made an examination of her.

After some correspondence and verbal conferences between Roald Amundsen and the dockyard, the latter, on March 9, 1909, made a tender for the repairs and alterations to the *Fram*. The repairs consisted of making good the damage to the topsides referred to above.

The alterations were due in the first instance to the circumstance that the steam-engine and boiler (the latter had had its flues burnt out on Sverdrup's expedition) were to be replaced by an oil-motor; as a consequence of this the coal-bunkers would disappear, while, on the other hand, a large number of oil-tanks, capable of containing about 90 tons of oil, were to be put in.

It was also considered desirable to rig square-sails on the foremast in view of the great distances that were to be sailed on the proposed expedition.

The present arrangement of the vessel will best be followed by referring to the elevation and plan (Figs. 1 and 2).

In the extreme after-part of the lower hold is placed the 180 horse-power Diesel engine, surrounded by its auxiliary machinery and air-reservoirs.

In addition, some of the tanks containing the fuel itself are placed in the engine-room (marked O); the other tanks shown in the engine-room (marked 9) serve for storing lubricating oil. The existing engine-room was formerly the engine and boiler room, with coal-bunkers on both sides in the forward part. Forward of the watertight bulkhead of the engine-room we have, in the lower hold, the main store of oil-fuel, contained in tanks (marked O) of various sizes, on account of their having to be placed among the numerous diagonal stays. The tanks are filled and emptied by means of a pump and a petroleum hose through a manhole in the top, over which, again, are hatches in the deck above; no connecting pipes are fitted between the different tanks, for fear they might be damaged by frost or shock, thus involving a risk of losing oil. The main supply tank for fuel is placed over the forward side of the engine-room, where it is supported on strong steel girders; inside this tank, again, there are two smaller ones—settling tanks— from which the oil is conveyed in pipes to the engine-pumps. The main tank is of irregular shape—as will be seen from the drawing—since a square piece is taken out of its starboard after-corner for a way down into the engine-room. Besides this way down, an emergency way leads up from the engine-room, right aft, to one of the after-cabins. The oil hold is closed forward by a watertight bulkhead, which goes up to the main-deck. The hold forward of the oil-supply is unaltered, and serves for stowing cargo (mainly provisions), as does the hold above the oil-supply and below the main-deck.

On the main-deck right aft we now find a space arranged on each side of the well for the propeller and rudder; the lower part of this space is occupied by two tanks for lamp-oil, and above the tanks is a thin partition, which forms the floor of two small sail-rooms, with hatches to the deck above. Around the mizzenmast is the after-saloon, with eight cabins leading out of it. From the forward end of the after-saloon two passages lead to the large workroom amidships. These passages run past what were formerly coal-bunkers, but are now arranged as cabins, intended only to be used in milder climates, as they are not provided with any special insulation. From the port passage a door leads to the engine-room companion. In the after-part of the large workroom is the galley. This room is entirely lined with zinc, both on walls and ceiling (on account of the danger of fire), while the deck is covered with lead, on which tiles are laid in cement. Forward of the galley is the main hatch, and two large water-tanks are fitted here, one on each side. The remainder of the workroom affords space for carpenter's benches, turning-lathes, a forge, vices, etc. From the workroom two doors lead into the fore-saloon with its adjoining cabins. Amundsen's cabin is the farthest forward on the starboard side, and communicates with an instrument-room. From the fore-saloon a door leads out forward, past a sixth cabin.

In the space forward on the main-deck we have the fore-hatch, and by the side of this a room entirely lined with zinc plates, which serves for storing furs. Forward of the fur store is fitted a 15 horse-power one-cylinder Bolinder motor for working the capstan; the main features of its working will be seen in the drawing. There are two independent transmissions: by belt and by chain. The former is usually employed. The chain transmission was provided as a reserve, since it was feared that belt-driving might prove unserviceable in a cold climate. This fear, however, has hitherto been ungrounded.

Forward of the motor there is a large iron tank to supply water for cooling it. In the same space are chain-pipes to the locker below and the heel of the bowsprit. This space also serves as cable-tier.

On the upper deck we find aft the opening of the rudder-well and that of the propeller-well, covered with gratings. A piece was added to the lower part of the rudder to give more rudder area.

Forward of the propeller-well comes the reserve steering-gear, almost in the same position formerly occupied by the only steering-gear; the ordinary steering-gear is now moved to the bridge. The old engine-room companion aft is now removed, and forward of the after-wheel is only the skylight of the after-saloon. Up through the latter comes the exhaust-pipe of the main engine. Forward of and round the mizzenmast is the bridge, which is partly formed by the roofs of the large chart-house and labora-tory amidships and the two houses on each side. The chart-house occupies the place of the old boiler-room ventilator, and abuts on the fore-deck. (It is thus a little aft of the place occupied by the chart-house on Nansen's expedition.) It is strongly built of timbers standing upright, securely bolted to the deck. On both sides of this timber work there are panels, 2 inches thick on the outside and 1 inch on the inside, and the space between is filled with finely-divided cork. Floor and roof are insulated in a similar way, as is also the door; the windows are double, of thick plate-glass. Inside the chart-house, besides the usual fittings for its use as such, there is a companion-way to the engine-room, and a hatch over the manhole to the main supply tank for oil-fuel. The open-ing in the deck has a hatch, made like the rest of the deck (in two thicknesses, with cork insulation between); the intention is to cut off the engine-room altogether, and remove the entrance of this companion during the drift in the ice through the Polar sea. The side houses are constructed of iron, and are not panelled; they are intended for w.c. and lamp-room. On the roof of the chart-house are the main steering-gear and the engine-room tele-graph. On the port side, on the forward part of the after-deck,

a Downton pump is fitted, which can either be worked by hand or
by a small motor, which also serves to drive the sounding-machine,
and is set up on the after-deck. Forward of the starboard side
house is the spare rudder, securely lashed to deck and bulwarks.
On each side of the chart-house a bridge leads to the fore-deck,
with ways down to the workroom and fore-saloon. On the fore-
deck, a little forward of the mainmast, we find the two ship's
pumps proper, constructed of wood. The suction-pipe is of wood,
covered on the outside with lead, so as to prevent leakage through
possible cracks in the wood; the valves are of leather, and the
piston of wood, with a leather covering. The pump-action is the
usual nickel action, that was formerly general on our ships, and is
still widely used on smacks. These simple pumps have been shown
by experience to work better than any others in severe cold. The
fore-deck also has skylights over the fore-saloon, the main and
fore hatches, and finally the capstan. This is of the ordinary
horizontal type, from Pusnes Engineering Works; it is driven by
the motor below, as already mentioned. The capstan can also be
used as a winch, and it can be worked by hand-power.

The *Fram* carries six boats: one large decked boat (29 × 9 ×
4 feet)—one of the two large boats carried on Nansen's expedition—
placed between the mainmast and the foremast, over the skylight;
three whale-boats (20 × 6 feet), and one large and one small
pram; the two last are carried on davits as shown in the drawing.
One of these whale-boats was left behind on the Ice Barrier, where
it was buried in snow when the ship left. It was brought ashore
that the wintering party might have a boat at their disposal after
the *Fram* had sailed.

For warming the vessel it is intended to use only petroleum.
For warming the laboratory (chart-house) there is an arrangement
by which hot air from the galley is brought up through its forward
wall.

The vessel was provided with iron chain plates bolted to the
timbers above the ice-skin. The mizzenmast is new. There was a

crack in the beam that forms the support for the mizzenmast; it was therefore strengthened with two heavy iron plates, secured by through-bolts. Two strong steel stanchions were also placed on each side of the engine, carried down to the frame-timbers. The old mizzenmast has been converted into a bowsprit and jib-boom in one piece. There are now standing gaffs on all three masts. The sail area is about 6,640 square feet.

All the cabins are insulated in the same way as before, though it has been found possible to simplify this somewhat. In general the insulation consists of:

1. In the cabins, against the ship's side and under the upper deck, there is first a layer of cork, and over that a double panelling of wood with tarred felt between.

2. Above the orlop deck aft there is a layer of cork, and above this a floor of boards covered with linoleum.

3. Under the orlop deck forward there is wooden panelling, with linoleum over the deck.

Bulkheads abutting on parts of the ship that are not warmed consist of three thicknesses of boards or planks with various non-conducting materials, such as cork or felt, between them.

When the vessel was docked before leaving Horten, the zinc sheathing was removed, as already stated, since fears were entertained that it would be torn by the ice, and would then prevent the ice from slipping readily under the bottom during pressure. The vessel has two anchors, but the former port anchor has been replaced by a considerably heavier one (1 ton $1\frac{1}{2}$ hundredweight), with a correspondingly heavier chain-cable. This was done with a special view to the voyage round Cape Horn.

In order to trim the ship as much as possible by the stern, which was desirable on account of her carrying a weather helm, a number of heavy spare stores, such as the old port anchor and its cable, were stowed aft, and the extreme after-peak was filled with cement containing round pieces of iron punched out of plates.

Along the railing round the fore-deck strong netting has been placed to prevent the dogs falling overboard. For the upper deck a loose wooden grating has been made, so that the dogs shall not lie on the wet deck. Awnings are provided over the whole deck, with only the necessary openings for working the ship. In this way the dogs have been given dry and, as far as possible, cool quarters for the voyage through the tropics. It is proposed to use the ship's spars as supports for a roof of boards, to be put up during the drift through the ice as a protection against falling masses of ice.

The *Fram's* new engine is a direct reversible Marine-Polar-Motor, built by the Diesel Motor Co., of Stockholm. It is a Diesel engine, with four working and two air-pump cylinders, and develops normally at 280 revolutions per minute 180 effective horse-power, with a consumption of oil of about $7\frac{3}{4}$ ounces per effective horse-power per hour. With this comparatively small consumption, the *Fram's* fuel capacity will carry her much farther than if she had a steam-engine, a consideration of great importance in her forth-coming long voyage in the Arctic Sea. With her oil capacity of about 90 tons, she will thus be able to go uninterruptedly for about 2,273 hours, or about 95 days. If we reckon her speed under engine power alone at $4\frac{1}{2}$ knots, she will be able to go about 10,000 nautical miles without replenishing her oil-supply. It is a fault in the new engine that its number of revolutions is very high, which necessitates the use of a propeller of small diameter (5 feet 9 inches), and thus of low efficiency in the existing conditions. This is the more marked on account of the unusual thickness of the *Fram's* propeller-post, which masks the propeller to a great extent. The position of the engine will be seen in Fig. 1. The exhaust gases from the engine are sent up by a pipe through the after-saloon, through its skylight, and up to a large valve on the bridge; from this valve two horizontal pipes run along the after side of the bridge, one to each side. By means of the valve the gases can be diverted to one side or the other, according to the direction of the wind,

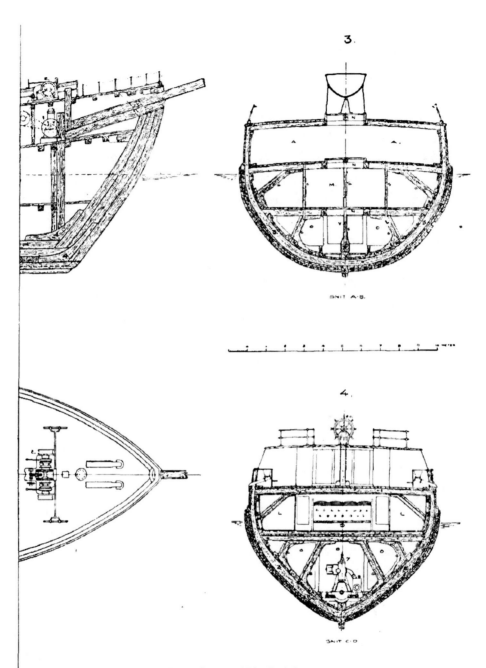

3.

ВИТ A-B.

4.

ВИТ C-D.

DSHIPS.   FIG. 4.—SECTION AT THE ENGINE-ROOM.

r cooling.

12. Exhaust-pipe.
13. Bilge-pump.
14. Skylight.
15. Engine-room companion.
16. Piano.
17. Sofa.
18. Propeller-well.
19. Rudder-well.
20. Steering-gear.
21. Store for paraffin-tanks below and sail-room above.

Besides the usual auxiliary engines, the main engine drives a large centrifugal bilge-pump, an ordinary machine bilge-pump, and a fan for use in the tropics.

When the *Fram* left Christiania in the spring of 1910, after taking her cargo on board, she drew 17 feet forward and 19 feet 5 inches aft. This corresponds to a displacement (measured outside the ice-skin) of about 1,100 tons. The ice-skin was then $12\frac{1}{2}$ inches above the waterline amidships.

APPENDIX II

REMARKS ON THE METEOROLOGICAL OBSERVA-
TIONS AT FRAMHEIM

By B. J. Birkeland

On account of the improvised character of the South Polar Expedition, the meteorological department on the *Fram* was not so
complete as it ought to have been. It had not been possible to
provide the aerological outfit at the time of sailing, and the
meteorologist of the expedition was therefore left behind in
Norway. But certain things were wanting even to complete the
equipment of an ordinary meteorological station, such as minimum
thermometers and the necessary instructions that should have
accompanied one or two of the instruments. Fortunately, among
the veterans of the expedition there were several practised observers,
and, notwithstanding all drawbacks, a fine series of observations was
obtained during ten months' stay in winter-quarters on the Antarctic
continent. These observations will provide a valuable supplement
to the simultaneous records of other expeditions, especially the
British in McMurdo Sound and the German in Weddell Sea, above
all as regards the hypsometer observations (for the determination of
altitude) on sledge journeys. It may be hoped, in any case, that it
will be possible to interpolate the atmospheric pressure at sea-level
in all parts of the Antarctic continent that were traversed by the
sledging expeditions. For this reason the publication of a provisional working out of the observations is of great importance at
the present moment, although the general public will, perhaps, look

upon the long rows of figures as tedious and superfluous. The complete working out of these observations can only be published after a lapse of some years.

As regards the accuracy of the figures here given, it must be noted that at present we know nothing about possible alterations in the errors of the different instruments, as it will not be possible to have the instruments examined and compared until we arrive at San Francisco next year. We have provisionally used the errors that were determined at the Norwegian Meteorological Institute before the expedition sailed; it does not appear, however, that they have altered to any great extent.

The meteorological outfit on the *Fram* consisted of the following instruments and apparatus :

Three mercury barometers, namely:
> One normal barometer by Fuess, No. 361.
> One Kew standard barometer by Adie, No. 839.
> One Kew marine barometer by Adie, No. 764.

Five aneroid barometers :
> One large instrument with thermometer attached, without name or number.
> Two pocket aneroids by Knudsen, Copenhagen, one numbered 1,503.
> Two pocket aneroids by Cary, London, Nos. 1,367 and 1,368, for altitudes up to 5,000 metres (16,350 feet).
> Two hypsometers by Casella, with several thermometers.

Mercury thermometers :
> Twelve ordinary standard (psychrometer-) thermometers, divided to fifths of a degree (Centigrade).
> Ten ordinary standard thermometers, divided to degrees.
> Four sling thermometers, divided to half degrees.
> Three maximum thermometers, divided to degrees.
> One normal thermometer by Mollenkopf, No. 25.

Toluene thermometers :

    Eighteen sling thermometers, divided to degrees.

    Three normal thermometers—by Tounelot, No. 4,993, and
      Baudin, Nos. 14,803 and 14,804.

Two torsion hair hygrometers of Russeltvedt's construction,
    Nos. 12 and 14.

One cup and cross anemometer of Professor Mohn's construc-
    tion, with spare cross.

One complete set of precipitation gauges, with Nipher's shield,
    gauges for snow density, etc.

Registering instruments :

    Two barographs.

    Two thermographs.

    One hair hygrograph.

    A number of spare parts, and a supply of paper and ink
      for seven years.

In addition, various books were taken, such as Mohn's "Meteorol-
ogy," the Meteorological Institute's "Guide," psychrometric tables,
Wiebe's steam-pressure tables for hypsometer observations, etc.

The marine barometer, the large aneroid, and one of the
barographs, the four mercury sling thermometers, and two whole-
degree standard thermometers, were kept on board the *Fram*,
where they were used for the regular observations every four hours
on the vessel's long voyages backwards and forwards.

As will be seen, the shore party was thus left without mercury
sling thermometers, besides having no minimum thermometers; the
three maximum thermometers proved to be of little use. There
were also various defects in the clockwork of the registering instruments. The barographs and thermographs have been used on all
the Norwegian Polar expeditions; the hygrograph is also an old
instrument, which, in the course of its career, has worked for over
ten years in Christiania, where the atmosphere is by no means

merciful to delicate instruments. Its clockwork had not been cleaned before it was sent to the *Fram*, as was done in the case of the other four instruments. The barographs worked irreproachably the whole time, but one of the thermographs refused absolutely to work in the open air, and unfortunately the spindle pivot of the other broke as early as April 17. At first the clockwork of the hygrograph would not go at all, as the oil had become thick, and it was not until this had been removed by prolonged severe heating (baking in the oven for several days) that it could be set going; but then it had to be used for the thermograph, the mechanism of which was broken, so that no registration was obtained of the humidity of the air.

The resulting registrations are then as follows: from Framheim, one set of barograms and two sets of thermograms, of which one gives the temperature of the air and the other the temperature inside the house, where the barometers and barograph were placed; from the *Fram* we have barograms for the whole period from her leaving Christiania, in 1910, to her arrival at Buenos Aires for the third time, in 1912.

Of course, none of these registrations can be taken into account in the provisional working out, as they will require many months' work, which, moreover, cannot be carried out with advantage until we have ascertained about possible changes of error in the instruments. But occasional use has been made of them for purposes of checking, and for supplying the only observation missing in the ten months.

The meteorological station at Framheim was arranged in this way: the barometers, barograph, and one thermograph hung inside the house; they were placed in the kitchen, behind the door of the living-room, which usually stood open, and thus protected them from the radiant heat of the range. A thermometer, a hygrometer, and the other thermograph were placed in a screen on high posts, and with louvred sides, which stood at a distance of fifteen yards to the south-west of the house. A little way beyond the screen, again, stood the wind-vane and anemometer. At the end of September the screen had to be moved a few yards to the east; the snow had drifted about it until it was only 2½ feet above the surface, whereas it ought to stand at the height of a man. At the same time the wind-vane was moved. The screen was constructed by Lindström from his recollection of the old *Fram* screen.

The two mercury barometers, the Fuess normal, and the Adie standard barometer, reached Framheim in good condition; as has been said, they were hung in the kitchen, and the four pocket aneroids were hung by the side of them. All six were read at the daily observations at 8 a.m., 2 p.m., and 8 p.m. The normal barometer, the instructions for which were missing, was used as a siphon barometer, both the mercury levels being read, and the bottom screw being locked fast; the usual mode of reading it, on the other hand, is to set the lower level at zero on the scale by turning the bottom screw at every observation, whereupon the upper level only is set and read. The Adie standard barometer is so arranged that it is only necessary to read the summit of the mercury. It appears that there is some difference between the atmospheric pressure values of the two instruments, but this is chiefly due to the difficult and extremely variable conditions of temperature. There may be a difference of as much as five degrees (Centigrade) between the thermometers of the two barometers, in spite of their hanging side by side at about the same height from the floor. On the other hand, the normal barometer is not suited to daily observations, especially in the Polar regions, and the double reading entails greater liability of error. That the Adie barometer is rather less sensitive than the other is of small importance, as the variations of atmospheric pressure at Framheim were not very great.

In the provisional working out, therefore, the readings of the Adie barometer alone have been used; those of the normal barometer, however, have been experimentally reduced for the first and last months, April and January. The readings have been corrected for the temperature of the mercury, the constant error of the instrument, and the variation of the force of gravity from the normal in latitude 45°. The reduction to sea-level, on the other hand, has not been made; it amounts to 1·1 millimetre at an air temperature of −10° Centigrade.

The observations show that the pressure of the atmosphere is throughout low, the mean for the ten months being 29·07 inches (738·6 millimetres). It is lower in winter than in summer, July having 28·86 inches (733·1 millimetres), and December 29·65 inches (753·3 millimetres), as the mean for the month, a difference of 20·2 millimetres. The highest observation was 30·14 inches (765·7 millimetres) on December 9, and the lowest 28·02 inches (711·7 millimetres) on May 24, 1911; difference, 54 millimetres.

AIR TEMPERATURE AND THERMOMETERS.

As has already been stated, minimum thermometers and mercury sling thermometers were wanting. For the first six months only toluene sling thermometers were used. Sling thermometers are short, narrow glass thermometers, with a strong loop at the top; before being read they are briskly swung round at the end of a string about half a yard long, or in a special apparatus for the purpose. The swinging brings the thermometer in contact with a great volume of air, and it therefore gives the real temperature of the air more readily than if it were hanging quietly in the screen.

From October 1 a mercury thermometer was also placed in the screen, though only one divided to whole degrees; those divided to fifths of a degree would, of course, have given a surer reading. But it is evident, nevertheless, that the toluene thermometers used are correct to less than half a degree (Centigrade), and even this difference may no doubt be explained by one thermometer being slung while the other was fixed. The observations are, therefore, given without any corrections. Only at the end of December was exclusive use made of mercury thermometers. The maximum thermometers taken proved of so little use that they were soon discarded ; the observations have not been included here.

It was due to a misunderstanding that mercury thermometers were not also used in the first half-year, during those periods when the temperature did not go below the freezing-point of mercury (−39° C.). But the toluene thermometers in use were old and good instruments, so that the observations for this period may also be regarded as perfectly reliable. Of course, all the thermometers had been carefully examined at the Norwegian Meteorological Institute, and at Framheim the freezing-point was regularly tested in melting snow.

The results show that the winter on the Barrier was about 12° C. (21·6° F.) colder than it usually is in McMurdo Sound, where the British expeditions winter. The coldest month is August, with a mean temperature of −44·5° C. (−48·1° F.) ; on fourteen days during this month the temperature was below −50° C. (−58° F.). The lowest temperature occurred on August 13 : −58·5° C. (−73·3° F.) ; the warmest day in that month had a temperature of −24° C. (−11·2° F.).

In October spring begins to approach, and in December the temperature culminates with a mean for the month of −6·6° C. (+20·1° F.), and a highest maximum temperature of −0·2° C. (+31·6° F.). The temperature was thus never above freezing-point, even in the warmest part of the summer.

The daily course of the temperature—warmest at noon and coldest towards morning—is, of course, not noticeable in winter, as the sun is always below the horizon. But in April there is a sign of it, and from September onward it is fairly marked, although the difference between 2 p.m. and the mean of 8 a.m. and 8 p.m. only amounts to 2° C. in the monthly mean.

HUMIDITY OF THE AIR.

For determining the relative humidity of the air the expedition had two of Russeltvedt's torsion hygrometers. This instrument has been accurately described in the *Meteorologische Zeitschrift*, 1908, p. 396. It has the advantage that there are no axles or sockets to be rusted or soiled, or filled with rime or drift-snow.

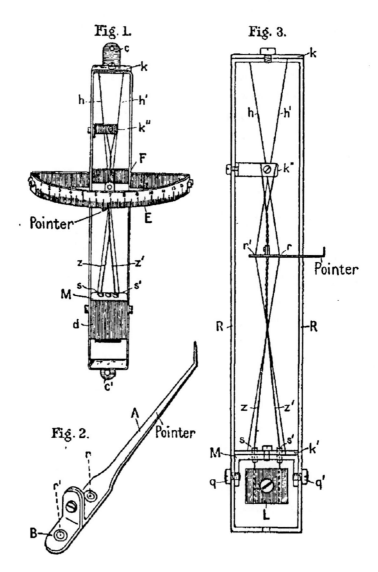

Fig. 1.

Fig. 3.

Fig. 2.

The two horsehairs (*h*, *h'*) that are used, are stretched tight by a torsion clamp (Z, Z', and L), which also carries the pointer; the position of the pointer varies with the length of the hairs, which, again, is dependent on the degree of humidity of the air. (See the diagrams.) These instruments have been in use in Norway for several years, especially at inland stations, where the winter is very cold, and they have shown themselves superior to all others in accuracy and durability; but there was no one on the *Fram* who knew anything about them, and there is therefore a possibility that they were not always in such good order as could be wished. On September 10, especially, the variations are very remarkable; but on October 13 the second instrument, No. 12, was hung out, and there can be no doubt of the correctness of the subsequent observations.

It is seen that the relative humidity attains its maximum in winter, in the months of July and August, with a mean of 90 per cent. The driest air occurs in the spring month of November, with a mean of 73 per cent. The remaining months vary between 79 and 86 per cent., and the mean of the whole ten months is 82 per cent. The variations quoted must be regarded as very small. On the other hand, the figures themselves are very high, when the low temperatures are considered, and this is doubtless the result of there being open water not very far away. The daily course of humidity is contrary to the course of the temperature, and does not show itself very markedly, except in January.

The absolute humidity, or partial pressure of aqueous vapour in the air, expressed in millimetres in the height of the mercury in the same way as the pressure of the atmosphere, follows in the main the temperature of the air. The mean value for the whole period is only 0·8 millimetre (0·031 inch); December has the highest monthly mean with 2·5 millimetres (0·097 inch), August the lowest with 0·1 millimetre (0·004 inch). The absolutely highest observation occurred on December 5 with 4·4 millimetres (0·173 inch), while the lowest of all is less than 0·05 millimetre, and can therefore only be expressed by 0·0; it occurred frequently in the course of the winter.

PRECIPITATION.

Any attempt to measure the quantity of precipitation—even approximately—had to be abandoned. Snowfall never occurred in still weather, and in a wind there was always a drift that entirely filled the gauge. On June 1 and 7 actual snowfall was observed, but it was so insignificant that it could not be measured; it was, however, composed of genuine flakes of snow. It sometimes happened that precipitation of very small particles of ice was noticed; these grains of ice can be seen against the observation lantern, and heard on the observer's headgear; but on returning to the house, nothing can be discovered on the clothing. Where the sign for snow occurs in the column for Remarks, it means drift; these days are included among days of precipitation. Sleet was observed only once, in December. Rain never.

CLOUDINESS.

The figures indicate how many tenths of the visible heavens are covered by clouds (or mist). No instrument is used in these observations; they depend on personal estimate. They had to be abandoned during the period of darkness, when it is difficult to see the sky.

WIND.

For measuring the velocity of the wind the expedition had a cup and cross anemometer, which worked excellently the whole time. It consists of a horizontal cross with a hollow hemisphere on each of the four arms of the cross; the openings of the hemispheres are all turned towards the same side of the cross-arms, and the cross can revolve with a minimum of friction on a vertical axis at the point of junction. The axis is connected with a recording mechanism, which is set in motion at each observation and stopped after a lapse of half a minute, when the figure is read off. This figure denotes the velocity of the wind in metres per second, and is directly transferred to the tables (here converted into feet per second).

The monthly means vary between 1·9 metres (6·2 feet) in May, and 5·5 metres (18 feet) in October; the mean for the whole ten months is 3·4 metres (11·1 feet) per second. These velocities may be characterized as surprisingly small; and the number of stormy days agrees with this low velocity. Their number for the whole period is only 11, fairly evenly divided between the months; there are, however, five stormy days in succession in the spring months October and November.

The frequency of the various directions of the wind has been added up for each month, and gives the same characteristic distribution throughout the whole period. As a mean we have the following table, where the figures give the percentage of the total number of wind observations:

N.	N.E.	E.	S.E.	S.	S.W.	W.	N.W.	Calm.
1·9	7·8	31·9	6·9	12·3	14·3	2·6	1·1	21·3

Almost every third direction is E., next to which come S.W. and S. Real S.E., on the other hand, occurs comparatively rarely. Of N., N.W., and W. there is hardly anything. It may be interesting to see what the distribution is when only high winds are taken into account—that is, winds with a velocity of 10 metres (32·8 feet) per second or more. We then have the following table of percentages:

N.	N.E.	E.	S.E.	S.	S.W.	W.	N.W.
7	12	51	10	4	10	2	4

Here again, E. is predominant, as half the high winds come from this quarter. W. and N.W. together have only 6 per cent.

The total number of high winds is 51, or 5·6 per cent. of the total of wind observations.

The most frequent directions of storms are also E. and N.E.

The Aurora Australis.

During the winter months auroral displays were frequently seen—altogether on sixty-five days in six months, or an average of every third day—but for want of apparatus no exhaustive observations could be attempted. The records are confined to brief notes of the position of the aurora at the times of the three daily observations.

The frequency of the different directions, reckoned in percentages of the total number of directions given, as for the wind, will be found in the following table:

N.	N.E.	E.	S.E.	S.	S.W.	W.	N.W.	Zenith.
18	17	16	9	8	3	8	13	8

N. and N.E. are the most frequent, and together make up one-third of all the directions recorded; but the nearest points on either side of this maximum—E. and N.W.—are also very frequent, so that these four points together—N.W., N., N.E., E.—have 64 per cent. of the whole. The rarest direction is S.W., with only 3 per cent. (From the position of the Magnetic Pole in relation to Framheim, one would rather have expected E. to be the most frequent, and W. the rarest, direction.) Probably the material before us is somewhat scanty for establishing these directions.

METEOROLOGICAL RECORD FROM FRAMHEIM.

APRIL, 1911—JANUARY, 1912.

Height above sea-level, 36 feet.
Gravity correction, ·072 inch at 29·89 inches.
Latitude, 78° 38′ S.
Longitude, 163° 37′ W.

EXPLANATION OF SIGNS IN THE TABLES.

✶ signifies snow.
≡ ,, mist.
⌣ ,, aurora.
⊕ ,, large ring round the sun.
▽ ,, ,, ,, ,, moon.
ꓼ\ ,, storm.
sq. ,, squalls.
a. ,, a.m.
p. ,, p.m.
I., II., III., signify respectively 8 a.m., 2 p.m., and 8 p.m.
° (e.g., ✶°) signifies slight.
² (e.g., ✶²) ,, heavy.

Times of day are always in local time.
The date was not changed on crossing the 180th meridian

APRIL, 1911.

Date	Barometer, Normal Gravity (Inches) 8 a.m.	2 p.m.	8 p.m.	Temperature of the Air (Fahrenheit) 8 a.	2 p.	8 p.	Absolute Humidity (Inch) 8 a.	2 p.	8 p.	Relative Humidity (per Cent.) 8 a.	2 p.	8 p.	Wind 8 a.	2 p.	8 p.	Cloud 8 a.	2 p.	8 p.	Remarks
1	28·81	28·87	28·91	−25·2	−19·3	−25·6	—	—	—	—	—	—	0·0	0·0	5·9 E.S.E.	9≡	10	1	—
2	28·98	29·05	29·06	−14·1	−9·4	−7·6	—	—	—	—	—	—	0·6 S.E.	4·2 S.	6·8 S.	9✻	10✻	10✻	—
3	29·04	29·00	28·94	−29·2	−16·8	−18·4	—	—	—	—	—	—	0·0 S.	1·3 S.	7·5 S.	8	10≡	10≡	—
4	28·81	28·79	28·75	−22·0	−0·4	−18·4	—	—	—	—	—	—	10·4 S.	9·8 S.	3·2 S.	10≡	10	10	—
5	28·78	28·84	28·81	−13·9	−10·5	−9·6	—	—	—	—	—	—	4·2 S.	0·9	0·0	10✻	10	10✻	—
6	28·69	28·74	28·74	−14·8	−13·0	−27·7	—	—	—	—	—	—	42·9 S.S.W.	17·3 S.	16·4 S.	7	6	7	—
7	28·77	28·90	29·02	−17·3	−13·3	−0·4	·019	·019	·019	74	79	78	0·0	0·0 E.	3·6	10	5	10	—
8	29·16	29·14	29·05	−10·1	−13·0	−11·5	·019	·019	·019	80	79	78	20·0 S.S.E.	13·7 E.	3·9 E.	10✻	10	7	✻° I.
9	28·92	28·93	28·92	−5·8	−6·5	−5·8	·027	·027	·027	80	79	80	1·3 S.E.	10·8	0·0	10✻	9	10✻	—
10	28·82	28·78	28·73	+12·2	+12·2	+2·9	·070	·066	·047	88	86	88	23·6 E.	17·0 N.E.	10·4 N.E.	6	9	6	—
11	28·80	28·91	28·98	+5·0	+5·0	+3·2	·051	·051	·035	90	88	88	26·8 N.W.	20·3 N.E.	17·3 N.E.	10	9	9	—
12	28·91	28·92	28·92	+1·4	+6·8	+7·9	·043	·051	·043	88	85	83	24·2 N.	17·3 N.	17·0	10	9	10	—
13	28·99	29·05	29·14	+10·4	+8·3	+17·5	·062	·051	·023	86	76	78	24·6 E.	19·3 N.E.	7·5	6	2	6	—
14	29·41	29·59	29·71	+11·2	−11·2	−13·0	·019	·019	·016	80	76	71	20·0 S.W.	23·9 S.W.	23·9 N.E.	10	10	0	—
15	29·77	29·80	29·75	−15·6	−15·1	−4·0	·016	·016	·019	83	78	80	10·4 S.E.	9·8 N.E.	17·0 S.W.	10✻	4	8	✻¹ I.
16	29·68	29·64	29·46	−14·8	+7·7	−20·5	·051	·051	·031	80	81	82	28·2 N.E.	19·6 E.	30·8 N.E.	10	6	10	—
17	28·97	29·11	29·09	+8·6	−24·1	−36·4	·055	·012	·012	84	79	81	4·2 N.W.	14·1 S.W.	14·1 N.W.	10	7	10	—
18	29·07	29·11	29·13	−25·2	−33·5	−22·0	·012	·008	·004	81	79	83	14·7 S.W.	0·0	0·0 S.W.	10	9	10	—
19	29·18	29·21	29·22	−25·6	−21·8	+0·9	·012	·012	·012	82	84	84	14·4 E.	11·1 E.N.E.	23·9	10	9	7	—
20	29·09	29·00	28·94	−12·1	−11·2	−25·9	·031	·023	·027	83	83	84	52·1 E.	29·5 E.	33·1 E.	10	5	10	✻¹ p.
21	28·83	28·84	28·81	+3·1	−1·3	−35·5	·031	·035	·039	84	83	80	25·2 E.S.E.	21·9 E.S.E.	28·8 E.S.E.	9	1	7	—
22	28·77	28·78	28·79	−12·3	−20·2	−12·6	·019	·012	·012	78	79	79	11·15 E.N.E. N.E.	9·1 N.E.	6·8 N.E.	3	10	9	—
23	28·73	28·74	28·78	−31·3	−31·0	−14·8	·008	·008	·008	79	79	82	0·0	0·0	0·0	2	10	—	—
24	28·87	28·90	28·92	−27·0	−16·0	−35·8	·023	·016	·019	80	81	80	0·0	20·3 E.	10·1 E.	10	1	10✻	—
25	29·08	29·24	29·37	−10·8	−16·9	−53·7	·008	·016	·019	84	83	82	0·0 E.	0·0 S.W.	0·0 S.W.	10	10	10	III.
26	29·45	29·43	29·41	−28·1	−32·1	−45·4	·004	·008	·008	76	79	80	0·0 S.	0·0 S.W.	3·2 S.W.	2	1	0	III.
27	29·50	29·54	29·54	−52·6	−54·4	−53·7	·004	·004	·004	76	77	76	5·9 S.W.	7·8 S.W.	0·0 S.S.W.	1	1	0	III.
28	29·42	29·33	29·28	−52·6	−46·8	−45·4	·004	·004	·004	77	77	78	7·8 S.S.W.	4·5 S.S.W.	0·0	1	10	0	III.
29	29·20	29·20	29·22	−37·1	−35·7	−34·6	·004	·004	·003	79	78	79	0·0 E.N.E.	7·2 E.	0·0	0	1	0	III.
30	29·23	29·20	29·16	−42·3	−38·2	−38·7	·004	·004	·004	79	79	79	0·0 S.W.	6·5 W.	1·9 W.	0	7	0	III.
Mean	29·06	29·09	29·09	−17·3	−15·7	−18·2	·023	·023	·019	81	80	81	12·4	10·8	9·8	7·8	7·5	6·3	

MAY, 1911.

Date	Barometer, Normal Gravity (Inches) 8 a.m.	2 p.m.	8 p.m.	Temperature of the Air (Fahrenheit) 8 a.	2 p.	8 p.	Absolute Humidity (Inch) 8 a.	2 p.	8 p.	Relative Humidity (per Cent.) 8 a.	2 p.	8 p.	Direction and Velocity of the Wind (Feet per Second) 8 a.	2 p.	8 p.	Cloud 8 a.	2 p.	8 p.	Remarks
1	29·14	29·17	29·19	−41·2	−44·3	−45·4	·004	·004	·004	78	78	77	S.E. 0·0	0·0	0·0	10	3	0	⌣ III.
2	29·24	29·23	29·23	−45·2	−37·5	−33·1	·004	·004	·008	77	78	78	0·0	0·0 S.S.W.	S.S.W. 4·2	2	2	10	—
3	29·24	29·24	29·19	−31·0	−38·5	−40·0	·008	·004	·004	79	78	78	S. 0·0	0·0 S.W.	S.W. 5·9	10	2	0	⌣ III.
4	29·05	29·04	28·98	−33·9	−35·1	−37·8	·008	·008	·004	79	78	78	S. 0·0	0·0	0·0	1	2	0	⌣ III.
5	28·95	29·05	29·16	−13·0	−17·3	−18·4	·019	·016	·016	83	82	82	S.S.W. 8·8	8·8	0·0	9	7	9	—
6	29·53	29·61	29·65	−4·0	−4·0	−4·2	·031	·031	·031	87	87	88	E. 6·5	6·5 E.	S. 8·2	10	9	10	—
7	29·66	29·66	29·60	−18·7	−24·1	−23·8	·016	·012	·012	83	82	79	S. 0·0	0·0 S.	4·9	0	4	0	⌣ III.
8	29·52	29·52	29·57	−30·6	−22·0	−23·4	·008	·008	·012	80	79	80	S.S.E. 5·9	5·9 S.S.W.	S. 4·9	—	—	—	⌣ I.
9	29·54	29·57	29·57	−27·4	−32·4	−35·1	·008	·008	·008	79	79	79	0·0	0·0	0·0	—	—	—	—
10	29·46	29·40	29·36	−30·1	−31·5	−32·8	·004	·008	·008	80	80	79	0·0	0·0	0·0	—	—	—	⌣ Zenith I.
11	29·37	29·42	29·44	−40·0	−33·0	−34·9	·004	·008	·008	78	79	80	S.S.E. 7·5	7·5 E.	E.S.E. 14·1	—	—	—	⌣ Zenith I., ꝺ III.
12	29·35	29·26	29·18	−11·2	−9·6	−5·8	·019	·023	·027	80	79	76	0·0	0·0 E.	0·0	—	—	—	⌣ III.
13	28·93	28·86	28·77	−35·5	−43·6	−39·3	·004	·004	·004	74	73	76	S. 0·0	4·2 E.	0·0	—	—	—	—
14	28·60	28·51	28·40	−34·9	−43·9	−33·5	·004	·004	·008	77	76	77	W.S.W. 20·3	3·9 S.W.	S.W. 13·1	—	—	—	—
15	28·39	28·59	28·72	−33·1	−40·3	−28·1	·008	·004	·008	77	76	80	E. 13·4	16·4 W.	0·0	—	—	—	—
16	29·01	29·17	29·27	6·9	−10·5	−16·6	·027	·023	·016	83	82	83	E. 13·4	21·6 E.S.E.	9·5	—	—	—	⌣ III.
17	29·16	29·07	29·04	−14·8	−21·6	−23·2	·019	·012	·012	83	82	81	E. 33·4	0·0	E.S.E. 0·6	—	—	—	ꝺ III.
18	29·12	29·16	29·19	−32·1	−38·2	−43·2	·008	·004	·008	83	82	78	0·0	0·0 S.S.W.	S.S.W. 19·6	—	—	—	ꝺ II., ꝺ III.
19	29·23	29·22	29·24	−43·2	−45·0	−38·2	·004	·004	·004	78	77	78	0·0	0·0 S.S.W.	S.W. 9·8	—	—	—	ꝺ I., ꝺ III.
20	29·20	29·09	28·98	−35·5	−42·9	−39·8	·004	·004	·004	79	76	77	W.S.W. 17·7	1·3 S.W.	S.W. 0·0	—	—	—	ꝺ II., ꝺ III.
21	28·90	28·89	28·86	−54·7	−52·6	−49·5	·004	·004	·004	73	75	75	S. 14·1	14·7 S.W.	0·0	—	—	—	ꝺ L., ꝺ I.
22	28·87	28·87	28·85	−50·8	−52·0	−53·7	·000	·004	·004	76	76	76	S. 0·0	14·1	0·0	—	—	—	ꝺ I.
23	28·71	28·50	28·31	−59·1	−55·5	−41·8	·000	·000	·004	74	76	76	0·0	0·0 S.	11·1	—	—	—	—
24	28·02	28·02	28·15	−56·2	−58·5	−18·9	·000	·000	·016	73	73	82	S. 7·2	7·2 S.E.	E. 14·4	—	—	—	⌣ III.
25	28·45	28·68	28·80	−16·9	−10·5	−40·5	·016	·023	·004	79	84	77	S.E. 14·1	17·3 E.	0·0 E. 8·2	—	—	—	—
26	28·87	28·99	29·15	−27·0	−30·6	−23·8	·012	·008	·012	80	80	83	N.E. 14·1	17·0 E.	12·4	—	—	—	—
27	29·39	29·41	29·36	−21·6	−21·1	−37·5	·012	·012	·012	82	82	79	E. 9·5	12·4 E.	7·5	—	—	—	—
28	29·07	28·94	28·87	−36·7	−36·4	−25·6	·004	·004	·004	82	82	82	0·0	0·0 S.W.	S.W. 18·0	—	—	—	—
29	28·71	28·62	28·55	−33·9	−25·6	−35·8	·008	·012	·012	80	82	77	S.S.W. 9·8	0·0 S.	12·4	—	*	*	⌣ I., III.
30	28·43	28·33	28·30	−31·0	−32·2	−9·4	·008	·008	·004	82	81	82	S.W. 0·0	11·1 S.W.	25·5	—	—	—	—
31	28·45	28·56	28·66	−30·6	−22·0	—	·008	·012	·023	80	80	82	E. 14·4	17·7 E.	19·0	—	—	—	⌣ III.
Mean	29·01	29·02	29·01	−31·7	−32·6	−31·7	·008	·008	·008	79	79	79	6·2	5·5	7·2	—	—	—	—

JUNE, 1911.

Date	Barometer, Normal Gravity (Inches)			Temperature of the Air (Fahrenheit)			Absolute Humidity (Inch)			Relative Humidity (per Cent.)			Direction and Velocity of the Wind (Feet per Second)			Cloud			Remarks
	8 a.m.	2 p.m.	8 p.m.	8 a.	2 p.	8 p.	8 a.	2 p.	8 p.	8 a.	2 p.	8 p.	8 a.	2 p.	8 p.	8 a.	2 p.	8 p.	
1	28·83	28·89	28·89	−1·3	−1·3	−2·7	·035	·039	·035	86	91	92	E. 0·0	E. 4·9	0·0	—	—	*	—
2	28·95	28·97	28·94	+0·3	−1·4	−1·1	·043	·043	·039	92	93	93	E. 15·7	E. 0·3	E.S.E. 11·1	—	—	—	III.
3	28·80	28·78	28·78	−5·9	−4·3	+0·7	·051	·047	·039	86	87	84	E. 44·6	E. 27·8	0·0	—	—	—	—
4	28·71	28·65	28·56	−7·6	−9·0	−10·9	·027	·023	·023	84	86	80	0·0	0·0	S.S.W. 7·2	—	—	—	III.
5	28·50	28·53	28·57	−27·4	−13·0	−2·2	·008	·019	·035	82	86	91	E. 10·8	E. 11·1	E. 11·1	—	**	*	L.
6	28·59	28·65	28·70	+5·7	+12·9	+12·2	·051	·078	·074	90	96	97	E. 26·8	E. 24·6	E. 15·0	—	—	*	—
7	28·69	28·60	28·54	+4·7	−5·9	−9·9	·055	·055	·066	95	93	94	7·2	0·0	0·0	—	*	*	I.
8	28·58	28·63	28·63	−11·2	−14·8	−21·6	·023	·019	·012	88	85	84	S. 13·4	S. 6·5	0·0	—	—	—	I.
9	28·54	28·53	28·54	−5·8	−5·1	−3·8	·031	·031	·035	89	85	90	E. 17·0	E. 11·1	E. 12·4	—	—	—	—
10	28·58	28·61	28·67	−7·6	−8·5	−11·4	·027	·027	·023	88	88	88	E. 13·1	E. 19·6	E. 15·0	—	—	—	—
11	28·77	28·83	28·87	−11·2	−9·9	−13·0	·023	·023	·019	87	86	87	E. 7·5	E. 9·8	E. 5·2	—	—	—	I.
12	28·86	28·88	28·90	−30·6	−37·8	−43·6	·008	·008	·004	86	80	79	S.S.E. 0·0	S.S.E. 3·2	0·0	—	—	—	—
13	28·95	29·01	29·02	−24·7	−24·1	−29·2	·012	·012	·008	83	83	82	E. 8·2	E. 13·1	E. 13·7	—	—	—	III.
14	29·05	29·08	29·08	−38·2	−38·2	−41·8	·004	·004	·004	80	80	79	E. 19·6	E. 24·2	E. 21·9	—	—	—	L., II.
15	28·97	28·90	28·83	−33·3	−38·2	−43·6	·008	·004	·004	80	86	86	E.S.E. 5·9	0·0	0·0	—	—	—	L., II.
16	28·73	28·70	28·74	−54·4	−58·0	−61·2	·004	·000	·000	83	83	82	S. 4·9	0·0	0·0	—	—	—	—
17	28·91	29·09	29·26	−53·1	−14·8	−11·7	·004	·019	·023	83	90	91	N.W. 14·4	N.N.W. 5·9	N. 6·5	—	—	—	—
18	29·45	29·52	29·54	−13·0	−17·8	−14·1	·019	·016	·019	90	90	92	E. 10·4	E. 17·3	E. 17·3	—	—	—	—
19	29·47	29·33	29·20	−30·6	−27·4	−40·0	·008	·012	·004	87	88	86	E.N.E. 4·5	0·0	S.W. 11·1	—	—	—	—
20	29·00	29·10	29·05	−49·7	−54·0	−34·2	·004	·004	·008	84	84	87	S.S.W. 8·5	S.W. 0·0	0·0	—	—	—	—
21	28·77	28·64	28·55	−23·8	−20·7	−32·4	·012	·016	·008	87	88	86	S.S.W. 17·7	S.S.W. 26·2	**S.S.W. 36·0**	—	—	—	I., III.
22	28·60	28·66	28·73	−50·8	−55·3	−51·1	·004	·004	·004	82	82	82	W.S.W. 12·1	0·0	0·0	—	—	—	I., III.
23	28·79	28·80	28·80	−52·6	−50·4	−48·8	·004	·004	·004	82	82	82	E. 21·3	E. 22·3	E. 20·6	—	—	—	L., II., III.
24	28·84	28·86	28·89	−51·1	−60·7	−64·8	·004	·000	·000	83	82	82	0·0	0·0	0·0	—	—	—	III.
25	28·84	28·78	28·72	−72·7	−70·9	−58·0	·000	·000	·000	82	81	82	0·0	S. 3·6	W.S.W. 6·5	—	—	—	III.
26	28·77	28·80	28·84	−62·8	−56·2	−52·6	·004	·000	·004	83	82	83	0·0	E. 22·3	E. 19·6	—	—	—	—
27	28·96	29·02	29·15	−42·1	−33·3	−43·6	·004	·008	·004	84	85	84	N.E. 15·7	E. 29·5	E. 13·7	—	—	—	I., III.
28	29·36	29·39	29·37	−59·8	−65·2	−63·9	·000	·000	·000	82	82	82	E. 18·0	E.N.E. 13·1	0·0	—	—	—	—
29	29·28	29·18	29·11	−68·8	−63·4	−52·6	·000	·000	·000	81	82	79	0·0	S. 0·0	S. 3·9	—	—	—	sq. a. and p.
30	28·95	28·85	28·77	−49·0	−41·8	−37·6	·004	·004	·004	82	82	80	S.W. 0·0	S.W. 12·4	S.S.W. 22·3	—	—	—	—
Mean	28·87	28·87	28·87	−30·6	−28·8	−29·2	·016	·016	·016	85	86	86	10·4	10·1	9·1	—	—	—	—

JULY, 1911.

Date	Barometer, Normal Gravity (Inches).			Temperature of the Air (Fahrenheit).			Absolute Humidity (Inch).			Relative Humidity (per Cent.).			Direction and Velocity of the Wind (Feet per Second).			Cloud.			Remarks.
	8 a.m.	2 p.m.	8 p.m.	8 a.	2 p.	8 p.	8 a.	2 p.	8 p.	8 a.	2 p.	8 p.	8 a.	2 p.	8 p.	8 a.	2 p.	8 p.	
1	28·82	28·98	29·03	−53·5	−64·5	−53·5	·004	·000	·004	81	79	80	S.W. 4·5	S.W. 0·0	0·0	—	—	—	◁ L., II., III.
2	29·17	29·26	29·32	−29·2	−35·5	−37·3	·008	·008	·008	82	86	86	0·0	S.S.W. 17·7	S.S.W. 28·2	—	—	—	◁ III.
3	29·48	29·51	29·46	−49·7	−52·6	−54·4	·004	·004	·008	83	84	84	S.W. 25·2	S.E. 0·0	E.S.E. 11·8	—	—	—	◁ L., II., III.
4	29·22	29·07	28·93	−31·9	−36·4	−29·5	·008	·008	·008	87	86	88	E.S.E. 15·0	E. 4·9	S.E. 14·1	—	*	—	◁ L.
5	28·64	28·46	28·40	−21·8	−27·0	−35·3	·012	·012	·008	87	88	86	E. 10·8	S.S.W. 5·5	S.S.W. 20·3	—	—	—	—
6	28·53	28·69	28·79	−33·5	−35·7	−45·4	·008	·008	·004	86	87	84	W.S.W. 11·4	S. 8·2	10·1	—	—	—	Ɵ II.
7	28·99	29·14	29·23	−45·0	−43·2	−43·6	·004	·004	·004	87	87	87	S.S.W. 9·8	S. 0·0	6·2	—	—	—	—
8	29·20	28·99	28·88	−29·2	−11·9	−13·7	·008	·023	·023	90	91	92	E. 20·6	E.S.E. 49·2	E. 30·8	—	—	—	—
9	28·73	28·66	28·63	+4·7	+0·9	+0·9	·055	·047	·047	97	99	98	E. 36·7	E. 24·6	E. 24·2	—	—	—	—
10	28·59	28·46	28·39	−4·0	+10·4	+0·7	·035	·070	·047	97	93	98	S. 8·2	E.S.E. 18·0	E. 39·3	—	—	—	—
11	28·33	28·26	28·24	−15·7	−23·8	−28·3	·019	·012	·012	98	93	94	E. 0·0	E. 15·0	E. 6·5	—	—	—	Ɵ III.
12	28·30	28·38	28·40	−4·0	+1·4	+1·4	·035	·047	·008	97	97	93	E. 17·0	S. 0·0	6·5	—	—	—	Ɵ III.
13	28·42	28·36	28·33	−5·8	−24·1	−33·7	·031	·012	·008	97	94	95	0·0	E.S.E. 24·2	6·5	—	—	—	Ɵ II., Ɵ III.
14	28·42	28·56	28·64	−46·1	−38·2	−22·0	·004	·004	·016	90	91	92	W.S.W. 3·6	S. 11·1	0·0	—	—	—	—
15	28·80	28·85	28·85	−34·6	−43·6	−34·6	·008	·004	·012	92	90	92	E. 30·8	W.N.W. 12·4	W.N.W. 19·6	—	—	—	Ɵ
16	28·80	28·77	28·77	−22·2	−20·2	−24·7	·012	·004	·012	95	92	92	0·0	E. 20·3	E. 16·4	—	—	—	Ɵ
17	28·94	28·98	29·00	−42·9	−16·6	−23·4	·004	·004	·023	88	83	86	E.S.E. 19·6	E. 0·0	E. 8·8	—	—	—	◁ II.
18	28·91	28·81	28·58	−23·1	−50·1	−55·8	·012	·019	·004	90	90	88	W.S.W. 18·0	E.S.E. 23·9	S.W. 30·5	—	—	—	◁ L., Ɵ III.
19	28·58	28·59	28·58	−48·4	−54·7	−56·2	·004	·004	·016	87	87	87	0·0	W.S.W. 13·3	S.W. 22·9	—	—	—	Ɵ L., sq. W.S.W. a.
20	28·59	28·55	28·42	−51·1	−45·7	−22·0	·000	·004	·000	84	88	87	W.S.W. 15·0	S.S.W. 18·3	E.N.E. 8·5	—	—	—	◁ II., III.
21	28·35	28·43	28·55	−56·2	−27·0	−32·8	·019	·012	·008	94	92	92	N.E. 26·8	E.N.E. 0·0	E. 15·0	*	—	*	◁ L., II.
22	28·79	28·90	28·95	−14·6	−19·8	−29·7	·016	·012	·008	88	92	89	E.N.E. 19·0	E. 22·3	E. 14·1	—	—	—	◁ III.
23	28·91	28·94	29·02	−18·4	−19·8	−23·8	·012	·016	·008	88	89	90	E. 9·8	E. 22·9	E.N.E. 16·7	—	—	—	◁ III.
24	29·17	29·19	29·18	−25·2	−22·2	−17·8	·012	·012	·012	90	90	90	E. 11·8	E.N.E. 11·4	E.S.E. 28·2	—	—	—	—
25	29·11	29·08	29·08	−27·4	−16·4	−49·0	·016	·019	·016	91	92	91	E.S.E. 7·8	E.S.E. 11·8	E. 16·4	—	—	—	—
26	29·16	29·23	29·25	−40·3	−59·4	−65·2	·000	·004	·004	91	92	88	0·0	E. 5·9	0·0	—	—	—	◁ L., III.
27	29·29	29·29	29·28	−59·8	−54·4	−39·4	·000	·000	·000	83	89	91	7·2	E.S.E. 3·9	7·2	—	—	—	◁ L., III.
28	29·22	29·20	29·16	−61·6	−43·9	−49·0	·004	·004	·004	89	89	91	S.S.E. 16·7	S.E. 3·9	0·0	—	—	—	◁ L.
29	29·13	29·09	29·03	−39·4	−46·8	−54·4	·000	·004	·004	91	91	89	S. 0·0	2·6	0·0	—	—	—	—
30	28·87	28·88	28·96	−40·6	−46·8	−54·4	·004	·004	·004	87	90	88	S.W. 10·8	0·0	—	—	—	◁ L., III.
31	29·14	29·18	29·15	−52·6	−52·9	−54·0	·004	·004	·004	88	88	88	S.S.W. 6·5	W.S.W. 3·9	—	—	—	◁ L., III.
Mean	28·86	28·86	28·86	−32·2	−33·5	−33·3	·012	·012	·012	90	90	90	11·1	12·1	13·4	—	—	—	

AUGUST, 1911.

Date.	Barometer, Normal Gravity (Inches) 8 a.m.	2 p.m.	8 p.m.	Temperature of the Air (Fahrenheit) 8 a.	2 p.	8 p.	Absolute Humidity (Inch) 8 a.	2 p.	8 p.	Relative Humidity (per Cent.) 8 a.	2 p.	8 p.	Wind 8 a.	2 p.	8 p.	Cloud 8 a.	2 p.	8 p.	Remarks.
1	29·06	28·96	28·87	62·1	63·4	58·3	·000	·000	·000	86	84	84	S.W. 23·6	S.W. 29·5	S.S.W. 6·5	—	—	—	☽ L, III.
2	28·54	28·60	28·69	13·0	13·0	35·5	·019	·019	·008	84	92	92	W.S.W. 37·7	W.S.W. 40·8	W.S.W. 28·2	—	—	—	Ɒ III.
3	28·77	28·72	28·60	29·2	32·8	27·4	·008	·008	·012	90	90	92	W.S.W. 7·8	E. 14·7	E.S.E. 15·7	—	—	—	—
4	28·61	28·72	28·80	54·9	59·8	58·3	·004	·004	·000	88	88	87	S.S.W. 10·8	S.W. 16·4	0·0	—	—	—	—
5	28·99	29·08	29·19	58·7	48·1	49·0	·004	·004	·004	88	90	89	E. 14·4	E. 15·7	E. 6·5	—	3	—	—
6	29·28	29·41	29·37	36·4	49·0	49·7	·008	·004	·004	92	91	90	0·0	0·0	0·0	—	6	—	III.
7	29·46	29·43	29·36	56·2	56·2	50·1	·004	·004	·004	88	87	88	0·0	0·0	0·0	—	9	—	—
8	29·20	29·07	29·01	52·2	54·7	52·2	·004	·004	·004	89	92	89	E. 3·2	E. 14·4	W.S.W. 6·5	—	6	—	Ɒ III.
9	28·89	28·83	28·84	56·2	58·0	58·0	·004	·004	·000	88	88	88	0·0	W. 0·0	S. 8·8	—	2	—	Ɒ Ɒ L.
10	28·95	29·04	29·09	61·2	68·8	58·0	·000	·000	·000	88	87	88	S. 0·0	S. 1·6	E. 19·0	—	—	—	—
11	29·12	29·09	29·02	40·9	40·0	43·6	·004	·004	·004	92	91	91	E. 24·9	E. 19·3	0·0	—	5	—	☀¹ II.
12	28·86	28·82	28·83	59·1	66·1	68·8	·000	·000	·000	88	88	88	0·0	S.W. 13·7	S.W. 9·8	—	2	—	Ɒ L, III.
13	28·83	28·82	28·78	73·3	69·3	58·0	·000	·000	·000	84	87	88	S.W. 0·0	E. 1·6	E. 19·6	—	2	—	—
14	28·77	28·81	28·83	64·3	52·6	49·0	·000	·000	·004	88	87	89	S.E. 5·9	S.S.E. 5·9	E. 16·4	—	2	—	☽ ☽ III.
15	28·91	29·07	29·20	31·0	65·2	64·6	·008	·004	·000	93	91	88	E.N.E. 9·8	W. 7·2	0·0	—	1 ≡	—	☽ III.
16	29·09	28·93	28·81	67·0	67·0	61·6	·000	·000	·000	88	88	88	0·0	0·0	0·0	—	2	—	☽ III.
17	28·79	28·87	29·01	71·5	50·8	63·4	·000	·000	·000	86	90	91	S.W. 19·6	S.W. 5·5	N.W. 1·9	—	5 ≡	—	—
18	29·07	29·11	29·11	51·1	46·3	40·5	·004	·004	·004	88	91	91	E. 16·4	E. 19·6	E. 16·4	—	2	—	☽ ☽ III.
19	29·06	29·02	28·98	36·4	68·2	50·2	·008	·004	·000	91	91	88	E. 16·4	N.E. 6·5	S. 3·2	—	5 ≡	—	☽ III.
20	28·84	28·82	28·77	70·9	68·8	71·7	·000	·000	·000	91	88	88	S.W. 4·5	S. 1·6	0·0	—	0	—	—
21	28·72	28·69	28·62	70·6	68·8	63·9	·000	·000	·000	88	87	88	0·0	0·0	E. 12·4	1	1	—	—
22	28·73	28·78	28·74	12·3	18·0	47·2	·023	·019	·004	95	94	92	E. 37·0	E. 30·1	S.S.W. 11·8	8	5	—	☀¹ L.
23	28·81	28·82	28·77	34·6	43·6	49·0	·004	·004	·004	91	93	94	0·0	E.N.E. 4·2	S.S.W. 19·6	0 ≡	2	—	—
24	28·81	28·87	28·87	32·8	34·2	43·6	·008	·008	·004	91	92	91	E.N.E. 18·0	E. 21·3	0·0	—	0	—	☽ III.
25	28·76	28·73	28·70	29·7	41·1	23·8	·008	·004	·012	93	92	93	0·0	E. 0·0	E. 13·1	10 ≡	10 ≡	—	—
26	28·81	28·91	29·04	33·5	26·7	18·4	·008	·012	·016	93	93	94	E.N.E. 18·3	E.N.E. 12·1	E. 15·4	8	10	—	—
27	29·31	29·42	29·46	11·2	16·9	25·2	·023	·019	·012	94	96	93	N. 7·8	N.E. 7·5	N.E. 6·5	0	10	—	—
28	29·43	29·32	29·22	43·6	39·1	36·4	·004	·004	·008	91	92	92	N.E. 15·0	N.E. 8·8	N.E. 13·7	—	8	—	—
29	29·00	28·82	28·72	62·5	62·5	58·0	·000	·000	·000	88	88	88	S.E. 0·0	S. 3·9	S. 2·6	1	8	—	—
30	28·57	28·51	28·52	62·5	59·1	38·2	·000	·000	·004	87	88	91	S. 4·2	0·0	0·0	4	3	—	—
31	28·82	29·00	29·03	14·6	28·5	38·2	·019	·012	·004	95	93	92	N.W. 40·3	N. 12·4	E. 22·9	—	3	—	☀¹ L, Ɒ III.
Mean	28·93	28·94	28·93	46·8	48·8	48·6	·004	·004	·004	90	90	90	10·8	11·1	8·8	—	4·4	—	—

389

SEPTEMBER, 1911.

Date	Barometer, Normal Gravity (Inches) 8 a.m.	2 p.m.	8 p.m.	Temperature of the Air (Fahrenheit) 8 a.	2 p.	8 p.	Absolute Humidity (Inch) 8 a.	2 p.	8 p.	Relative Humidity (per Cent.) 8 a.	2 p.	8 p.	Direction and Velocity of the Wind (Feet per Second) 8 a.	2 p.	8 p.	Cloud 8 a.	2 p.	8 p.	Remarks
1	29·04	29·05	29·09	−43·6	−48·1	−52·2	·004	·004	·004	91	92	90	N.E. 13·1	N.E. 10·8	0·0	5	3	1	☇ III.
2	29·05	29·10	29·13	−62·7	−53·7	−56·7	·000	·004	·000	88	88	88	0·0	S.W. 0·0	S.W. 1·9	3	1	1	☇ III.
3	29·17	29·24	29·26	−61·6	−55·5	−55·6	·000	·004	·004	88	88	88	17·0	0·0	0·0	0	1	1	
4	29·18	29·11	28·98	−47·2	−43·9	−47·2	·004	·004	·004	88	90	91	N.E. 14·1	N.E. 26·8	N.E. 24·6 ≡	10≡	10≡	10≡	
5	28·78	28·76	28·78	−45·4	−38·2	−32·8	·004	·008	·008	92	93	92	E. 17·3	E. 0·9	E. 17·3 ≡	8	10≡	10≡	
6	28·90	29·01	29·10	−23·8	−24·1	−20·5	·012	·012	·016	94	94	94	E. 27·2	E. 22·9	E. 20·6	10≡	7	10	⊕ III.
7	29·31	29·38	29·48	−25·6	−10·8	−7·6	·012	·027	·031	93	96	97	E. 0·9	E. 30·5	E. 37·3 ≡	10	10≡	10	
8	29·41	29·34	29·26	−29·2	−32·8	−41·8	·008	·008	·004	93	93	93	E.N.E. 10·4	E. 17·0	N.E. 0·3	6	2	6	
9	29·02	29·00	28·88	−45·7	−42·7	−44·5	·004	·004	·004	91	92	88	N.E. 0·0	N.E. 0·0	0·0	4	2	6	
10	28·84	28·87	28·90	−43·6	−41·8	−50·8	·004	·004	·000	91	91	88	N.E. 0·3	N.E. 0·3	S. 7·5	10	2	6≡	☇ III.
11	28·93	28·91	28·89	−61·6	−59·8	−63·4	·000	·000	·000	41	44	43	S.W. 10·4	S.W. 10·4	0·0	0	6≡	4	☇ III.
12	28·66	28·63	28·62	−58·0	−52·9	−49·0	·000	·000	·000	43	54	51	S. 10·0	S. 0·0	S.W. 0·3	3≡	0	0	
13	28·69	28·67	28·61	−54·4	−56·2	−59·8	·000	·004	·004	56	54	55	S. 10·8	S. 4·5	S.W. 9·8	6	4	4≡	
14	28·56	28·63	28·69	−56·2	−49·0	−49·0	·004	·004	·000	59	60	62	W. 0·0	S.W. 13·7	E. 19·6	3	7	7	
15	28·79	28·87	28·99	−43·6	−36·4	−38·5	·004	·008	·004	62	68	72	N.E. 10·4	W. 11·1	N.E. 10·1	6	7	0	
16	28·95	28·99	28·60	−47·2	−52·6	−59·8	·000	·000	·000	71	72	73	N.E. 0·0	S.E. 0·3	E. 0·6	2	0	0	
17	28·78	28·72	28·70	−61·6	−56·2	−63·4	·000	·000	·004	74	73	73	0·0	S. 0·0	S.W. 0·9	0	0	0	
18	28·52	28·66	28·70	−57·1	−52·6	−49·0	·004	·004	·004	73	74	74	N.E. 7·5	N.E. 0·0	0·0	1	0	2	
19	28·90	29·08	29·13	−46·3	−44·7	−52·6	·004	·012	·012	79	78	77	S.W. 14·1	S.W. 8·8	3·2	8	4	7	
20	29·19	29·28	29·35	−25·9	−22·0	−24·1	·012	·019	·016	83	84	86	N.E. 17·0	E. 14·4	E. 19·0	10	10	8	
21	29·41	29·43	29·45	−12·3	−15·0	−20·5	·023	·019	·016	88	87	88	E. 34·4	E. 21·6	E. 26·5	10	2	7	
22	29·45	29·43	29·40	−13·2	−32·8	−43·6	·008	·008	·004	88	87	87	E. 4·9	0·0	E. 4·2	7	1	1	
23	29·30	29·18	29·07	−43·2	−29·0	−42·9	·004	·008	·004	87	90	87	S. 8·8	0·0	0·0	7	7	5	
24	28·83	28·65	28·64	−27·4	−22·9	−36·4	·012	·012	·008	91	90	91	0·0	0·0	S.W. 6·8	10≡	10≡	10≡	
25	28·61	28·60	28·55	−30·6	−27·0	−18·4	·008	·012	·016	88	88	90	E. 9·8	E.N.E. 11·1	N.E. 16·4	10	10≡	10≡	
26	28·73	28·73	28·76	−17·3	−0·4	−0·7	·019	·043	·043	92	96	98	N. 7·5	N. 19·6	N.N.E. 21·6	10*≡	10*≡	10≡	
27	28·60	28·53	28·55	−3·1	−1·6	−2·2	·039	·039	·039	96	96	95	E. 28·5	E. 35·0	E. 26·2	10	10	10	
28	28·54	28·44	28·21	+6·8	+11·1	+15·8	·058	·074	·094	97	97	100	S.E. 22·9	S.E. 16·4	S.E. 32·8	10*	5	10*	* L, III.
29	28·46	28·58	28·59	+15·8	+10·1	+5·7	·094	·070	·055	100	97	93	N.E. 62·3	N.N.E. 45·9	E. 16·4	10	8	0	* L.
30	28·30	28·18	28·04	+9·3	+11·3	+3·2	·066	·070	·051	98	95	96	E. 3·2	0·0	0·0	9	10	10*	
Mean	28·90	28·90	28·89	−35·8	−32·4	−35·3	·012	·016	·016	83	83	82	11·4	11·1	10·8	6·6	5·1	5·8	

Date	Barometer, Normal Gravity (Inches).			Temperature of the Air (Fahrenheit).			Absolute Humidity (Inch).			Relative Humidity (per Cent.).			Direction and Velocity of the Wind (Feet per Second).			Cloud.			Remarks.
	8 a.m.	2 p.m.	8 p.m.	8 a.	2 p.	8 p.	8 a.	2 p.	8 p.	8 a.	2 p.	8 p.	8 a.	2 p.	8 p.	8 a.	2 p.	8 p.	
1	28·15	28·35	28·56	+8·6	+5·4	+9·2	·066	·055	·066	97	94	95	N. 34·1	N.E. 28·8	N.N.E. 21·9	—	—	10	✱ I. II.
2	28·68	28·58	28·51	−0·6	+7·0	+7·4	·043	·058	·058	94	96	97	E.S.E. 40·6	E. 36·0	E.S.E. 22·9	—	10✱	10	✱✱ I.
3	28·35	28·33	28·33	+11·0	+10·6	+6·3	·070	·070	·058	98	97	96	E.S.E. 30·1	E. 39·3	E. 18·0	10✱	7	10	✱✱ II.
4	28·44	28·45	28·44	+1·8	+5·4	+2·5	·028	·031	·035	92	90	91	N.E. 12·1	E. 13·7	E. 13·7	10✱	7	10	
5	28·19	28·10	28·15	+0·5	−19·8	−26·7	·039	·031	·012	79	84	84	S.S.W. 14·4	S. 13·1	S. 4·5	1	10≡	5	
6	28·22	28·26	28·33	−36·4	−29·5	−32·4	·035	·008	·008	82	80	82	S. 7·2	0·0	0·0	2	3	7	
7	28·50	28·58	28·60	−27·4	−25·8	−26·7	·008	·008	·012	80	78	82	N.E. 6·5	S.E. 8·2	S.E. 0·6	2	2	3	⊕ I.
8	28·60	28·61	28·61	−32·8	−25·9	−40·3	·008	·012	·004	82	83	82	N.E. 6·5	E. 4·5	2	1	1	
9	28·63	28·64	28·58	−25·4	−16·6	−22·3	·012	·012	·012	84	81	84	E.N.E. 29·5	E. 25·5	E. 19·6	7	8	4	
10	28·48	28·49	28·48	−16·6	−17·3	−30·3	·016	·016	·008	78	79	80	E. 43·6	S.E. 0·0	0·0	1	1	4	
11	28·52	28·55	28·57	−38·5	−34·6	−40·2	·004	·008	·004	82	86	84	S.S.W. 0·0	S.W. 6·5	S.W. 5·5	10	10	10	
12	28·64	28·69	28·79	−37·6	−27·4	−29·2	·012	·012	·008	83	65	72	E.N.E. 9·8	E.N.E. 22·3	E.N.E. 21·6	10	10	8≡	
13	29·00	29·15	29·29	−23·1	−16·6	−17·5	·012	·012	·016	73	74	73	E.N.E. 18·3	E. 13·1	E. 11·8	10	10	10≡	
14	29·62	29·66	29·59	−13·5	−17·7	−13·0	·016	·016	·016	77	72	74	S.W. 2·2	E.N.E. 2·2	E. 20·3	8	10	10	
15	29·36	29·13	28·87	−25·6	−19·6	−22·0	·008	·012	·019	75	75	74	E. 16·4	E.S.E. 16·4	E.S.E. 14·7	6	10	10	
16	28·54	28·47	28·38	−12·8	−16·6	−27·7	·012	·016	·012	73	73	72	S.W. 4·5	S. 11·1	S.S.W. 11·4	6≡	6≡	9	
17	28·30	28·47	28·69	−25·2	−23·4	−14·1	·008	·012	·008	72	70	75	S.W. 20·3	W.S.W. 37·7	W.S.W. 14·4	10≡	10≡	4	
18	28·99	29·01	28·92	+2·0	+4·7	+2·4	·031	·043	·027	66	66	65	N.E. 13·1	E.S.E. 24·2	E.S.E. 36·7	10	10	10	
19	28·44	28·32	28·26	+1·4	+4·0	+5·6	·035	·023	·023	70	72	73	E.N.E. 54·4	E.N.E. 33·7	0·0	10	10	10	
20	28·37	28·48	28·54	−16·2	+6·1	−15·7	·016	·023	·016	69	72	68	S.E. 7·5	N.E. 9·8	N.E. 17·3	9	6	2	
21	28·41	28·24	28·29	−2·2	+4·7	−14·8	·031	·039	·016	75	72	75	S.E. 26·8	S. 33·4	S. 14·4	0	6	8	
22	28·37	28·44	28·41	+1·4	+1·4	+6·8	·035	·035	·047	75	74	75	E. 27·5	S.E. 20·3	E. 30·8	10	6	4	I. II.
23	28·23	28·27	28·43	−11·2	−15·7	−22·0	·019	·016	·012	74	71	71	S.W. 40·6	S.W. 42·9	S.W. 14·4	0	6	2	✱ I. II.
24	28·66	28·59	28·48	+3·2	+6·8	+1·4	·035	·047	·035	70	76	71	N.E. 10·8	N.E. 23·9	N.E. 16·7	10	10	6	✱ I. II. III.
25	28·38	28·41	28·61	+1·4	+1·4	+7·6	·035	·035	·023	72	76	75	S.W. 10·4	S.W. 20·6	S.W. 20·0	4	6	8	
26	28·79	28·89	28·91	−20·2	+9·4	−14·1	·012	·019	·016	70	70	75	S. 0·0	10·1	0	4	6	
27	28·91	28·93	28·72	−21·1	−15·5	+10·4	·012	·019	·051	66	71	72	E. 0·5	E. 4·2	E. 40·0	0	4	8	III.
28	28·30	28·16	28·10	+10·1	+15·8	+10·4	·051	·074	·058	70	83	83	S.E. 33·7	S.E. 17·7	0·0	10	10	10✱	I. II.
29	28·29	28·43	28·66	−13·0	+3·2	+10·4	·019	·039	·062	73	75	84	S.W. 30·1	W. 19·6	W. 19·6	10	10	10✱	✱ I. II. III.
30	28·92	29·05	29·11	+12·2	+6·8	+8·3	·066	·051	·055	86	83	83	N. 50·1	N. 50·5	N. 27·2	10	10	10✱	✱ I. II. II.
31	29·08	29·05	29·02	−0·7	+5·7	+4·0	·031	·039	·027	72	64	72	E. 33·7	0·0	0·0	2	6	4	—
Mean	28·60	28·61	28·62	−11·4	−8·8	−11·7	·027	·027	·027	78	78	79	20·6	19·0	14·4	7·2	7·8	7·4	

NOVEMBER, 1911.

Date.	Barometer, Normal Gravity (Inches).			Temperature of the Air (Fahrenheit).			Absolute Humidity (Inch).			Relative Humidity (per Cent.).			Direction and Velocity of the Wind (Feet per Second).			Cloud.			Remarks.
	8 a.m.	2 p.m.	8 p.m.	8 a.	2 p.	8 p.	8 a.	2 p.	8 p.	8 a.	2 p.	8 p.	8 a.	2 p.	8 p.	8 a.	2 p.	8 p.	
1	29·11	29·22	29·25	−18·4	−7·6	−4·9	·012	·023	·027	72	75	72	E. 1·3	S. 16·4	S.E. 16·4	5	0	2	—
2	29·25	29·12	29·09	−0·4	+2·9	−6·3	·031	·043	·019	75	80	61	E. 47·2	E. 53·7	S. 3·2	0	0	1	* I., II.
3	29·08	29·08	29·13	−14·8	−6·1	−7·6	·016	·023	·023	64	64	74	S. 0·3	S. 0·6	S.W. 17·7	0	0	0	—
4	29·33	29·45	29·51	−5·8	+1·4	−5·8	·023	·035	·023	72	74	72	S. 0·6	. 0·0	S.W. 19·6	0	0	0	—
5	29·47	29·51	29·51	+3·2	−2·2	+6·1	·043	·031	·023	81	75	75	S.W. 14·4	S. 19·6	S.W. 26·2	10	10	9	—
6	29·52	29·49	29·37	−11·2	−0·4	−3·6	·019	·035	·031	75	80	80	E. 3·9	E. 3·2	S.W. 0·0	2	2	3	* III.
7	29·28	29·29	29·29	+15·8	+15·8	+11·3	·066	·070	·051	72	75	70	E. 43·9	E. 53·7	E. 27·2	4	2	2	** I., II., III.
8	29·37	29·25	29·15	−0·4	−2·2	−2·2	·027	·027	·027	61	66	71	S. 19·6	S. 20·3	S.W. 25·5	0	0	0	—
9	29·12	29·12	29·12	−9·4	+1·4	−5·8	·019	·031	·023	68	68	68	S.W. 0·6	. 0·0	. 0·0	0	2	1	—
10	29·22	29·26	29·28	−4·0	+0·7	−0·4	·023	·031	·031	65	68	69	S.W. 10·4	S.W. 19·6	S.W. 7·2	1	1	2	—
11	29·30	29·33	29·36	−4·9	+3·2	+2·1	·027	·039	·035	72	72	70	S.E. 0·6	S.W. 16·7	S.W. 13·7	0	1	2	—
12	29·43	29·49	29·50	−2·2	+10·4	+2·7	·027	·051	·035	70	73	70	E. 13·7	N.E. 0·6	E. 0·0	1	0	2	—
13	29·54	29·56	29·52	−3·2	+3·2	+2·3	·039	·039	·039	68	66	75	E. 47·2	E. 1·3	E. 22·9	4	1	0	—
14	29·48	29·55	29·49	+1·4	+6·5	+1·1	·031	·039	·035	58	75	71	E. 14·1	S.E. 13·7	E. 48·6	1	0	2	* I., III.
15	29·50	29·56	29·54	+5·0	+8·3	+2·5	·031	·051	·035	66	65	68	E. 43·9	S.E. 22·9	E. 20·9	1	2	10	—
16	29·39	29·39	29·34	−4·3	+6·8	+5·0	·035	·039	·039	62	64	60	E. 43·9	N.E. 56·7	N.E. 59·9	10	4	2	* I., III.
17	29·28	29·24	29·24	+7·9	+10·4	+10·4	·039	·047	·043	75	75	81	E. 23·9	N.E. 17·3	N.E. 0·6	10	10	10	—
18	29·26	29·37	29·37	+7·9	+13·7	+15·1	·047	·062	·074	81	75	68	S. 0·0	S.W. 3·9	S.W. 13·4	8	8	9	—
19	29·41	29·43	29·44	+15·5	+17·6	+6·8	·074	·074	·043	64	64	73	E. 0·6	S.W. 0·9	S.W. 10·8	4	7	6	—
20	29·45	29·46	29·55	+6·1	+8·3	+1·2	·039	·043	·035	75	71	72	E. 4·2	S.W. 4·2	S.W. 4·5	5	0	6	—
21	29·61	29·67	29·69	+8·7	+0·3	+1·5	·023	·031	·031	72	81	73	S. 0·6	E. 10·1	S.W. 13·1	0	0	2	—
22	29·75	29·81	29·84	−2·9	+6·5	−0·6	·023	·043	·031	83	81	85	S. 10·8	E. 10·8	E. 7·5	6	10	10	—
23	29·88	29·93	29·98	+7·2	+15·8	+17·6	·047	·074	·082	63	90	70	E. 0·6	N.E. 10·8	N.E. 0·6	0	8	10	—
24	30·00	30·01	29·94	+17·6	+18·0	+15·5	·082	·082	·062	73	76	84	E. 0·0	E. 4·2	E. 0·0	8	10	6	—
25	29·80	29·72	29·63	+19·1	+19·1	+14·7	·066	·078	·062	77	72	80	E. 0·9	E. 0·9	N. 20·6	10*	8	10*	** I., II., III.
26	29·45	29·40	29·39	+19·4	+10·4	+20·3	·062	·105	·094	79	77	84	E. 11·1	N. 23·9	N.W. 40·3	10	10	10*	** II., III.
27	29·52	29·62	29·63	+17·6	+23·7	+20·5	·074	·094	·090	73	64	80	N.W. 10·4	N.W. 20·6	N.E. 0·6	8	8	9	—
28	29·80	29·88	29·87	+19·1	+17·3	+8·6	·082	·070	·055	77	72	81	W. 0·3	S.W. 0·3	N.E. 10·1	10*	7	4	—
29	29·80	29·80	29·78	+15·1	+18·3	+12·0	·070	·082	·062	79	77	82	E. 3·6	E. 3·6	E. 4·2	8	8	9	—
30	29·75	29·76	29·79	+16·2	+20·5	+13·7	·066	·070	·062	73	64	75	S.E. 0·6	E. 0·0	. 0·0	6	4	4	—
Mean	29·47	29·49	29·49	+3·6	+8·4	+4·7	·043	·051	·043	72	73	73	11·4	14·1	14·4	4·6	3·9	4·5	

DECEMBER, 1911.

Date	Barometer, Normal Gravity (Inches) 8 a.m.	2 p.m.	8 p.m.	Temperature of the Air (Fahrenheit) 8 a.	2 p.	8 p.	Absolute Humidity (Inch) 8 a.	2 p.	8 p.	Relative Humidity (per Cent.) 8 a.	2 p.	8 p.	Direction and Velocity of the Wind (Feet per Second) 8 a.	2 p.	8 p.	Cloud 8 a.	2 p.	8 p.	Remarks
1	29·78	29·80	29·78	+12·9	+14·0	+6·5	·062	·066	·047	75	77	77	E. 11·1	S. 6·8	S. 14·4	8	6	3	—
2	29·80	29·79	29·73	+10·1	+9·7	+4·7	·047	·051	·043	68	72	75	0·3	S.E. 0·6	S.E. 0·9	0	0	0	—
3	29·60	29·72	29·78	+1·8	+10·1	+5·0	·039	·055	·047	81	75	95	S.W. 11·1	S.E. 0·9	S.E. 3·9	0	0	0	—
4	29·70	29·50	29·38	+12·2	+19·4	+29·9	·055	·090	·157	72	86	72	S.E. 37·0	E. 42·9	N.E. 27·2	10*	10*	10*	* L., II., III.
5	29·33	29·33	29·25	+31·7	+31·7	+28·8	·157	·173	·113	86	98	93	N.E. 33·7	N.E. 50·1	N.E. 60·2	10*	10*	10*	—
6	29·28	29·30	29·30	+28·4	+28·1	+28·1	·109	·118	·145	72	77	81	N.E. 27·1	E. 29·8	E. 29·8	10*	10*	10*	—
7	29·55	29·73	29·82	+27·3	+30·2	+24·8	·113	·094	·109	76	57	93	S.W. 14·1	0·0	0·9	10	10	9	—
8	29·91	29·98	30·01	+20·9	+26·6	+26·6	·086	·109	·118	76	76	81	0·0	0·0	W. 0·9	8	10	4	Sleet III
9	30·14	30·02	29·82	+18·5	+26·6	+28·4	·097	·134	·149	93	91	95	0·0	W. 4·5	W. 16·7	10≡	10*	10*	* L., II.
10	29·54	29·45	29·56	+24·8	+23·9	+20·3	·101	·086	·086	76	81	80	S. 26·5	S.W. 29·8	S.W. 33·1	8	2	2	* * I.
11	29·36	29·34	29·30	+16·2	+20·1	+17·6	·078	·082	·082	76	74	74	S.W. 23·6	S.W. 20·6	0·0	9	2	10*	* I.
12	29·20	29·24	29·25	+19·4	+16·5	+19·1	·082	·082	·074	80	85	75	0·0	E. 7·8	E. 22·9	10	6	0	—
13	29·26	29·27	29·25	+17·6	+20·9	+19·4	·082	·090	·074	72	79	70	E. 19·6	S.E. 22·9	S.E. 3·6	6	9	2	* I.
14	29·26	29·28	29·26	+20·1	+20·9	+16·2	·078	·097	·090	85	85	86	0·0	E. 7·5	E. 9·8	0	5	5	—
15	29·35	29·46	29·56	+16·2	+19·1	+23·0	·109	·109	·094	85	85	92	E. 13·7	E. 17·7	E. 20·9	4	10	10	* III.
16	29·72	29·80	29·82	+23·0	+28·1	+26·3	·109	·141	·134	87	90	86	E. 10·1	E. 0·0	E. 0·0	0	10	10	* I.
17	29·76	29·72	29·67	+24·5	+28·4	+20·5	·109	·109	·097	85	70	83	E. 10·1	E. 10·1	E. 0·0	0	3	4	—
18	29·63	29·61	29·62	+22·7	+24·5	+23·7	·105	·109	·105	86	85	83	E. 10·8	E. 13·7	E. 0·0	0	10	10	—
19	29·71	29·78	29·82	+18·3	+21·6	+26·1	·105	·097	·105	93	71	93	S.W. 14·1	E. 3·9	E. 23·5	6	10	10	—
20	29·86	29·85	29·80	+23·0	+24·8	+19·4	·105	·113	·090	85	92	83	N.E. 14·1	N.E. 7·5	E. 10·8	8	10	10*	* L., III.
21	29·70	29·73	29·72	+18·5	+25·5	+23·7	·090	·130	·122	86	79	93	E. 26·8	E. 14·1	E. 13·7	10	10	10	—
22	29·69	29·68	29·64	+26·6	+25·9	+20·5	·128	·109	·082	86	71	71	E. 14·1	S.E. 16·7	E. 0·0	8	10	10	—
23	29·67	29·74	29·78	+19·4	+24·8	+26·1	·101	·101	·101	93	82	87	E. 17·0	E. 16·7	E. 13·7	10	10	10	—
24	29·80	29·81	29·79	+25·5	+27·3	+20·1	·113	·122	·094	82	79	83	E. 10·4	E. 13·4	E. 13·4	8	4	8	—
25	29·74	29·73	29·72	+30·2	+20·1	+23·9	·105	·090	·109	63	75	82	0·0	S. 0·0	S. 17·0	10	10	8	—
26	29·77	29·79	29·82	+11·9	+24·8	+19·1	·055	·090	·082	68	73	75	S. 6·8	* 0·0	0·0	0	0	0	—
27	29·89	29·91	29·90	+14·7	+22·7	+22·7	·058	·090	·097	68	85	85	0·0	S.W. 7·8	S.W. 6·5	2	2	1	—
28	29·88	29·89	29·87	+13·1	+18·5	+15·5	·062	·086	·078	79	81	85	S.E. 7·5	E. 9·8	E. 6·8	8	2	2	—
29	29·84	29·84	29·83	+13·7	+21·2	+20·5	·070	·094	·097	86	82	86	E. 17·0	E. 17·3	E. 17·0	0	10	8	—
30	29·80	29·78	29·74	+19·4	+22·7	+22·1	·090	·101	·101	86	84	84	E. 13·7	E.N.E. 11·1	E. 4·2	2	10	10	—
31	29·66	29·62	29·63	+20·1	+26·3	+18·9	·094	·126	·082	86	88	79	E. 11·1	E.N.E. 6·8	S.E. 9·8	0	10	9	—
Mean	29·65	29·66	29·65	+19·4	+22·7	+20·7	·090	·101	·097	80	81	83	13·1	12·7	11·8	7·6	6·8	6·3	

JANUARY, 1912.

Date.	Barometer, Normal Gravity (Inches). 8 a.m.	2 p.m.	8 p.m.	Temperature of the Air (Fahrenheit). 8 a.	2 p.	8 p.	Absolute Humidity (Inch). 8 a.	2 p.	8 p.	Relative Humidity (per Cent.). 8 a.	2 p.	8 p.	Direction and Velocity of the Wind (Feet per Second). 8 a.	2 p.	8 p.	Cloud. 8 a.	2 p.	8 p.	Remarks.
1	29·62	29·60	29·59	+18·9	+26·6	+13·1	·094	·101	·066	90	72	82	9·8 S.W.	9·8 S.W.	4·5 S.W.	9	8	2	—
2	29·54	29·52	29·52	+14·9	+25·5	+15·8	·074	·094	·070	83	68	75	0·0	0·0 S.W.	20·3 S.W.	10*	2	8	—
3	29·47	29·46	29·46	+8·3	+17·3	+15·1	·055	·082	·078	83	81	83	13·4 S.W.	10·4 S.W.	13·4 S.W.	1	0	0	—
4	29·54	29·52	29·57	+13·7	+14·4	+14·0	·066	·074	·070	81	86	84	6·8 S.E.	14·1 E.	4·2 E.	1	2	6	—
5	29·56	29·60	29·59	+8·6	+15·5	+8·1	·055	·070	·051	86	82	80	3·9	3·9 N.	1·6 N.E.	2	0	1	—
6	29·59	29·56	29·46	+9·0	+15·8	+14·0	·055	·086	·074	83	93	88	0·0 S.W.	10·8 S.W.	7·2 E.	10≡	10≡	10	—
7	29·28	29·13	29·14	+15·1	+19·4	+17·6	·078	·097	·082	88	92	83	19·6 S.E.	7·5 S.E.	3·9 S.	10	10	10	—
8	29·03	29·03	29·01	+19·4	+19·4	+15·8	·086	·086	·074	80	79	87	4·2 E.	0·0	0·0	6	4	5	—
9	29·10	29·20	29·22	+19·9	+16·7	+16·5	·066	·078	·082	84	83	79	6·5 E.	20·9 E.	20·6 E.	10	8	10	—
10	29·33	29·36	29·36	+20·9	+26·3	+20·1	·097	·122	·090	86	85	75	10·1 E.	11·1 E.	13·1 E.S.E.	5	4	4	—
11	29·25	29·18	29·17	+19·4	+24·5	+22·3	·090	·109	·090	81	83	92	20·9 E.	17·7 E.	20·3 E.	10	8	4	—
12	29·14	29·18	29·13	+22·7	+23·0	+17·3	·097	·090	·086	79	76	92	0·0	0·0	4·2 E.N.E.	9	9	9	—
13	29·02	29·02	29·01	+18·4	+20·3	+19·1	·090	·090	·086	88	81	81	17·0 E.	20·3 E.	14·1 E.	6	2	0	—
14	29·06	29·25	29·33	+17·4	+24·5	+20·9	·070	·082	·094	92	62	81	0·0	0·0 S.W.	3·9 S.W.	0	8	10	—
15	29·42	29·47	29·52	+16·2	+18·0	+17·3	·086	·086	·078	92	84	81	11·1 S.W.	10·1	0·0	10	1	2	—
16	29·51	29·46	29·40	+13·3	+20·3	+20·9	·066	·094	·094	81	83	81	0·0	0·9 E.	0·0	10	2	10	—
17	29·32	29·33	29·37	+22·1	+27·5	+17·6	·097	·122	·078	83	79	77	4·2 W.	0·0	3·9 S.E.	8	0	0	—
18	29·38	29·39	29·32	+14·0	+19·1	+19·1	·062	·086	·082	74	75	75	0·0	30·5 E.	0·0	0	0	6	—
19	29·31	29·35	29·36	+16·2	+16·2	+10·1	·066	·066	·055	68	69	75	0·0 S.	20·3 S.S.W.	19·6 S.S.W.	6	0	0	—
20	29·42	29·41	29·36	+7·7	+13·7	+10·1	·055	·066	·058	84	79	82	6·8 W.S.W.	10·1 S.W.	3·9 S.W.	0	9	10	—
21	29·34	29·40	29·40	+6·1	+14·0	+20·5	·047	·066	·105	79	80	95	3·2 E.	3·9 E.	20·9 E.	0	10	0	—
22	29·48	29·47	29·54	+19·1	+23·0	+20·9	·086	·105	·097	83	86	85	4·2 E.	13·4 E.	0·0	6	10	10	⊕ III.
23	29·58	29·59	29·57	+21·2	+17·6	+17·6	·097	·094	·094	83	94	94	0·0 N.E.	11·1 N.E.	17·3 E.N.E.	10	10	10	—
24	29·59	29·59	29·60	+11·3	+9·3	+5·0	·062	·051	·043	81	76	77	10·1 S.	14·1 S.	7·5 S.	8	10	10	—
25	29·43	29·35	29·21	+1·4	+1·4	+8·3	·039	·039	·058	81	79	88	10·4 S.W.	11·1 S.S.W.	27·5 W.S.W.	10	8	10	—
26	29·22	29·22	29·23	+11·1	+17·3	+8·6	·058	·058	·047	79	61	68	17·0 S.E.	7·5 E.	4·2 S.E.	2	0	0	—
27	29·28	29·27	29·18	+9·5	+15·5	+13·3	·055	·062	·070	79	70	85	3·9 E.	6·8 S.	7·5 E.	0	0	0	—
28	29·27	29·28	29·23	+15·5	+15·3	+10·1	·062	·055	·055	70	61	79	6·8 S.	7·8 E.	0·0	0	0	10	—
29	29·27	29·29	29·31	+16·7	+18·2	+14·0	·082	·082	·078	85	82	94	3·2 S.E.	13·1 S.	0·0	10	10	10	—
Mean	29·36	29·36	29·35	+14·6	+18·5	+15·3	·074	·082	·074	82	79	82	6·5	9·8	8·5	5·9	4·3	5·4	

394

APPENDIX III

GEOLOGY

Provisional Remarks on the Examination of the Geological Specimens brought by Roald Amundsen's South Polar Expedition from the Antarctic Continent (South Victoria Land and King Edward VII. Land). By J. Schetelig, Secretary of the Mineralogical Institute of Christiania University

The collection of specimens of rocks brought back by Mr. Roald Amundsen from his South Polar expedition has been sent by him to the Mineralogical Institute of the University, the Director of which, Professor W. C. Brögger, has been good enough to entrust to me the work of examining this rare and valuable material, which gives us information of the structure of hitherto untrodden regions.

Roald Amundsen himself brought back altogether about twenty specimens of various kinds of rock from *Mount Betty*, which lies in lat. 85° 8′ S. Lieutenant Prestrud's expedition to King Edward VII. Land collected in all about thirty specimens from *Scott's Nunatak*, which was the only mountain bare of snow that this expedition met with on its route. A number of the stones from Scott's Nunatak were brought away because they were thickly overgrown with lichens. These specimens of lichens have been sent to the Botanical Museum of the University.

A first cursory examination of the material was enough to show that the specimens from Mount Betty and Scott's Nunatak consist exclusively of granitic rocks and crystalline schists. There were no specimens of sedimentary rocks which, by possibly containing fossils, might have contributed to the determination of the age of these mountains. Another thing that was immediately apparent was the striking agreement that exists between the rocks from these two places, lying so far apart. The distance from Mount Betty to Scott's Nunatak is between seven and eight degrees of latitude.

I have examined the specimens microscopically.

From *Mount Betty* there are several specimens of *white granite*, with dark and light mica ; it has a great resemblance to the white granites from Sogn, the Dovre district, and Nordland, in Norway. There is one very beautiful specimen of shining white, fine-grained *granite aplite*, with small, pale red garnets. These granites show in their exterior no sign of pressure structure. The remaining rocks from Mount Betty are *gneissic granite*, partly very rich in dark mica, and *gneiss* (granitic schist) ; besides *mica schist*, with veins of quartz.

From *Scott's Nunatak* there are also several specimens of *white granite*, very like those from Mount Betty. The remaining rocks from here are richer in lime and iron, and show a series of gradual transitions from *micacious granite*, through *grano-diorite* to *quartz diorite*, with considerable quantities of dark mica and green hornblende. In one of the specimens the quantity of free quartz is so small that the rock is almost a quartz-free *diorite*. The quartz diorites are : some medium-grained, some coarse-grained (quartz-diorite-pegmatite), with streaks of black mica. The schistose rocks from Scott's Nunatak are streaked, and, in part, very fine-grained *quartz diorite schists*. Mica schists do not occur among the specimens from this mountain.

Our knowledge of the geology of South Victoria Land is mainly due to Scott's expedition of 1901-1904, with H. T. Ferrar as geologist, and Shackleton's expedition of 1907-08, with Professor David and R. Priestley as geologists. According to the investigations of these expeditions, South Victoria Land consists of a vast, ancient complex of crystalline schists and granitic rocks, large extents of which are covered by a sandstone formation ("Beacon Sandstone," Ferrar), on the whole horizontally bedded, which is at least 1,500 feet thick, and in which Shackleton found seams of coal and fossil wood (a coniferous tree). This, as it belongs to the Upper Devonian or Lower Carboniferous, determines a lower limit for the age of the sandstone formation. Shackleton also found in lat. 85° 15′ S. beds of limestone, which he regards as underlying and being older than the sandstone. In the limestone, which is also on the whole horizontally bedded, only radiolaria have been found. The limestone is probably of older Palæozoic age (? Silurian). It is, therefore, tolerably certain that the underlying older formation of gneisses, crystalline schists and granites, etc., is of Archæan age, and belongs to the foundation rocks.

Volcanic rocks are only found along the coast of Ross Sea and on a range of islands parallel to the coast. Shackleton did not find volcanic rocks on his ascent from the Barrier on his route towards the South Pole.

G. T. Prior, who has described the rocks collected by Scott's expedition, gives the following as belonging to the complex of foundation rocks: gneisses, granites, diorites, banatites, and other eruptive rocks, as well as crystalline limestone, with chondrodite. Professor David and R. Priestley, the geologists of Shackleton's expedition, refer to Ferrar's and Prior's description of the foundation rocks, and state that according to their own investigations the foundation rocks consist of banded gneiss, gneissic granite, granodiorite, and diorite rich in sphene, besides coarse crystalline limestone as enclosures in the gneiss.

This list of the most important rocks belonging to the foundation series of the parts of South Victoria Land already explored agrees so closely with the rocks from Mount Betty and Scott's Nunatak, that there can be no doubt that the latter also belong to the foundation rocks.

From the exhaustive investigations carried out by Scott's and Shackleton's expeditions it appears that South Victoria Land is a plateau land, consisting of a foundation platform, of great thickness and prominence, above which lie remains, of greater or less extent, of Palæozoic formations, horizontally bedded. From the specimens of rock brought home by Roald Amundsen's expedition it is established that the plateau of foundation rocks is continued eastward to Amundsen's route to the South Pole, and that King Edward VII. Land is probably a northern continuation, on the eastern side of Ross Sea, of the foundation rock plateau of South Victoria Land.

CHRISTIANIA,
September 26, 1912.

APPENDIX IV

THE ASTRONOMICAL OBSERVATIONS AT THE POLE

NOTE BY PROFESSOR H. GEELMUYDEN

CHRISTIANIA,
September 16, 1912.

WHEN requested this summer to receive the astronomical observations from Roald Amundsen's South Pole Expedition, for the purpose of working them out, I at once put myself in communication with Mr. A. Alexander (a mathematical master) to get him to undertake this work, while indicating the manner in which the materials could be best dealt with. As Mr. Alexander had in a very efficient manner participated in the working out of the observations from Nansen's *Fram* Expedition, and since then had calculated the astronomical observations from Amundsen's *Gjöa* Expedition, and from Captain Isachsen's expeditions to Spitzbergen, I knew by experience that he was not only a reliable and painstaking calculator, but that he also has so full an insight into the theoretical basis, that he is capable of working without being bound down by instructions.

(*Signed*) H. GEELMUYDEN,
Professor of Astronomy,
The Observatory of the University,
Christiania.

MR. ALEXANDER'S REPORT.

CAPTAIN ROALD AMUNDSEN,

At your request I shall here give briefly the result of my examination of the observations from your South Pole Expedition. My calculations are based on the longitude for Framheim given to me by Lieutenant Prestrud, 163° 37′ W. of Greenwich. He describes this longitude as provisional, but only to such an extent that the final result cannot differ appreciably from it. My own results may also be somewhat modified on a final treatment of the material. But these modifications, again, will only be immaterial, and, in any case, will not affect the result of the investigations given below as to the position of the two Polar stations.

At the first Polar station, on December 15, 1911, eighteen altitudes of the sun were taken in all with each of the expedition's sextants. The latitude calculated from these altitudes is, on an average of both sextants, very near 89° 54′, with a mean error of ±2′. The longitude calculated from the altitudes is about 7ᵗ (105°) E.; but, as might be expected in this high latitude, the aberrations are very considerable. We may, however, assume with great certainty that this station lies between lat. 89° 52′ and 89° 56′ S., and between long. 90° and 120° E.

The variation of the compass at the first Polar station was determined by a series of bearings of the sun. This gives us the absolute direction of the last day's line of route. The length of this line was measured as five and a half geographical miles. With the help of this we are able to construct for Polheim a field of the same form and extent as that within which the first Polar station must lie.

At Polheim, during a period of twenty-four hours (December 16-17), observations were taken every hour with one of the sextants. The observations show an upper culmination altitude of 23° 19·2′, and a resulting lower culmination altitude of 23° 17·4′. These

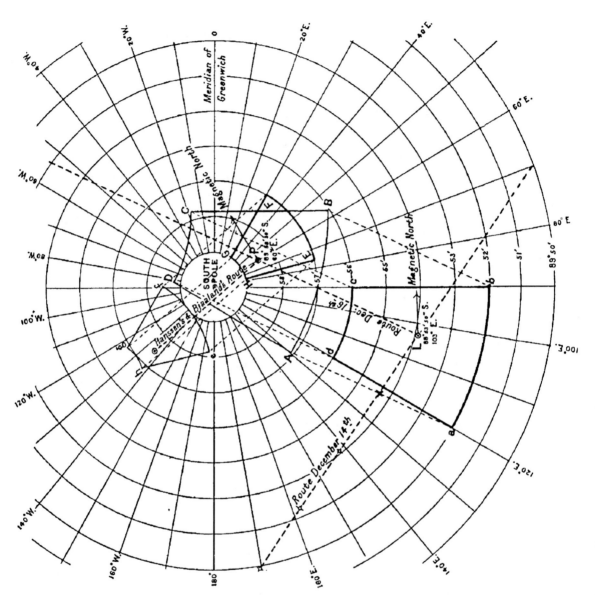

altitudes are one or two minutes of arc too low. This is not more than may be accounted for by uncertainty in the determination of the error of the instrument; but that atmospheric anomalies were also present is shown by the series of observations as a whole. In

combining the above two altitudes, an equal error on the same side
in each will have no influence on the result. The combination
gives a latitude of 89° 58·6'. That this result must be nearly
correct is confirmed by the considerable displacement of the periods
of culmination which is indicated by the series of observations, and
which in the immediate neighbourhood of the Pole is caused by the
change in the sun's declination. On the day of the observations
this displacement amounted to thirty minutes in 89° 57', forty-six
minutes in 89° 58', and over an hour and a half in 89° 59'. The
upper culmination occurred so much too late, and the lower
culmination so much too early. The interval between these two
periods was thus diminished by double the amount of the displace-
ments given. Now the series of observations shows that the interval
between the upper and the lower culmination amounted at the
most to eleven hours; the displacement of the periods of culmination was thus at least half an hour. It results that Polheim must
lie south of 89° 57', while at the same time we may assume that it
cannot lie south of 89° 59'. The moments of culmination could,
of course, only be determined very approximately, and in the same
way the observations as a whole are unserviceable for the determination of longitude. It may, however, be stated with some certainty
that the longitude must be between 30° and 75° E. The latitude,
as already mentioned, is between 89° 57' and 89° 59', and the
probable position of Polheim may be given roughly as lat. 89°
58·5' S., and long. 60° E.

On the accompanying sketch-chart the letters *abcd* indicate the
field within which the first Polar station must lie; *ABCD* is the
field which is thereby assigned to Polheim; *EFGH* the field within
which Polheim must lie according to the observations taken on the
spot itself; *P* the probable position of Polheim, and *L* the resulting
position of the first Polar station. The position thus assigned to
the latter agrees as well as could be expected with the average
result of the observations of December 15. According to this,
Polheim would be assumed to lie one and a half geographical

miles, or barely three kilometres, from the South Pole, and certainly not so much as six kilometres from it.

From your verbal statement I learn that Helmer Hanssen and Bjaaland walked four geographical miles from Polheim in the direction taken to be south on the basis of the observations.   On the chart the letters *efgh* give the field within which the termination of their line of route must lie.   It will be seen from this that they passed the South Pole at a distance which, on the one hand, can hardly have been so great as two and a half kilometres, and on the other, hardly so great as two kilometres ; that, if the assumed position of Polheim be correct, they passed the actual Pole at a distance of between 400 and 600 metres ; and that it is very probable that they passed the actual Pole at a distance of a few hundred metres, perhaps even less.

I am, etc.,

(Signed)   ANTON ALEXANDER.

CHRISTIANIA,
September 22, 1912.

APPENDIX V

OCEANOGRAPHY

REMARKS ON THE OCEANOGRAPHICAL INVESTIGATIONS CARRIED OUT BY THE "FRAM" IN THE NORTH ATLANTIC IN 1910 AND IN THE SOUTH ATLANTIC IN 1911. BY PROFESSOR BJÖRN HELLAND-HANSEN AND PROFESSOR FRIDTJOF NANSEN

IN the earliest ages of the human race the sea formed an absolute barrier. Men looked out upon its immense surface, now calm and bright, now lashed by storms, and always mysteriously attractive ; but they could not grapple with it. Then they learned to make boats ; at first small, simple craft, which could only be used when the sea was calm. But by degrees the boats were made larger and more perfect, so that they could venture farther out and weather a storm if it came. In antiquity the peoples of Europe accomplished the navigation of the Mediterranean, and the boldest maritime nation was able to sail round Africa and find the way to India by sea. Then came voyages to the northern waters of Europe, and far back in the Middle Ages enterprising seamen crossed from Norway to Iceland and Greenland and the north-eastern part of North America. They sailed straight across the North Atlantic, and were thus the true discoverers of that ocean.

Even in antiquity the Greek geographers had assumed that the greater part of the globe was covered by sea, but it was not till the beginning of the modern age that any at all accurate idea arose of the extent of the earth's great masses of water. The

404

knowledge of the ocean advanced with more rapid steps than ever before. At first this knowledge only extended to the surface, the comparative area of oceans, their principal currents, and the general distribution of temperature. In the middle of the last century Maury collected all that was known, and drew charts of the currents and winds for the assistance of navigation. This was the beginning of the scientific study of the oceanic waters; at that time the conditions below the surface were still little known. A few investigations, some of them valuable, had been made of the sea fauna, even at great depths, but very little had been done towards investigating the physical conditions. It was seen, however, that there was here a great field for research, and that there were great and important problems to be solved; and then, half a century ago, the great scientific expeditions began, which have brought an entire new world to our knowledge.

It is only forty years since the *Challenger* sailed on the first great exploration of the oceans. Although during these forty years a quantity of oceanographical observations has been collected with a constant improvement of methods, it is, nevertheless, clear that our knowledge of the ocean is still only in the preliminary stage. The ocean has an area twice as great as that of the dry land, and it occupies a space thirteen times as great as that occupied by the land above sea-level. Apart from the great number of soundings for depth alone, the number of oceanographical stations—with a series of physical and biological observations at various depths—is very small in proportion to the vast masses of water; and there are still extensive regions of the ocean of the conditions of which we have only a suspicion, but no certain knowledge. This applies also to the Atlantic Ocean, and especially to the South Atlantic.

Scientific exploration of the ocean has several objects. It seeks to explain the conditions governing a great and important part of our earth, and to discover the laws that control the immense masses of water in the ocean. It aims at acquiring a knowledge of its varied fauna and flora, and of the relations between this infinity of organisms and the medium in which they live. These were the principal problems for the solution of which the voyage of the *Challenger* and other scientific expeditions were undertaken. Maury's leading object was to explain the conditions that are of practical importance to navigation; his investigations were, in the first instance, applied to utilitarian needs.

But the physical investigation of the ocean has yet another very important bearing. The difference between a sea climate and a continental climate has long been understood; it has long been known that the sea has an equalizing effect on the temperature of the air, so that in countries lying near the sea there is not so great a difference between the heat of summer and the cold of winter as on continents far from the sea-coast. It has also long been understood that the warm currents produce a comparatively mild climate in high latitudes, and that the cold currents coming from the Polar regions produce a low temperature. It has been known for centuries that the northern arm of the Gulf Stream makes Northern Europe as habitable as it is, and that the Polar currents on the shores of Greenland and Labrador prevent any richer development of civilization in these regions. But it is only recently that modern investigation of the ocean has begun to show the intimate interaction between sea and air; an interaction which makes it probable that we shall be able to forecast the main variations in climate from year to year, as soon as we have a sufficiently large material in the shape of soundings.

In order to provide new oceanographical material by modern methods, the plan of the *Fram* expedition included the making of a number of investigations in the Atlantic Ocean. In June, 1910, the *Fram* went on a trial cruise in the North Atlantic to the west of the British Isles. Altogether twenty-five stations were taken in this region during June and July before the *Fram's* final departure from Norway.

The expedition then went direct to the Antarctic and landed

the shore party on the Barrier. Neither on this trip nor on the *Fram's* subsequent voyage to Buenos Aires were any investigations worth mentioning made, as time was too short; but in June, 1911, Captain Nilsen took the *Fram* on a cruise in the South Atlantic, and made in all sixty valuable stations along two lines between South America and Africa.

An exhaustive working out of the very considerable material collected on these voyages has not yet been possible. We shall here only attempt to set forth the most conspicuous results shown by a preliminary examination.

Besides the meteorological observations and the collection of plankton—in fine silk tow-nets—the investigations consisted of taking temperatures and samples of water at different depths The temperatures below the surface were ascertained by the best modern reversing thermometers (Richter's); these thermometers are capable of giving the temperature to within a few hundredths of a degree at any depth. Samples of water were taken for the most part with Ekman's reversing water-sampler; it consists of a brass tube, with a valve at each end. When it is lowered the valves are open, so that the water passes freely through the tube. When the apparatus has reached the depth from which a sample is to be taken, a small slipping sinker is sent down along the line. When the sinker strikes the sampler, it displaces a small pin, which holds the brass tube in the position in which the valves remain open. The tube then swings over, and this closes the valves, so that the tube is filled with a hermetically enclosed sample of water. These water samples were put into small bottles, which were afterwards sent to Bergen, where the salinity of each sample was determined. On the first cruise, in June and July, 1910, the observations on board were carried out by Mr. Adolf Schröer, besides the permanent members of the expedition. The observations in the South Atlantic in the following year were for the most part carried out by Lieutenant Gjertsen and Kutschin.

The Atlantic Ocean is traversed by a series of main currents, which are of great importance on account of their powerful influence on the physical conditions of the surrounding regions of sea and atmosphere.   By its oceanographical investigations in 1910 and 1911 the *Fram* expedition has made important contributions to our knowledge of many of these currents.   We shall first speak of the investigations in the North Atlantic in 1910, and afterwards of those in the South Atlantic in 1911.

INVESTIGATIONS IN THE NORTH ATLANTIC IN JUNE AND JULY, 1910.

The waters of the Northern Atlantic Ocean, to the north of lats. 30° and 40° N., are to a great extent in drifting motion north-eastward and eastward from the American to the European side.   This drift is what is popularly called the Gulf Stream.   To the west of the Bay of Biscay the eastward flow of water divides into two branches, one going south-eastward and southward, which is continued in the Canary Current, and the other going north-eastward and northward outside the British Isles, which sends comparatively warm streams of water both in the direction of Iceland and past the Shetlands and Faroes into the Norwegian Sea and north-eastward along the west coast of Norway.   This last arm of the Gulf Stream in the Norwegian Sea has been well explored during the last ten or fifteen years; its course and extent have been charted, and it has been shown to be subject to great variations from year to year, which again appear to be closely connected with variations in the development and habitat of several important species of fish, such as cod, coal-fish, haddock, etc., as well as with variations in the winter climate of Norway, the crops, and other important conditions.   By closely following the changes in the Gulf Stream from year to year, it looks as if we should be able to predict a long time in advance any great changes in the cod and haddock fisheries in the North Sea, as well as variations in the winter climate of North-Western Europe.

But the cause or causes of these variations in the Gulf Stream are at present unknown. In order to solve this difficult question we must be acquainted with the conditions in those regions of the Atlantic itself through which this mighty ocean current flows, before it sends its waters into the Norwegian Sea. But here we are met by the difficulty that the investigations that have been made hitherto are extremely inadequate and deficient; indeed, we have no accurate

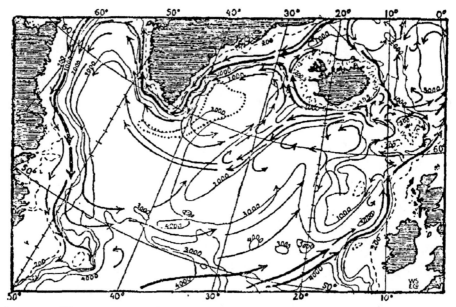

FIG. 1.—HYPOTHETICAL REPRESENTATION OF THE SURFACE CURRENTS IN THE NORTHERN ATLANTIC IN APRIL.

After Nansen, in the *Internationale Revue der gesamten Hydrobiologie und Hydrographie*, 1912.

knowledge even of the course and extent of the current in this ocean. A thorough investigation of it with the improved methods of our time is therefore an inevitable necessity.

As the Gulf Stream is of so great importance to Northern Europe in general, but especially to us Norwegians, it was not a mere accident that three separate expeditions left Norway in the same year, 1910—Murray and Hjort's expedition in the *Michael Sars*, Amundsen's trial trip in the *Fram*, and Nansen's voyage in the gunboat *Frithjof*—all with the object of investigating the conditions in the North Atlantic. The fact that on these three voyages observations were made approximately at the same time in different parts of the ocean increases their value in a great degree, since they can thus be directly compared; we are thus able to obtain, for instance, a reliable survey of the distribution of temperature and salinity, and to draw important conclusions as to the extent of the currents and the motion of the masses of water.

Amundsen's trial trip in the *Fram* and Nansen's voyage in the *Frithjof* were made with the special object of studying the Gulf Stream in the ocean to the west of the British Isles, and by the help of these investigations it is now possible to chart the current and the extent of the various volumes of water at different depths in this region at that time.

A series of stations taken within the same region during Murray and Hjort's expedition completes the survey, and provides valuable material for comparison.

After sailing from Norway over the North Sea, the *Fram* passed through the English Channel in June, 1910, and the first station was taken on June 20, to the south of Ireland, in lat. 50° 50′ N. and long. 10° 15′ W., after which thirteen stations were taken to the westward, to lat. 53° 16′ N. and long. 17° 50′ W., where the ship was on June 27. Her course then went in a northerly direction to lat. 57° 59′ N. and long. 15° 8′ W., from which point a section of eleven stations (Nos. 15-25) was made straight across the Gulf Stream to the bank on the north of Scotland, in lat. 59° 33′ N. and long. 4° 44′ W. The voyage and the stations are represented in Fig. 2. Temperatures and samples of water were taken at all the twenty-four stations at the following depths: surface, 5, 10, 20, 30, 40, 50, 75, 100, 150, 200, 300, 400, and 500 metres (2·7, 5·4, 10·9, 16·3, 21·8, 27·2, 40·8, 54·5, 81·7, 109, 163·5, 218, and 272·5 fathoms)—or less, where the depth was not so great.

The *Fram's* southerly section, from Statio 1 to 13 (see Fig. 3) is divided into two parts at Station 10, on the Porcupine Bank, south-west of Ireland. The eastern part, between Stations 1 and 10, extends over to the bank south of Ireland, while the three stations of the western part lie in the deep sea west of the Porcupine Bank.

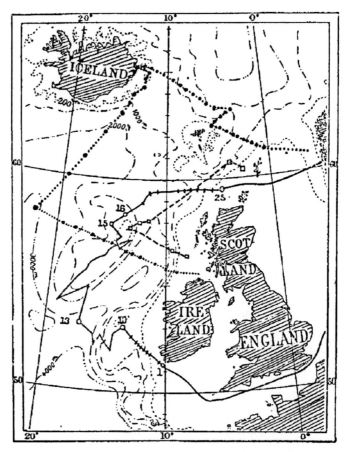

FIG. 2.—THE "FRAM'S" ROUTE FROM JUNE 20 TO JULY 7, 1910 (GIVEN IN AN UNBROKEN LINE—THE FIGURES DENOTE THE STATIONS).

The dotted line gives the *Frithjof's* route, and the squares give five of the *Michael Sars's* stations.

In both parts of this section there are, as shown in Fig. 3, two great volumes of water, from the surface down to depths greater than 500 metres, which have salinities between 35·4 and 35·5 per mille. They have also comparatively high temperatures; the isotherm for 10° C. goes down to a depth of about 500 metres in both these parts.

It is obvious that both these comparatively salt and warm volumes of water belong to the Gulf Stream. The more westerly of them, at Stations 11 and 12, and in part 13, in the deep sea to the west of the Porcupine Bank, is probably in motion towards the north-east along the outside of this bank and then into Rockall Channel—between Rockall Bank and the bank to the west of the

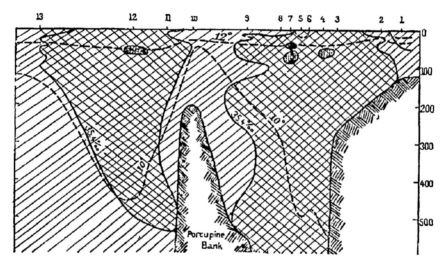

FIG. 3.—TEMPERATURE AND SALINITY IN THE "FRAM'S" SOUTHERN SECTION, JUNE, 1910.

British Isles—where a corresponding volume of water, with a somewhat lower salinity, is found again in the section which was taken a few weeks later by the *Frithjof* from Ireland to the west-north-west across the Rockall Bank. This volume of water has a special interest for us, since, as will be mentioned later, it forms the main part of that arm of the Gulf Stream which enters the Norwegian Sea, but which is gradually cooled on its way and mixed with fresher water, so that its salinity is constantly decreasing. This fresher water is evidently derived in great measure directly from precipitation, which is here in excess of the evaporation from the surface of the sea.

The volume of Gulf Stream water that is seen in the eastern part (east of Station 10) of the southern *Fram* section, can only flow north-eastward to a much less extent, as the Porcupine Bank is connected with the bank to the west of Ireland by a submarine ridge (with depths up to about 300 metres), which forms a great obstacle to such a movement.

The two volumes of Gulf Stream water in the *Fram's* southern section of 1910 are divided by a volume of water, which lies over the Porcupine Bank, and has a lower salinity and also a somewhat lower average temperature. On the bank to the south of Ireland (Stations 1 and 2) the salinity and average temperature are also comparatively low. The fact that the water on the banks off the coast has lower salinities, and in part lower temperatures, than the water outside in the deep sea, has usually been explained by its being mixed with the coast water, which is diluted with river water from the land. This explanation may be correct in a great measure; but, of course, it will not apply to the water over banks that lie out in the sea, far from any land. It appears, nevertheless, on the Porcupine Bank, for instance, and, as we shall see later, on the Rockall Bank, that the water on these ocean banks is—in any case in early summer—colder and less salt than the surrounding water of the sea. It appears from the *Frithjof* section across the Rockall Bank, as well as from the two *Fram* sections, that this must be due to precipitation combined with the vertical currents near the surface, which are produced by the cooling of the surface of the sea in the course of the winter. For, as the surface water cools, it becomes heavier than the water immediately below, and must then sink, while it is replaced by water from below. These vertical currents extend deeper and deeper as the cooling proceeds in the course of the winter, and bring about an almost equal temperature and salinity in the upper waters of the sea during the winter, as far down as this vertical circulation reaches. But as the precipitation in these regions is constantly decreasing the salinity of the surface water, this vertical circulation must bring about a diminution of salinity in the underlying waters, with which the sinking surface water is mixed into a homogeneous volume of water. The *Frithjof* section in particular seems to show that the vertical circulation in these regions reaches to a depth of 500 or 600 metres at the close of the winter. If we consider, then, what must happen over a bank in the ocean, where the depth is less than this, it is obvious that the vertical circulation will here be prevented by the bottom from reaching the depth it otherwise would, and there will be a smaller volume of water to take part in this circulation and to be mixed with the cooled and diluted surface water. But as the cooling of the surface and the precipitation are the same there as in the surrounding regions, the consequence must be that the whole of this volume of water over the bank will be colder and less salt than the surrounding waters. And as this bank water, on account of its lower temperature, is heavier than the water of the surrounding sea, it will have a tendency to spread itself outwards along the bottom, and to sink down along the slopes from the sides of the bank. This obviously contributes to increase the opposition that such banks offer to the advance of ocean currents, even when they lie fairly deep.

These conditions, which in many respects are of great importance, are clearly shown in the two *Fram* sections and the *Frithjof* section.

The Northern *Fram* section went from a point to the north-west of the Rockall Bank (Station 15), across the northern end of this bank (Station 16), and across the northern part of the wide channel (Rockall Channel) between it and Scotland. As might be expected, both temperature and salinity are lower in this section than in the southern one, since in the course of their slow northward movement the waters are cooled, especially by the vertical circulation in winter already mentioned, and are mixed with water containing less salt, especially precipitated water. While in the southern section the isotherm for 10° C. went down to 500 metres, it here lies at a depth of between 50 and 25 metres. In the comparatively short distance between the two sections, the whole volume of water has been cooled between 1° and 2° C. This represents a great quantity of warmth, and it is chiefly given off to the air, which is thus warmed over a great area. Water contains more than 3,000 times as much warmth as the same volume of air at the same temperature. For example, if 1 cubic metre of water is cooled 1°, and the whole quantity of warmth thus taken from the water is given

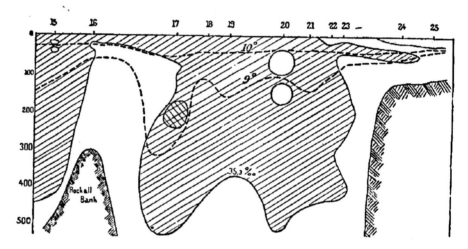

FIG. 4.—TEMPERATURE AND SALINITY IN THE " FRAM'S " NORTHERN SECTION, JULY, 1910.

to the air, it is sufficient to warm more than 3,000 cubic metres of air 1°, when subjected to the pressure of one atmosphere. In other words, if the surface water of a region of the sea is cooled 1° to a depth of 1 metre, the quantity of warmth thus taken from the sea is sufficient to warm the air of the same region 1° up to a height of much more than 3,000 metres, since at high altitudes the air is subjected to less pressure, and consequently a cubic metre there contains less air than at the sea-level. But it is not a depth of 1 metre of the Gulf Stream that has been cooled 1° between these two sections; it is a depth of about 500 metres or more, and it has been cooled between 1° and 2° C. It will thus be easily understood that this loss of warmth from the Gulf Stream must have a profound influence on the temperature of the air over a wide area; we see how it comes about that warm currents like this are capable of rendering the climate of countries so much milder, as is the case in Europe; and we see further how comparatively slight variations in the temperature of the current from year to year must bring about considerable variations in the climate; and how we must be in a position to predict these latter changes when the temperature of the currents becomes the object of extensive and continuous investigation. It may be hoped that this is enough to show that far-reaching problems are here in question.

The salinity of the Gulf Stream water decreases considerably between the *Fram's* southern and northern sections. While in the former it was in great part between 35·4 and 35·5 per mille, in the latter it is throughout not much more than 35·3 per mille. In this section, also, the waters of the Gulf Stream are divided by an accumulation of less salt and somewhat colder bank water, which here lies over the Rockall Bank (Station 16). On the west side of this bank there is again (Station 15) salter and warmer Gulf Stream water, though not quite so warm as on the east. From the *Frithjof* section, a little farther south, it appears that this western volume of Gulf Stream water is comparatively small. The investigations of the *Fram* and the *Frithjof* show that the part of the Gulf Stream which penetrates into the Norwegian Sea comes in the main through the Rockall Channel, between the Rockall Bank and the bank to the west of the British Isles; its width in this region is thus considerably less than was usually supposed. Evidently this is largely due to the influence of the earth's rotation, whereby currents in the northern hemisphere are deflected to the right, to a greater degree the farther north they run. In this way the ocean currents, especially in northern latitudes, are forced against banks and coasts lying to the right of them, and frequently follow the edges, where the coast banks slope down to the deep. The conclusion given above, that the Gulf Stream comes through the Rockall Channel, is of importance to future investigations; it shows that an annual investigation of the water of this channel would certainly contribute in a valuable way to the understanding of the variations of the climate of Western Europe.

We shall not dwell at greater length here on the results of the *Fram's* oceanographical investigations in 1910. Only when the observations then collected, as well as those of the *Frithjof's* and *Michael Sars's* voyages, have been fully worked out shall we be able to make a complete survey of what has been accomplished.

INVESTIGATIONS IN THE SOUTH ATLANTIC, JUNE TO AUGUST, 1911.

In the South Atlantic we have the southward Brazil Current on the American side, and the northward Benguela Current on the African side. In the southern part of the ocean there is a wide current flowing from west to east in the west wind belt. And in its northern part, immediately south of the Equator, the South Equatorial Current flows from east to west. We have thus in the South Atlantic a vast circle of currents, with a motion contrary to that of the hands of a clock. The *Fram* expedition has now made two full sections across the central part of the South Atlantic; these sections take in both the Brazil Current and the Benguela Current, and they lie between the eastward current on the south and the westward current on the north. This is the first time that such complete sections have been obtained between South America and Africa in this part of the ocean. And no doubt a larger number of stations were taken on the *Fram's* voyage than have been taken — with the same amount of detail — in the whole South Atlantic by all previous expeditions put together.

When the *Fram* left Buenos Aires in June, 1911, the expedition went eastward through the Brazil Current. The first station was taken in lat. 36° 13′ S. and long. 43° 15′ W.; this was on June 17. Her course was then north-east or east until Station 32 in lat. 20° 30′ S. and long. 8° 10′ E.; this station lay in the Benguela Current, about 300 miles from the coast of Africa, and it was taken on July 22. From there she went in a gentle curve

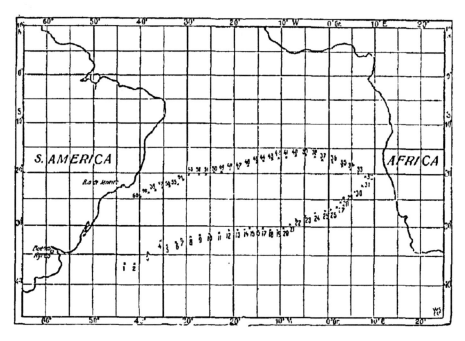

Fig. 5.—The "Fram's" Stations in the South Atlantic (June–August, 1911).

past St. Helena and Trinidad back to America. The last station (No. 60) was taken on August 19 in the Brazil Current in lat. 24° 39′ S. and about long. 40° W.; this station lay about 200 miles south-east of Rio de Janeiro.

There was an average distance of 100 nautical miles between one station and the next. At nearly all the stations investigations were made at the following depths: surface, 5, 10, 25, 50, 100, 150,

200, 250, 300, 400, 500, 750, and 1,000 metres (2·7, 5·4, 13·6, 27·2, 54·5, 81·7, 109, 136·2, 163·5, 218, 272·5, and 545 fathoms). At one or two of the stations observations were also taken at 1,500 and 2,000 metres (817·5 and 1,090 fathoms).

The investigations were thus carried out from about the middle of July to the middle of August, in that part of the southern winter which corresponds to the period between the middle of

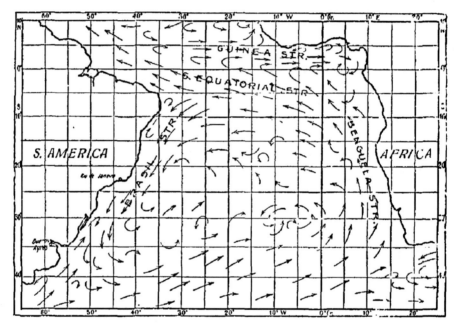

FIG. 6.—CURRENTS IN THE SOUTH ATLANTIC (JUNE–AUGUST, 1911).

December and the middle of February in the northern hemisphere We must first see what the conditions were on the surface in those regions in the middle of the winter of 1911.

It must be remembered that the currents on the two sides of the ocean flow in opposite directions. Along the coast of Africa we have the Benguela Current, flowing from south to north; on the American side the Brazil Current flows from the tropics southward. The former current is therefore comparatively cold and the latter comparatively warm. This is clearly seen on the chart, which shows the distribution of temperatures and salinities on the surface. In lat. 20° S. it was only about 17° C. off the African coast, while it was about 23° C. off the coast of Brazil.

The salinity depends on the relation between evaporation and the addition of fresh water. The Benguela Current comes from

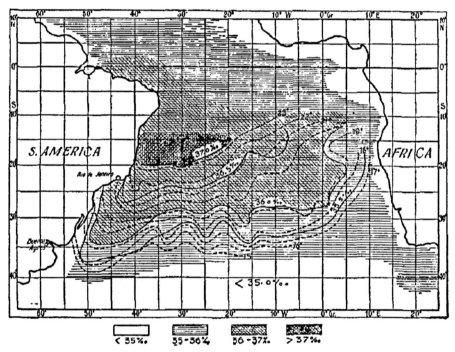

| < 35‰. | 35-36‰ | 36-37‰ | > 37‰ |

FIG. 7.—SALINITIES AND TEMPERATURES AT THE SURFACE IN THE SOUTH ATLANTIC (JUNE–AUGUST, 1911).

regions where the salinity is comparatively low; this is due to the acquisition of fresh water in the Antarctic Ocean, where the evaporation from the surface is small and the precipitation comparatively large. A part of this fresh water is also acquired by the sea in the form of icebergs from the Antarctic Continent. These icebergs melt as they drift about the sea.

Immediately off the African coast there is a belt where the

salinity is under 35 per mille on the surface; farther out in the Benguela Current the salinity is for the most part between 35 and 36 per mille. As the water is carried northward by the current, evaporation becomes greater and greater; the air becomes comparatively warm and dry. Thereby the salinity is raised. The Benguela Current is then continued westward in the South Equatorial Current; a part of this afterwards turns to the north-west, and crosses the Equator into the North Atlantic, where it joins the North Equatorial Current. This part must thus pass through the belt of calms in the tropics. In this region falls of rain occur, heavy enough to decrease the surface salinity again. But the other part of the South Equatorial Current turns southward along the coast of Brazil, and is then given the name of the Brazil Current. The volume of water that passes this way receives at first only small additions of precipitation; the air is so dry and warm in this region that the salinity on the surface rises to over 37 per mille. This will be clearly seen on the chart; the saltest water in the whole South Atlantic is found in the northern part of the Brazil Current. Farther to the south in this current the salinity decreases again, as the water is there mixed with fresher water from the South. The River La Plata sends out enormous quantities of fresh water into the ocean. Most of this goes northward, on account of the earth's rotation; the effect of this is, of course, to deflect the currents of the southern hemisphere to the left, and those of the northern hemisphere to the right. Besides the water from the River La Plata, there is a current flowing northward along the coast of Patagonia—namely, the Falkland Current. Like the Benguela Current, it brings water with lower salinities than those of the waters farther north; therefore, in proportion as the salt water of the Brazil Current is mixed with the water from the River La Plata and the Falkland Current, its salinity decreases. These various conditions give the explanation of the distribution of salinity and temperature that is seen in the chart.

Between the two long lines of section there is a distance of between ten and fifteen degrees of latitude. There is, therefore, a considerable difference in temperature. In the southern section the average surface temperature at Stations 1 to 26 (June 17 to July 17) was 17·9° C.; in the northern section at Stations 36 to 60 (July 26 to August 19) it was 21·6° C. There was thus a difference of 3·7° C. If all the stations had been taken simultaneously, the difference would have been somewhat greater; the northern section was, of course, taken later in the winter, and the temperatures were therefore proportionally lower than in the southern section. The difference corresponds fairly accurately with that which Krümmel has calculated from previous observations.

We must now look at the conditions below the surface in that part of the South Atlantic which was investigated by the *Fram* Expedition.

The observations show in the first place that both temperatures and salinities at every one of the stations give the same values from the surface downward to somewhere between 75 and 150 metres (40·8 and 81·7 fathoms). This equalization of temperature and salinity is due to the vertical currents produced by cooling in winter; we shall return to it later. But below these depths the temperatures and salinities decrease rather rapidly for some distance.

The conditions of temperature at 400 metres (218 fathoms) below the surface are shown in the next little chart. This chart is based on the *Fram* Expedition, and, as regards the other parts of the ocean, on Schott's comparison of the results of previous expeditions. It will be seen that the *Fram's* observations agree very well with previous soundings, but are much more detailed.

The chart shows clearly that it is much warmer at 400 metres (218 fathoms) in the central part of the South Atlantic than either farther north—nearer the Equator—or farther south. On the Equator there is a fairly large area where the temperature is only 7° or 8° C. at 400 metres, whereas in lats. 20° to 30° S. there are large regions where it is above 12° C.; sometimes above 13° C., or even 14° C. South of lat. 30° S. the temperature decreases again rapidly; in the chart no lines are drawn for temperatures below 8° C., as we have not sufficient observations to show the course of these lines properly. But we know that the temperature at 400 metres sinks to about 0° C. in the Antarctic Ocean.

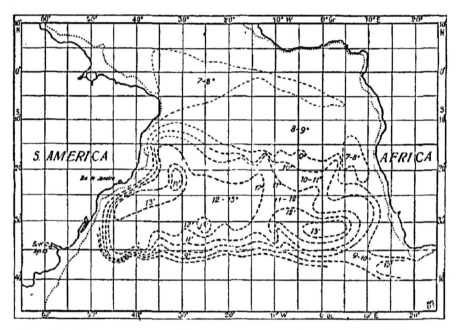

FIG. 8.—TEMPERATURES (CENTIGRADE) AT A DEPTH OF 400 METRES (218 FATHOMS).

At these depths, then, we find the warmest water within the region investigated by the *Fram*. If we now compare the distribution of temperature at 400 metres with the chart of currents in the South Atlantic, we see that the warm region lies in the centre of the great circulation of which mention was made above. We see that there are high temperatures on the left-hand side of the currents, and low on the right-hand side. This, again, is an effect of the earth's rotation, for the high temperatures mean as a rule that the water is comparatively light, and the low that it is comparatively heavy. Now, the effect of the earth's rotation in the southern hemisphere is that the light (warm) water from above is forced somewhat down on the left-hand side of the current, and that the heavy (cold) water from below is raised somewhat. In the northern hemisphere the contrary is the case. This explains the cold water at a depth of 400 metres on the Equator; it also explains the fact that the water immediately off the coasts of Africa and South America is considerably colder than farther out in the ocean. We now have data for studying the relation between the currents and the distribution of warmth in the volumes of water in a way which affords valuable information as to the movements themselves. The material collected by the *Fram* will doubtless be of considerable importance in this way when it has been finally worked out.

Below 400 metres (218 fathoms) the temperature further decreases everywhere in the South Atlantic, at first rapidly to a depth between 500 and 1,000 metres (272·5 and 545 fathoms), afterwards very slowly. It is possible, however, that at the greatest depths it rises a little again, but this will only be a question of hundredths, or, in any case, very few tenths of a degree.

It is known from previous investigations in the South Atlantic, that the waters at the greatest depths, several thousand metres below the surface, have a temperature of between 0° and 3° C. Along the whole Atlantic, from the extreme north (near Iceland) to the extreme south, there runs a ridge about half-way between Europe and Africa on the one side, and the two American continents on the other. A little to the north of the Equator there is a slight elevation across the ocean floor between South America and Africa. Farther south (between lats. 25° and 35° S.) another irregular ridge runs across between these continents. We therefore have four deep regions in the South Atlantic, two on the west (the Brazilian Deep and the Argentine Deep) and two on the east (the West African Deep and the South African Deep). Now it has been found that the " bottom water " in these great deeps— the bottom lies more than 5,000 metres (2,725 fathoms) below the surface—is not always the same. In the two western deeps, off South America, the temperature is only a little above 0° C. We find about the same temperatures in the South African Deep, and farther eastward in a belt that is continued round the whole earth. To the south, between this belt and Antarctica, the temperature of the great deeps is much lower, below 0° C. But in the West African Deep the temperature is about 2° C. higher; we find there the same temperatures of between 2° and 2·5° C. as are found everywhere in the deepest parts of the North Atlantic. The explanation of this must be that the bottom water in the western part of the South Atlantic comes from the south, while in the north-eastern part it comes from the north. This is connected with the earth's rotation, which has a tendency to deflect currents to the left in the southern hemisphere. The bottom water coming from the south goes to the left—that is, to the South American side; that which comes from the north also goes to the left—that is, to the African side.

The salinity also decreases from the surface downward to 600 to 800 metres (about 300 to 400 fathoms), where it is only a little over 34 per mille, but under 34·5 per mille; lower down it rises to about 34·7 per mille in the bottom water that comes from the south, and to about 34·9 per mille in that which comes from the North Atlantic.

We mentioned that the Benguela Current is colder and less salt at the surface than the Brazil Current. The same thing is found in those parts of the currents that lie below the surface. This is clearly shown in Fig. 9, which gives the distribution of temperature at Station 32 in the Benguela Current, and at Station 60 in the Brazil Current; at the various depths down to 500 metres (272·5 fathoms) it was between 5° and 7° C. colder in the former than in the latter. Deeper down the difference becomes less, and at 1,000 metres (545 fathoms) there was only a difference of one or two tenths of a degree.

Fig. 10 shows a corresponding difference in salinities; in the first 200 metres below the surface the water was about

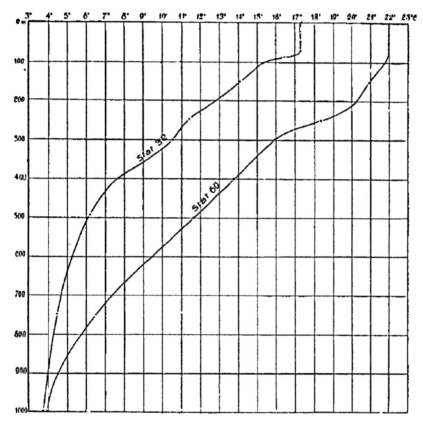

FIG. 9.—TEMPERATURES AT STATION 32 (IN THE BENGUELA CURRENT, JULY 22, 1911), AND AT STATION 60 (IN THE BRAZIL CURRENT, AUGUST 19, 1911).

1 per mille more saline in the Brazil Current than in the Benguela Current. Both these currents are confined to the upper waters; the former probably goes down to a depth of about 1,000 metres (545 fathoms), while the latter does not reach a depth of much more than 500 metres. Below the two currents the

conditions are fairly homogeneous, and there is no difference worth
mentioning in the salinities.

The conditions between the surface and a depth of 1,000 metres
along the two main lines of course are clearly shown in the two
sections (Figs. 11 and 12). In these the isotherms for every second
degree are drawn in broken lines. Lines connecting points with
the same salinity (isohalins) are drawn unbroken, and, in addition,
salinities above 35 per mille are shown by shading. Above is a
series of figures, giving the numbers of the stations. To understand

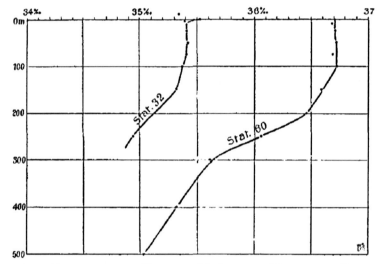

FIG. 10.—SALINITIES AT STATION 32 (IN THE BENGUELA CURRENT,
JULY 22, 1911), AND AT STATION 60 (IN THE BRAZIL
CURRENT, AUGUST 19, 1911).

the sections rightly it must be borne in mind that the vertical scale
is 2,000 times greater than the horizontal.

Many of the conditions we have already mentioned are clearly
apparent in the sections : the small variations between the surface
and a depth of about 100 metres at each station ; the decrease of
temperature and salinity as the depth increases ; the high values
both of temperature and salinity in the western part as compared
with the eastern. We see from the sections how nearly the
isotherms and isohalins follow each other. Thus, where the

temperature is 12° C., the water almost invariably has a salinity very near 35 per mille. This water at 12° C., with a salinity of 35 per mille, is found in the western part of the area (in the Brazil Current) at a depth of 500 to 600 metres, but in the eastern part (in the Benguela Current) no deeper than 200 to 250 metres (109 to 136 fathoms).

We see further in both sections, and especially in the southern one, that the isotherms and isohalins often have an undulating course, since the conditions at one station may be different from those at the neighbouring stations. To point to one or two examples: at Station 19 the water a few hundred metres down was comparatively warm; it was, for instance, 12° C. at about 470 metres (256 fathoms) at this station; while the same tempera-ture was found at about 340 metres (185 fathoms) at both the neighbouring stations, 18 and 20. At Station 2 it was relatively cold, as cold as it was a few hundred metres deeper down at Stations 1 and 3.

These undulating curves of the isotherms and isohalins are familiar to us in the Norwegian Sea, where they have been shown in most sections taken in recent years. They may be explained in more than one way. They may be due to actual waves, which are transmitted through the central waters of the sea. Many things go to show that such waves may actually occur far below the surface, in which case they must attain great dimensions; they must, indeed, be more than 100 metres high at times, and yet— fortunately—they are not felt on the surface. In the Norwegian Sea we have frequently found these wave-like rises and falls. Or the curves may be due to differences in the rapidity and direction of the currents. Here the earth's rotation comes into play, since, as mentioned above, it causes zones of water to be depressed on one side and raised on the other; and the degree of force with which this takes place is dependent on the rapidity of the current and on the geographical latitude. The effect is slight in the tropics, but great in high latitudes. This, so far as it goes, agrees with the

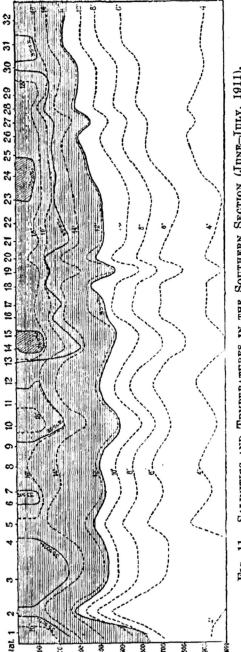

Fig. 11.—Salinities and Temperatures in the Southern Section (June–July, 1911).

Salinities between 35 per mille and 36 per mille is shown by horizontal shading; above 36 per mille by cross-hatching.

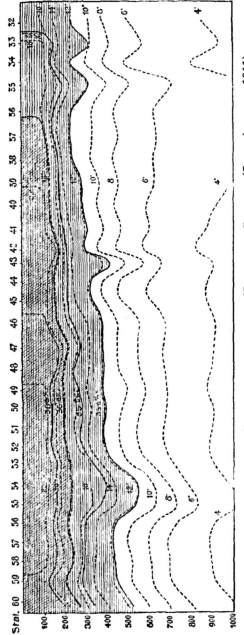

Fig. 12.—Salinities and Temperatures in the Northern Section (July–August, 1911)

fact that the curves of the isotherms and isohalins are more marked in the more southerly of our two sections than in the more northerly one, which lies 10 or 15 degrees nearer the Equator.

But the probability is that the curves are due to the formation of eddies in the currents. In an eddy the light and warm water will be depressed to greater depths if the eddy goes contrary to the hands of a clock and is situated in the southern hemisphere. We appear to have such an eddy around Station 19, for example. Around Station 2 an eddy appears to be going the other way; that is, the same way as the hands of a clock. On the chart of currents we have indicated some of these eddies from the observations of the distribution of salinity and temperature made by the *Fram* Expedition.

While this, then, is the probable explanation of the irregularities shown by the lines of the sections, it is not impossible that they may be due to other conditions, such as, for instance, the submarine waves alluded to above. Another possibility is that they may be a consequence of variations in the rapidity of the current, produced, for instance, by wind. The periodical variations caused by the tides will hardly be an adequate explanation of what happens here, although during Murray and Hjort's Atlantic Expedition in the *Michael Sars* (in 1910), and recently during Nansen's voyage to the Arctic Ocean in the *Veslemöy* (in 1912), the existence of tidal currents in the open ocean was proved. It may be hoped that the further examination of the *Fram* material will make these matters clearer. But however this may be, it is interesting to establish the fact that in so great and deep an ocean as the South Atlantic very considerable variations of this kind may occur between points which lie near together and in the same current.

As we have already mentioned in passing, the observations show that the same temperatures and salinities as are found at the surface are continued downward almost unchanged to a depth of between 75 and 150 metres; on an average it is about

100 metres. This is a typical winter condition, and is due to the vertical circulation already mentioned, which is caused by the surface water being cooled in winter, thus becoming heavier than the water below, so that it must sink and give place to lighter water which rises. In this way the upper zones of water become mixed, and acquire almost equal temperatures and salinities. It thus appears that the vertical currents reached a depth of about 100 metres in July, 1911, in the central part of the South Atlantic. This cooling of the water is a gain to the air, and what happens is that not only the *surface* gives off warmth to the air, but also the *sub-surface waters*, to as great a depth as is reached by the vertical circulation. This makes it a question of enormous values.

This state of things is clearly apparent in the sections, where the isotherms and isohalins run vertically for some way below the surface. It is also clearly seen when we draw the curves of distribution of salinity and temperature at the different stations, as we have done in the two diagrams for Stations 32 and 60 (Fig. 9). The temperatures had fallen several degrees at the surface at the time the *Fram's* investigations were made. And if we are to judge from the general appearance of the station curves, and from the form they usually assume in summer in these regions, we shall arrive at the conclusion that the whole volume of water from the surface down to a depth of 100 metres must be cooled on an average about 2° C.

As already pointed out, a simple calculation gives the following : if a cubic metre of water is cooled 1° C., and the whole quantity of warmth thus taken from the water is given to the air, it will be sufficient to warm more than 3,000 cubic metres of air 1° C. A few figures will give an impression of what this means. The region lying between lats. 15° and 35° S. and between South America and Africa—roughly speaking, the region investigated by the *Fram* Expedition—has an area of 13,000,000 square kilometres. We may now assume that this part of the ocean gave off so much warmth to the air that a zone of water 100 metres in depth was thereby cooled on an average 2° C. This zone of water weighs about 1·5 trillion kilogrammes, and the quantity of warmth given off thus corresponds to about 2·5 trillion great calories.

It has been calculated that the whole atmosphere of the earth weighs 5·27 trillion kilogrammes, and it will require something over 1 trillion great calories to warm the whole of this mass of air 1° C. From this it follows that the quantity of warmth which, according to our calculation, is given off to the air from that part of the South Atlantic lying between lats. 15° and 35° S., will be sufficient to warm the whole atmosphere of the earth about 2° C., and this is only a comparatively small part of the ocean. These figures give one a powerful impression of the important part played by the sea in relation to the air. The sea stores up warmth when it absorbs the rays of the sun ; it gives off warmth again when the cold season comes. We may compare it with earthenware stoves, which continue to warm our rooms long after the fire in them has gone out. In a similar way the sea keeps the earth warm long after summer has gone and the sun's rays have lost their power.

Now it is a familiar fact that the average temperature of the air for the whole year is a little lower than that of the sea ; in winter it is, as a rule, considerably lower. The sea endeavours to raise the temperature of the air ; therefore, the warmer the sea is, the higher the temperature of the air will rise. It is not surprising, then, that after several years' investigations in the Norwegian Sea we have found that the winter in Northern Europe is milder than usual when the water of the Norwegian Sea contains more than the average amount of warmth. This is perfectly natural. But we ought now to be able to go a step farther and say beforehand whether the winter air will be warmer or colder than the normal after determining the amount of warmth in the sea.

It has thus been shown that the amount of warmth in that part of the ocean which we call the Norwegian Sea varies from year to year. It was shown by the Atlantic Expedition of the *Michael Sars* in 1910 that the central part of the North Atlantic was considerably colder in 1910 than in 1873, when the *Challenger* Expedition made investigations there; but the temperatures in 1910

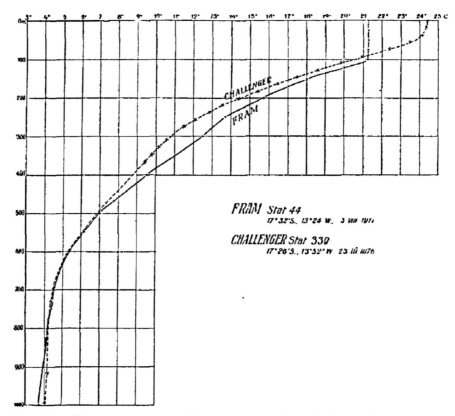

FIG. 13.—TEMPERATURES AT ONE OF THE "FRAM'S" AND ONE OF THE "CHALLENGER'S' STATIONS, TO THE SOUTH OF THE SOUTH EQUATORIAL CURRENT.

were about the same as those of 1876, when the *Challenger* was on her way back to England.

We can now make similar comparisons as regards the South Atlantic. In 1876 the *Challenger* took a number of stations in about the same region as was investigated by the *Fram*. The *Challenger's* Station 339 at the end of March, 1876, lies near the point where the *Fram's* Station 44 was taken at the beginning of August, 1911. Both these stations lay in about lat. 17·5° S., approximately half-way between Africa and South America—that is, in the region where a relatively slack current runs westward, to the south of the South Equatorial Current. We can note the difference in Fig. 13, which shows the distribution of temperature at the two stations. The *Challenger's* station was taken during the autumn and the *Fram's* during the winter. It was therefore over 3° C. warmer at the surface in March, 1876, than in August, 1911. The curve for the *Challenger* station shows the usual distribution of temperature immediately below the surface in summer; the temperature falls constantly from the surface downward. At the *Fram's* station we see the typical winter conditions; we there find the same temperature from the surface to a depth of 100 metres, on account of cooling and vertical circulation. In summer, at the beginning of the year 1911, the temperature curve for the *Fram's* station would have taken about the same form as the other curve; but it would have shown higher temperatures, as it does in the deeper zones, from 100 metres down to about 500 metres. For we see that in these zones it was throughout 1° C. or so warmer in 1911 than in 1876; that is to say, there was a much greater store of warmth in this part of the ocean in 1911 than in 1876. May not the result of this have been that the air in this region, and also in the east of South America and the west of Africa, was warmer during the winter of 1911 than during that of 1876? We have not sufficient data to be able to say with certainty whether this difference in the amount of warmth in the two years applied generally to the whole ocean, or only to that part which surrounds the position of the station; but if it was general, we ought probably to be able to find a corresponding difference in the climate of the neighbouring regions. Between 500 and 800 metres (272 and 436 fathoms) the temperatures were exactly the same in both years, and at 900 and 1,000 metres (490 and 545 fathoms) there was only a

difference of two or three tenths of a degree. In these deeper
parts of the ocean the conditions are probably very similar; we
have there no variations worth mentioning, because the warming
of the surface and sub-surface waters by the sun has no effect
there, unless, indeed, the currents at these depths may vary so

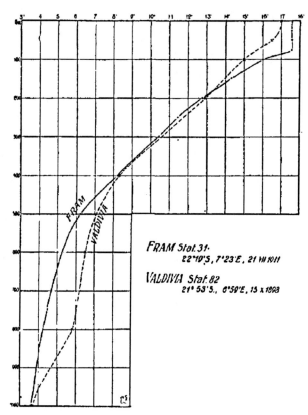

FRAM Stat. 31.
    22°10′S, 7°23′E, 21 VII 1911

VALDIVIA Stat. 82
    21° 53′S., 0°50′E, 15 x 1898

FIG. 14.—TEMPERATURES AT ONE OF THE "FRAM'S" AND ONE OF THE
"VALDIVIA'S" STATIONS, IN THE BENGUELA CURRENT.

much that there may be a warm current one year and a cold one
another year. But this is improbable out in the middle of the
ocean.

In the neighbourhood of the African coast, on the other hand, it
looks as if there may be considerable variations even in the deeper
zones below 500 metres (272 fathoms). During the *Valdivia*

Expedition in 1898 a station (No. 82) was taken in the Benguela Current in the middle of October, not far from the point at which the *Fram's* Station 31 lay. The temperature curves from here show that it was much warmer (over 1·5° C.) in 1898 than in 1911 in the zones between 500 and 800 metres (272 and 436 fathoms). Probably the currents may vary considerably here. But in the upper waters of the Benguela Current itself, from the surface down to 150 metres, it was considerably warmer in 1911 than in 1898; this difference corresponds to that which we found in the previous comparison of the *Challenger's* and *Fram's* stations of 1876 and 1911. Between 200 and 400 metres (109 and 218 fathoms) there was no difference between 1898 and 1911; nor was there at 1,000 metres (545 fathoms).

In 1906 some investigations of the eastern part of the South Atlantic were conducted by the *Planet*. In the middle of March a station was taken (No. 25) not far from St. Helena and in the neighbourhood of the *Fram's* Station 39, at the end of July, 1911. Here, also, we find great variations; it was much warmer in 1911 than in 1906, apart from the winter cooling by vertical circulation of the sub-surface waters. At a depth of only 100 metres (54·5 fathoms) it was 2° C. warmer in 1911 than in 1906; at 400 metres (218 fathoms) the difference was over 1°, and even at 800 metres (436 fathoms) it was about 0·75° C. warmer in 1911 than in 1906. At 1,000 metres (545 fathoms) the difference was only 0·3°.

From the *Planet's* station we also have problems of salinity, determined by modern methods. It appears that the salinities at the *Planet* station, in any case to a depth of 400 metres, were lower, and in part much lower, than those of the *Fram* Expedition. At 100 metres the difference was even greater than 0·5 per mille; this is a great deal in the same region of open sea. Now, it must be remembered that the current in the neighbourhood of St. Helena may be regarded as a continuation of the Benguela Current, which comes from the south and has relatively low salinities. It looks, therefore, as if there were yearly variations of salinity in these

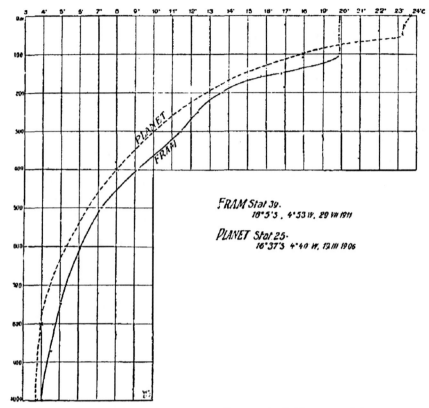

FIG 15.—TEMPERATURES AT THE " PLANET'S " STATION 25, AND THE
" FRAM'S " STATION 39—BOTH IN THE NEIGHBOURHOOD OF
ST. HELENA.

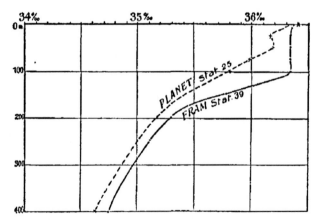

FIG. 16.—SALINITIES AT THE " PLANET'S " STATION 25 (MARCH 19, 1906),
AND THE " FRAM'S " STATION 39 (JULY 29, 1911).

regions. This may either be due to corresponding variations in the Benguela Current—partly because the relation between precipitation and evaporation may vary in different years, and partly because there may be variations in the acquisition of less saline water from the Antarctic Ocean. Or it may be due to the Benguela Current in the neighbourhood of St. Helena having a larger admixture of the warm and salt water to the west of it in one year than in another. In either case we may expect a relatively low salinity (as in 1906 as compared with 1911) to be accompanied by a relatively low temperature, such as we have found by a comparison of the *Planet's* observations with those of the *Fram.*

We require a larger and more complete material for comparison ; but even that which is here referred to shows that there may be considerable yearly variations both in the important, relatively cold Benguela Current, and in the currents in other parts of the South Atlantic. It is a substantial result of the observations made on the *Fram's* voyage that they give us an idea of great annual variations in so important a region as the South Atlantic Ocean. When the whole material has been further examined it will be seen whether it may also contribute to an understanding of the climatic conditions of the nearest countries, where there is a large population, and where, in consequence, a more accurate knowledge of the variations of climate will have more than a mere scientific interest.

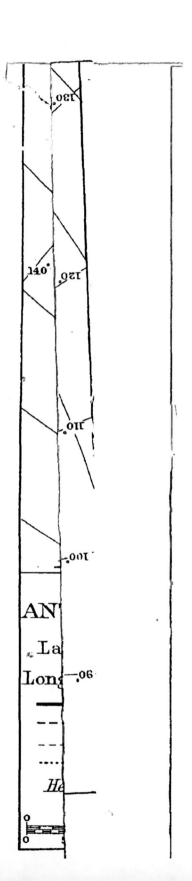

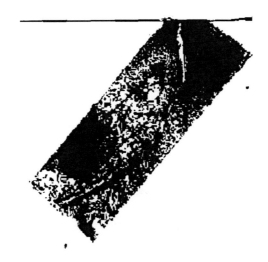

INDEX

THE END

BILLING AND SONS, LTD., PRINTERS, GUILDFORD

LaVergne, TN USA
22 June 2010
187076LV00003B/25/P